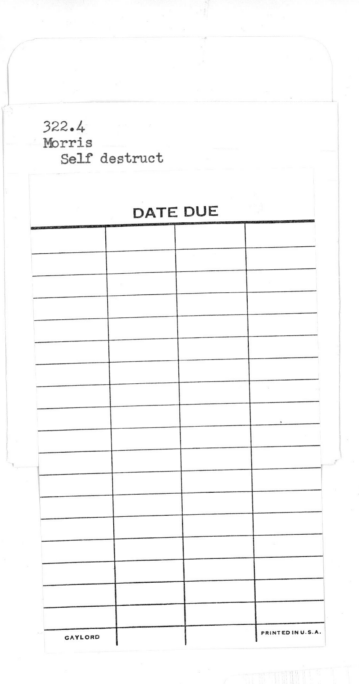

✦✦✦✦✦✦

ITS:

CHRISTIAN HIGH SCHOOL
San Diego, California

✦✦✦✦✦

SELF DESTRUCT

SELF DESTRUCT

Dismantling America's Internal Security

Robert Morris, 1914-

Arlington House

165 Huguenot Street, New Rochelle, New York 10801

P 10 9 8 7 6 5 4 3 2 1

Book design by Pat Slesarchik

Manufactured in the United States of America

Library of Congress Cataloging in Publication Data

Morris, Robert, 1914–
    Self-destruct.

    Includes index.
    1. Internal security—United States. 2. Subversive
activities—United States. 3. Communism—United States.
4. United States—National security. I. Title.
E839.8.M6   322.4'2'0973   78–31938
ISBN 0–87000–437–9

Dedication

This effort is dedicated to the memory of William B. Stephenson, Lyle H. Munson and Robert C. Hill who labored selflessly in the cause of this volume.

Acknowledgements

The author is grateful for the help he received from many people in compiling this volume: my wife Joan who gave continuing advice and collated and filed the physical ingredients; Irene Highley who dutifully performed the typing; Jay Sourwine, Nathaniel and Sylvia Weyl who rendered great editorial assistance; and my son Robert Jr. who did some of the research in Washington.

Contents

Foreword

IT IS FASHIONABLE nowadays to proceed on the assumption—preferably unstated, but articulated if necessary—that most Americans in the late 1940s and 1950s wildly overestimated the aggressive intentions and inimical behavior of the Soviet Union and its U.S. agents and admirers. One implicit corollary of this assumption is that, since the national consensus now favors a much more complacent view of these matters, the actual state of affairs in regard to them today is surely no worse than it was in those earlier years and quite possibly measurably better.

To both the assumption and its corollary, Robert Morris takes sharp exception. He believes, and in this book convincingly demonstrates, that the Soviet Union, from the end of World War II until today, has striven diligently and all too successfully to weaken the United States, with a view to its ultimate destruction and the arrival of that momentous day when, in the words of Communism's anthem, "The International Soviet shall be the human race."

Worse yet, he shows how this country, through blindness or willful indifference or poor leadership or deliberate deception, has again and again become a party to the on-going process of its own destruction. It is this melancholy fact that provides the book with its title.

Back and forth Morris moves, through both space and time,

playing the flashlight of his exposition on first one and then another aspect of Communism's multifaceted assault: the KGB's telephonic eavesdropping, the propaganda campaign against America's key security institutions, the uses of the American Communist Party, specific individual instances of Soviet espionage, the curious phenomenon of "Eurocommunism," the role of terror, and much else. I have no doubt that, before they have finished this book, many readers will want to protest, "No! It can't be as bad—as uniformly, almost monotonously bad—as that!" But Robert Morris goes implacably on, citing fact after fact from which we have—at grave peril—too long averted our eyes. If the record is appalling and the situation grim, that is scarcely his fault.

The reader is entitled, however, to inquire what credentials Robert Morris has for investigating, describing and evaluating the Communist threat to America. The answer is that his credentials are impeccable. No American alive today is better qualified to discuss the subject. As early as 1940, Morris was counsel to the Rapp-Coudert Committee which investigated the penetration of Communists into the New York state school system. During World War II he served as an officer in Naval Intelligence. Back in civilian life again, he was practicing law in New York City when the Republican senators on the Tydings Committee, which had been formed to investigate the early charges of Senator Joseph McCarthy, asked him to serve as their minority counsel. He acquitted himself so ably in that capacity that Senator Pat McCarran, in a rare gesture of non-partisan admiration, invited him in 1950 to become chief counsel to the newly-created Internal Security Subcommittee of McCarran's Senate Judiciary Committee. Morris accepted, and promptly won accolades for a brilliant series of investigations of Communist activity in the United States.

Retiring from that position in 1953, he served for a time as a municipal court justice in New York City. But the excitement and importance of congressional investigations of Communism still attracted him powerfully, and in 1956 he accepted the invitation of Senator James O. Eastland, the Internal Security

10

Subcommittee's new chairman, to resume his old job as chief counsel.

It was during his brief judicial career, from 1953 to 1956, that I first got to know Morris, and I eagerly accepted his offer to take me with him, in the capacity of associate counsel, when he returned to Washington and the Subcommittee. There, during 1956 and 1957, in the course of literally dozens of investigations and hundreds of hearings, I grew to admire him as a lawyer, as an investigator, and as a man. It implies no derogation of the fine work done by many others for the Subcommittee when I say that it was unquestionably the record compiled by Robert Morris as chief counsel that principally inspired the House of Delegates of the American Bar Association to commend the Subcommittee, in 1959, for its work over the years.

In the ensuing two decades, as public concern over the threat presented by Communism has dwindled steadily, Morris has turned to education and writing as means of supporting his growing family. But he has never for an instant ceased to monitor Communist activities, or to warn against the peril they pose.

It is this lifetime of detailed knowledge and first-hand experience on which Morris draws in the present volume. Some people may choose to scoff at his deep concern as dated or old-hat —but have they looked at the world around them? Since Morris last retired as chief counsel to the Internal Security Subcommittee in 1958, the Soviet Union has: (1) drawn at least abreast of the United States as a military superpower, (2) established a spacious island base just ninety miles off the coast of Florida, (3) come within inches of taking full control of Indonesia and Chile, (4) drawn India into its orbit, (5) quarterbacked the Communist conquest of Vietnam, Cambodia and Laos, (6) erupted with permanent naval forces and bases into both the Mediterranean and the Indian Ocean, (7) deployed at least 30,000 surrogate Cuban troops on half a dozen fronts all over Africa—and nonetheless persuaded bemused Republican and Democratic administrations alike to believe it is sincere about wanting "détente." If what we have been witnessing is "détente," no wonder the Russians want it!

Nowhere else will you find, in such clear and concentrated form, so comprehensive an overview of the threat, techniques and successes of Communism as is contained in the pages that follow. I wish every American would read and ponder them— while there is yet time to read, and we still have the God-given freedom to ponder.

William A. Rusher

Prologue

Here on the beach of Mantoloking where I write this volume, the world about me appears to be the same world that could be viewed back in early 1958 when I left Washington where I was immersed in internal security duties. White-crested waves roll over the sand bar that stretches before me much as they did just twenty years ago. So do sandpipers bravely chase each outgoing wave, only to retreat, timorously, before the incoming wave that inexorably follows. The rosy sun peers over the morning horizon with a glow of filtered light and, after warming the beaches and the children at play, sets with a fireball brilliance into Barnegat Bay behind us in the west.

If one did not cast a clear eye beyond the physical lineaments of this Atlantic Ocean scene, he would see the same world that my predecessors beheld some twenty years ago. But looking beyond what people, in the routine of their lives, reflect upon, and beyond the physical tranquillity, ominous signs loom about me, for the world is indeed different and times have indeed changed.

1

The Crumbling Ramparts of Freedom

WITHIN THE BRIEF time-interval of twenty years, the position of the United States has declined from that of the undisputed leader of a confident world alliance of free peoples to that of a beleaguered island in a rising sea of totalitarian despotism.

This headlong retreat from power and responsibility has several dimensions—among them, the erosion of decisive American military superiority into a military capability even inferior to that of the Soviet Union, and the emasculation and destruction of the internal security agencies of the United States.

Few, if any, nations have ever plunged from world leadership to political and military inferiority in such a short period of time.

When I left Washington early in 1958, security agencies were maintaining surveillance over subversives. Today the subversives are discrediting security agents. Colonel Rudolph Abel, the Soviet spy, was arrested and convicted then. Today former FBI officials L. Patrick Gray, W. Mark Felt, and Edward S. Miller are under indictment for measures undertaken to track down the terrorist Weathermen.

The United States then had an overwhelming nuclear superiority of 100-to-1 over the USSR, which was ringed by Western nuclear bases, Polaris submarines, and poised B-52s. Today the USSR has a clear superiority over the United States in nuclear might and is in the process of surrounding the United States.

15

Her fleets maneuver in the Gulf of Mexico and off the Hawaiian coasts, and a hundred Soviet submarines infest the Atlantic Ocean.[1]

The island of Cuba, ninety miles from our coastline, was a sunny tourist haven in 1958. Today Cuba is a Soviet military base of aggression which threatens not only the United States but also Jamaica, the Panama Canal, South America, and even far-off Africa.

In 1958 the United States was protected internally by the Committees of Congress, the Subversive Activities Control Board, the Internal Security Division of the Department of Justice, the counterintelligence departments of the army, navy, air force and coast guard, counterintelligence departments of law enforcement agencies including police departments, and of course the FBI and the CIA.

Today, the Committees of Congress, the Subversive Activities Control Board, and the Internal Security Division of the Department of Justice have been abolished, the counterintelligence departments of the armed forces and of law enforcement agencies have been emasculated, and many of our leaders are trying to strip the FBI of its intelligence-gathering function and to weaken the role of the CIA.

Nikita Khrushchev boasted then that he would conquer by decolonization, disarmament, and peaceful coexistence. We have been pressuring our allies to abandon their colonies. We have responded to Khrushchev's demands that we disarm by disarming. We have taken obliging steps toward peaceful coex-

[1]"Early in July 1977, Cuban warships joined a task force of four Soviet warships, including the 10,000-ton missile-firing cruiser *Vasily Chapayev,* for several days' naval maneuvers in the Gulf of Mexico. At one point the Communist warships steamed to within thirty miles of the western coast of Florida in open defiance of the newly-established 200-mile territorial limits of the United States, Cuba, and other maritime nations. The Soviet force was comprised also of two missile-firing destroyers, the *Rezki* and the *Rezvy,* each 5,000 tons, and of one naval support and supply ship. Perhaps so as not to appear to be helping to celebrate the American Fourth of July, the Soviet warships arrived in the Cuban port of Cienfuegos on July 5" (*America's Future,* August 12, 1977).

istence—unilaterally, but reassuring ourselves by calling it "détente."

Nationalist China was our ally then. Commanding as it does the Strait of Taiwan and the Bashi Channel, it formed a significant part of our defense perimeter. Today we are negotiating, by adhering to the Shanghai Communiqué, to turn over this strategic island to its enemy, Communist China.

In 1958, fresh from its aggressions in Korea and Tibet, the People's Republic of China was continuing its threats against the United States. Today, despite the unregenerate stance of the PRC, the United States is embracing the Chinese Communists, negotiating over the heads and against the interests of our Asian allies.

Communist guerrillas and terrorists were pariahs then. Today, wearing the disguise of "freedom fighters" or "patriotic fronts," vicious Soviet-trained and Soviet-armed guerrillas have the support of the Carter administration in their efforts to conquer Southern Africa and turn the area into Marxist-Leninist states.

Communist aggression was a specter that aroused deep American concern then. Today, our most strident voices call for cuts in our defense expenditures and for the dismantling of our security agencies. Today's villains are not Mao Tse-tung, who killed millions of his own people and waged aggressive war on the United States and the United Nations, nor the KGB, nor the Kremlin. Today's villains are the FBI, the CIA, and such "rightists" as the late J. Edgar Hoover, who devoted his life to defending the internal security of the United States without establishing a national political police.

Thus, on March 16, 1978, the perceptive syndicated Washington columnist Paul Scott wrote:

> Zbigniew Brzezinski, the chief foreign policy-maker of the Carter Administration, has confirmed the greatest fear of many of this country's long and trusted allies. In establishing its foreign policy priorities, the Carter administration has quietly downgraded the defense of the West as a major U.S. objec-

17

tive. This goal has now been replaced with a policy of collaborating with Moscow and other Communist governments to shape a new international community.[2]

This historic and potentially catastrophic change of policy direction was officially acknowledged in Brzezinski's October 25, 1977, address to a meeting of the Trilateral Commission in Bonn. Circulated by the White House in the spring of 1978 under the title *American Policy and Global Change*, the key paragraph reads:

> A concentrated foreign policy must give way to a complex foreign policy, no longer focused on a single dramatic task—such as the defense of the West. Instead we must engage ourselves in the distant and difficult task of giving shape to a world that has suddenly become politically awakened and socially restless.

Dr. Brzezinski then added that any "wider and more cooperative world system" must include that "one-third of mankind [that] now lives under Communist systems, and these states have to be assimilated into a wider fabric of global cooperation."

How did all this come about? Why cannot we see today what was so clearly visible then? Has someone conditioned us not to perceive our own danger?

One of the first purposes of a conspiracy is to convince its targets that no conspiracy exists. The misinformation, camouflage, and incessant propaganda of the Communist apparatus, neatly complemented by self-deception and gullibility on our own part, have conditioned us to accept with indifference the growth of a menace to our very existence.

And as this threat, now clear and unmistakable, becomes more proximate and more ominous, a strange response is set-

[2]Syndicated, March 16, 1978.

ting in. Instead of shoring up our defenses in the face of such a threat, we are dismantling our ramparts and treating as meddlesome extremists those who would halt that dismantling.

We must analyze this curious response and isolate and deal with its causes in order to regain the clear vision and healthy physical structure which we need in order to avert, as it can be averted, the triumph of what now appears to be an inexorable antagonist.

Much more is involved in the present problem than lapses and misjudgments. As we will show, deliberate subversion within our ranks and the activities of the Disinformation Department of the KGB have greatly supplemented the self-deception and gullibility of some of our political leaders. The result is that we are more likely today than ever before to make fatal blunders.

We have made mistakes in the past and survived despite them, but miscalculation and perfidy today, when the world is threatened by nuclear weapons of incalculable destructive power, could cause far more devastation than we experienced at Pearl Harbor.

December 7, 1941, propelled us into the most sanguinary war in our history. The holocaust at Pearl Harbor was made possible by a combination of failures that converged with destructive fury. Our intelligence was inadequate in assessing the enemy's strength and intentions. When it performed properly and broke the Japanese code, the communication of the intelligence information to the political and military decision-makers was shamefully delinquent. When a clear warning of the intended Japanese attack on Pearl Harbor was received in Washington, it was sent to the commanding officers in Hawaii by commercial channels and hence arrived too late to alert the Pacific fleet to the impending bombardment.

Intelligence and counterintelligence failures can cause disasters in our own day no less fatal than the legendary intelligence failure concerning the Trojan horse described in the *Iliad*.

We were able to go on to victory in World War II—a victory whose fruits we have largely cast away.

If the clouds of war do burst open again, the distressing

inadequacies we demonstrated then may seal our doom and bring this great nation and all of Western civilization, its treasures and its people, to death and destruction. There is, of course, an alternative to death and destruction: the subjugation that would be our lot if we should relinquish our will to resist. In that event, also, the United States would cease to exist as an independent nation.

Our historical commitment and our current strategic position make the United States the central redoubt of human liberty. If we fall, the lights of liberty will be extinguished all over the world for the foreseeable future. And those lights have already been extinguished or dimmed in more than half the countries of the world. More than a billion souls groan in darkness.

Yet the world today is concerned with human rights. Men and nations profess to espouse them. With some, the concern is a sham, because they systematically suppress them; nevertheless they invoke the concept. With a great flourish, the nations of the world signed the Human Rights Accord at Helsinki, Finland, in 1976. But even when this accord is invoked it is often being used to alienate nations who, with their imperfections, are trying to repel the Communist aggressors.

The United States must be strong. We must be strong in our military arsenal, continually developing both sophisticated nuclear weapons and conventional arms. We must have a powerful navy and merchant marine, and valor and discipline in the ranks of all our services.

We must forge alliances with men and nations who also respect and defend human rights. Strong as we may be, we cannot stand in stubborn isolation—or if we do, it should be as a last resort. In the councils of the world we must be true to the rule of law, for that rule is at once a fount and a measure of human rights.

But we must also be strong in our internal ramparts and in that protective circle that shields us in our sanctuary. We must protect that sanctuary, not only to safeguard our own existence, but also because that sanctuary is, in many respects, the center of influence and of communications, and its penetration and resulting defilement would have grievous consequences in all the nations of the world. The protection of that sanctuary we call internal security, and it is the subject of this volume.

Our internal security requires that we maintain an intelligence-gathering organization that can assess the strength, the motivation and the intentions of every real or potential enemy. We must also maintain a counterintelligence force that will preserve us from the misinformation of our enemies, from their penetration of our apparatus, and from the negligence, stupidity, and disloyalty of our own operatives. We need an education and information system, not only to inform our intelligence community, but also to induce a broad public understanding of the issues that prevail in the world of today.

2

The Threat

WHILE THE THREAT to the United States is many-pronged, the prime danger comes from the Soviet Union. An implacable ideology that brooks no compromise in its march toward world conquest powers that nation; a military force that is now superior in most respects to that of the United States buttresses it; and it is wired together by a secret police force, the KGB, that not only subjugates its own population but wraps its tentacles around the globe as well, in missions of aggression, intelligence, subversion, and terror. At the onset of World War II, this force was contained by the borders of the USSR. Today its power is spread by its satellites and its advance battalions throughout Europe, Asia, and Africa.

There are other dangers. Communist China came to power on the mainland of Asia by a combination of three forces. Those forces were the Chinese Communist armies, subversive activity among the policy planners in the United States, and the active assistance of the Soviet Union.

The Chinese Communist armies were led by Mao Tse-tung. Their successes were marked by severe discipline, undeviating ideology, superior public relations, and total devotion to inflexible purpose.

When they prevailed over the Nationalist forces, they were closely allied in the Comintern with the USSR. After the death in 1953 of Josef Stalin, whom Mao revered, cleavages began to appear in the alliance. When Khrushchev exposed Stalin's crimes in 1956, Mao began to show his resentment; and after increasingly acrimonious exchanges the alliance was terminated, in some areas, in 1960 when the Russians withdrew their nuclear installations.

There remain to this day, however, important areas where the Russians and the Chinese Communists are allied in purpose and in achievement.

The USSR worked unremittingly to have Communist China installed in the United Nations. Chinese, Cuban, and Russian Communists collaborated in 1963 to conquer Zanzibar off the coast of East Africa.

It was Mao Tse-tung's resentment of the treatment of Stalin by the latter's successors that caused the split that now exists. With the death of Mao, the reason for the cleavage may or may not have been removed. Josef Stalin still remains one of the heroes of Communist China, and his name is emblazoned, together with those of Marx, Engels, and Mao Tse-tung, as one of the glorious leaders of their revolution.

The Chinese Communists operate an intelligence and propaganda organization in the United States. It is centered in the People's Republic of China Mission to the United Nations and in the liaison office in Washington, D.C. It directs a vast espionage operation throughout the United States and deploys a propaganda effort that has been successfully urging the United States to normalize relations with the PRC under the terms of its version of the Shanghai Communiqué, which reads:

> Taiwan is a province of China which has long been returned to the motherland; the liberation of Taiwan is China's internal affair in which no other country has the right to interfere.

The threat of Castro's Cuba also grows. With the normalization of relations with Havana looming larger every day, the Soviet Union is assigning more and more military and espionage responsibilities to its junior partner in aggression. Cuban expeditionary forces are now scattered throughout Africa, and

Cuban police are on duty in several countries in the Caribbean, particularly Jamaica and Panama. The Cuban Intelligence (DGI) has been completely absorbed by the KGB, and because the former's agents are relatively more sanitized than the latter's, it is being given more responsibilities in the United States and Latin America.

We must also consider the dangers of the terrorist organizations operated by such affiliated and unaffiliated forces as the Palestine Liberation Organization, the Hanafis, the Puerto Rican Liberation Front, the Weathermen, the Irish Republican Army, the Venceremos Brigade, the Croatian Nationals, the Red Brigade, and literally scores of others.

All of these constitute real threats, in varying degrees, to the internal security of the United States of America.

Grievous as they are in their menacing thrusts, the most serious problem we have is the ineptitude (and worse) of our response to their aggression.

In 1945, the United States alone had the atom bomb. Our navy and the British navy dominated the seas of the world and our armies were superior. It was Winston Churchill who said at the time:

> The United States at this minute stand at the summit of the world. I rejoice that this is so. Let them act up to the level of their power and responsibility—not for themselves but for all men in all lands—and then a brighter day may dawn on human history.[1]

But it was not to be. Allen Drury, the perceptive author of many political volumes, has written:

> Through a combination of lapses, stupidities, over-idealism, and misjudgments, each at the time seemingly sound and justified, each in its moment capable of a rationale that had brought a majority to approve it, the United States had gotten herself into a posi-

[1]Winston Churchill, August 6, 1945.

24

tion vis-à-vis the Russians in which the issue was more and more rapidly narrowing down to a choice between fight and die now or compromise and die later.[2]

[2]Allen Drury, *Advise and Consent* (New York: Doubleday, 1959), p. 37.

3

The Failure of American Intelligence

THE CONFUSED RETREAT of the United States toward military vulnerability is illustrated by the progressive obsolescence of our navy at a time when the Soviet Union is engaged in building the most powerful fleet the world has ever seen.

Admiral S. G. Gorshkov boasted recently that the Red fleet was superior to the American navy in every category except carriers. He proclaimed that "the oceanic vastnesses are now the least secure in the United States' systems of defense." His conclusion: "The United States may become the theater of military operations."

This pessimistic appraisal was echoed by J. William Middendorf, secretary of the navy under Presidents Ford and Nixon:

> Today we face a Soviet threat far greater than any other threat this nation has ever faced in its two hundred years of existence. Which one of us will want to say to his child or grandchildren that when we had the opportunity to protect our freedoms and to rebuild our strength, we didn't do it?[1]

[1] *Washington Report,* May 1977 (American Security Council). In August of 1978, Mr. Middendorf updated this estimate and wrote for Paul Scott's syndicated column: "Recent years have seen such a severe erosion of our military and particularly our naval posture that the

As for the condition of the air force, the late General Daniel James, when he served as commander-in-chief of the North American Air Defense Command, warned: "I think the trend can be clearly seen when you consider that we've gone from 1,500 fighters down to 300 today. . . . We have no defense against ballistic missiles—no, we don't."

The same condition prevails with respect to our nuclear deterrent.

Lieutenant General Daniel O. Graham, the former head of the Defense Intelligence Agency, measured our status in 1977:

U.S. ability to deter and prevail is seriously threatened.

"The U.S. has become increasingly dependent on foreign supplies of vital raw materials, such as rubber, cobalt, chrome, manganese, and particularly oil. Since 99% of our foreign trade is carried by ship, the survival of our economy and our military security are inextricably tied to our ability to keep open the world's shipping lanes.

"As the Soviet navy has steadily gained in strength, it also has become more adventurous, showing the Soviet flag with increasing frequency at hot spots throughout the world. Routinely Soviet naval task forces sail the Mediterranean, the Indian Ocean, the Caribbean, and even the Gulf of Mexico.

". . . In every category except aircraft carriers the Soviet fleet far exceeds ours.

"In the key area of ballistic missile submarines, the Russians outnumber the U.S. fleet by better than two to one. Worse yet, the Soviet Delta class sub is equipped with 4200-mile-range missiles while the latest U.S. sub-based missile has a range of only 1700 miles.

"The Soviet Union has placed heavy emphasis on building a 'first strike' navy. To overcome the U.S. advantage in aircraft carriers, the Soviet Navy has 1250 land-based aircraft, 30 of which are the new 5000-mile-range BACKFIRE bombers. In addition, they vastly outnumber us in small, fast, and highly maneuverable attack boats equipped with nuclear missiles.

"In spite of the growing superiority of the Soviet Navy, powerful voices in this country continue to urge U.S. unilateral disarmament. And this advice is being followed within the Carter administration.

"Currently, our navy is smaller than at any time since before Pearl Harbor, yet the Carter administration has cut in half the navy's 5-year ship-building program."

By most standards of measuring military forces the Soviets have surpassed—or are surpassing—us, despite . . . the on-going Strategic Arms Limitations Talks (SALT). . . . During the past decade, the Soviets have gone from 224 intercontinental ballistic missiles (ICBMs) to more than 1,600. In sea-launched missiles (SLBMs) . . . from 29 to around 800; in nuclear warheads, from 390 to around 3,500. . . . America has fallen from being 600 ahead in ICBMs to about 600 behind. . . . Since 1972, the USSR has tested and deployed four new ICBMs—all of considerably heavier payload than ours. . . . The Soviets have not built up their forces, as we have, to deter a nuclear war. They have built their forces to fight a nuclear war.[2]

In the area of defensive capability, the inferiority is even more pronounced. The USSR has 12,000 surface to air missiles, the U.S. has none. The USSR has 64 ABM missile weapons, the U.S. has none. The USSR has 2,600 fighter interceptors, the U.S. has 300.

One of the most compelling critics of our current defense capabilities is Major General George Keegan. General Keegan resigned in 1977 as head of Air Force Intelligence to warn the nation of its peril. In a speech to an American Security Council press luncheon in Washington, D.C., he linked the United States' declining military position to deteriorating intelligence-gathering and analysis.

"During the past five years," he said, "I have watched at first hand the culmination of twenty-five years of consistent underestimation of the Soviet threat. . . . When I look back upon my experience with this nation's highest estimating body I have the impression of having taken part in a Charles Dickens novel. The sense of make-believe and unreality has to be experienced to be believed."

General Keegan's explanation for this dangerous atmo-

[2] *Washington Report*, American Security Council, April 1977.

sphere is a grim one. He suggests that our estimates of Soviet strength have been deliberately miniaturized and falsified to conform to what the politicians want to hear.

The effects of this politicization of the intelligence community, warns General Keegan, are as dangerous as its implications are disturbing. Intelligence has supported policy, rather than reflected data. Our planning is more and more based upon the idea that "if we could somehow assuage Soviet fears of the United States, we might induce them to behave in a non-belligerent manner." The guiding principle of Soviet forces, on the other hand, is that they "must be prepared to wage war at all conflict levels and emerge successfully."

The result of these attitudes, General Keegan reported, is a serious disparity in military strength and efficiency. The Soviets have recovered most of the ground they lost by their late entry into the industrial age and today make up in bulk what they may still lack in quality. He gave several examples of this disparity, some of them—for instance, the Backfire bomber and refirable ICBMs—never taken into account as threats by the United States' intelligence community. He concluded that this deliberate omission could only be explained by our policy "not to perturb SALT or détente."

Let me now pass to the details of some of General Keegan's charges:

> The intelligence community in general, and CIA in particular, has been wrong in its assessments of Soviet intentions—almost continuously since World War II. The community has erred about its judgments to the national leadership on whether the Soviets were pursuing superiority, whether they could afford to do so, or whether they could, in fact, pursue such superiority.
>
> The intelligence estimators—heavily dominated by the influence of CIA and the State Department—have been wrong about Soviet purposes in pursuing détente. They have been shockingly deficient in their

estimates of the risks and the advantages to the United States and the free world of the so-called "technology exchange" with the Soviet Union. . . .

Soviet defense expenditures were consistently understated. The Russian peasants, it was assumed, could not afford to strive for superiority. The rhetoric of the cold war was eliminated; and, finally, self-imposed restraint became the key to international security—premised on the naive belief that Soviet objectives were not dissimilar from our own, and that if we could somehow assuage Soviet fears of the United States, we might induce them to behave in a non-belligerent manner.

The Soviets have more staying power. They are far better able to protect their society, their forces, their economy, and their war-oriented industrial base. Their hot production base is capable of generating, and is now generating, a vastly superior quantity of high quality armaments for all levels of military application.

Soviet forces today are premised exclusively on the principle that they must be prepared to wage war at all conflict levels and emerge successfully. Such a strategic philosophy is totally different from our own.

U.S. strategic forces and policy, in contrast, have been premised on the view that nuclear war was so horrible that it could not be contemplated in any rational environment. Therefore, we have based our military preparations, at the strategic level at least, on the view that we must be prepared to deter such aggression. The Soviet view, in contrast, has been that they must be prepared to wage nuclear war if they are to satisfy their own security requirements. . . .

Oleg Penkovsky, you will recall, was the Soviet colonel who, in the early 1960s, supplied U.S. intelligence with a remarkable array of top secret documents regarding Soviet strategic planning—until he was arrested and shot. Regrettably, those remarkable documents—clearly reflecting Soviet long-term plans—have not yet been published and made available to the American people—for reasons which I am at a total loss to comprehend.

However, you don't have to have the Penkovsky documents in order to understand Soviet strategic planning. All you have to read is Soviet Marshal V. D. Sokolovsky's book *Military Strategy*, now in its third edition. It is all there. And what it provides is a detailed, unmistakable blueprint of how one prepares an economy and a society for the acceptance of total war—premised, of course, on the bedrock principle that such capabilities have one fundamental end in mind—namely, to help the Soviet political leadership impose its way of life over the rest of the world.

The Sokolovsky book is the single most comprehensive blueprint on the requirements and preparations incident to waging total war ever published.

As the first American translation of that all-important book was nearing completion, there were a number of high defense officials in this government who became very concerned about the possible impact of such a book on the American public. Accordingly, some of those officials went to considerable extremes to try to obscure the thrust of that book and to minimize its possible impact upon the evolving American strategic blueprint—as conceived under Mr. McNamara and others in the Kennedy administration.

Our greatest single deficiency today is in the strategic warning area. Since the Pearl Harbor attack, this country has spent tens of billions of dollars in order to assure that a surprise attack would never happen again. Yet today I submit that we are not much better off than we were on the eve of Pearl Harbor. Despite our vast technological achievements in the development of surveillance and warning technology and capabilities, and despite the vast organization of intelligence which we have created, most of the ills which existed on the eve of Pearl Harbor remain with us—increasingly so.

4

The Disintegration of Internal Security and the Decline of National Strength

AMERICAN INTERNAL SECURITY is deteriorating fast. The strength of the Free World is being eroded apace.

Our neglect of internal security leads directly to Communist gains around the world.

In a unanimous report that was adopted by the full Senate Judiciary Committee in 1952, the Senate Internal Security Subcommittee found that a small group of persons, some of them Communists, working in the Institute of Pacific Relations, a prestigious research foundation, and in the State Department, influenced United States Far Eastern policy so effectively that a major change was brought about that accommodated Communist purposes and objectives in China.[1]

The Soviet conquest of Cuba was accomplished in part by misinformation emanating from the State Department and the media, particularly one reporter on the *New York Times*, but primarily by a failure of internal security forces to transmit effectively and credibly the demonstrable fact that Fidel Castro was a Communist from the very time that he participated in riots and demonstrations against the Organization of American States conference in Bogotá, Colombia in 1948.

Despite this intelligence, since admitted by Castro, the self-

[1]*Institute of Pacific Relations*. Report of the Committee on the Judiciary, July 2, 1952.

33

deception on the part of the State Department was such that the Cuban dictator was effectively promoted and brought to power in Havana, with the policy makers in Washington even rejecting Ambassador Earl Smith's effort to form a coalition of all anti-Batista forces (except Castro) to replace the unacceptable Batista.

Similarly Yugoslavia fell—partly, it is true, as the result of Soviet military gains but also partly because of self-deception and faulty intelligence on the political make-up of Josip Tito. Tito's identity as a Communist was well documented by our intelligence agencies but minimized by our actual policy planners.

The nation has been seared by the long and tragic Vietnam War in which the United States was defeated for the first time in its history. The defeat was not a military one, for it was brought on by lamentable planning, by a policy that called for the gradual but predictable escalation on our part that enabled the Soviet Union and the People's Republic of China to escalate even more effectively, all the while generating a war weariness on the national scene that forced the untimely withdrawal of American forces.

During and before World War II, there were two hundred movies made in support of the United States in its struggle against the Nazis and the Fascists. During the Vietnam War, one would have to search diligently to find any that supported the effort of the United States to blunt aggression in Indochina. The overwhelming majority of the films derided our war effort, and some openly glamorized the current-day Tokyo Roses whose falsehoods and propaganda undermined the efforts of gallant men and made their sacrifice one for a hopeless cause.

The one episode that more than anything else dragged the United States into the quagmire of Vietnam was our support of the overthrow of President Diem in 1963, when he was winning the war against Communist insurgency. The counsel of Roger Hilsman, then assistant secretary of state for Far Eastern affairs, and of W. Averell Harriman, undersecretary for political affairs, prevailed with President Kennedy over that of Ambassador to Vietnam Frederick Nolting (whom they had recalled), CIA mission head John Richardson, and top military advisor General Paul Harkins. Despite the strong reports of the latter three, the United States policy supported the overthrow of Diem, creating a vacuum that resulted in the eventual extensive mobilization of American and Allied forces.

Father Raymond de Jaegher, a Catholic priest with years of intimate experience of Asia and great practical knowledge of Asian politics, was present at the shameful overthrow. He openly warned the American ambassador who had replaced Nolting and Duong Van Minh ("Big Minh"), the general who led the coup and engineered the subsequent assassination of President Diem and his brother, that what we had done in Saigon that day would create "a vacuum" that would have to be filled "by the lives of scores of thousands of American boys."

How prophetic that warning proved to be! When Diem was overthrown, his whole administration fell, and chaos ensued all over the nation. The leaders who succeeded Big Minh provided only confusion and indecision that paved the way for Communist successes until President Thieu came onto the scene. Then the forces of subversion here and around the world began to calumniate Thieu, as they had done in the case of Diem, with extraordinary success.

Ironically, the United Nations Investigating Team that conducted an inquiry in South Vietnam at the time that President Diem was assassinated disclosed in its report—after the overthrow—that there was no discrimination on the part of the butchered President—the charge that had provoked our intervention in the first place.

All during the Vietnam War there was almost no effective information campaign designed to instruct our armed forces and the American public about the nature of the enemy—Communism—and its effort to conquer Indochina as a base from which to extend its dominion over the rest of Asia.

The famous Fulbright Memorandum which effectively spiked the efforts of all military establishments to teach about the nature of Communism prevailed even during the Vietnam War.

During the most critical phase of this war, President Nixon

and his secretary of state openly wined and dined with the Communist dictators on the Chinese mainland, while in the rice paddies of Indochina our troops were fighting the subordinates of those dictators, dying, and languishing in cruel prisons. Think what that spectacle signifies: drinking with and exculpating the prime aggressors while sending men to die to thwart their aggressions. The whole cause thereby loses its purpose.

The same dangerous inconsistency can be observed today. The Soviet Union is now driving toward Southern Africa to conquer that strategic redoubt. The Cape of Good Hope is the gateway to the Indian Ocean, and the countries making up Southern Africa are pregnant with precious and essential minerals. Yet the misinformation emanating from high policy posts and the complete suppression of internal security relating to that current-day aggression hold sway. Internal security files bearing on the motives of some of the prime protagonists of the present policy are literally being suppressed.

And as we will detail later, Chinese Communist propaganda is strongly pressuring the United States to "normalize relations" with the People's Republic of China, to rescind the mutual defense treaty with the Republic of China, and to subjugate Taiwan to Communist dictatorship. Because aspects of this propaganda bear some of the characteristics of our policy, it is often difficult to distinguish and isolate it.

Even within the past year, in April of 1978, the USSR scored an impressive coup in overthrowing the Afghanistan government of President Daud and establishing Noor Mohammed Toraki, a former employee of the State Department and of the U.S. Overseas Mission, as its new head of state. Dispatches the next morning reported that the State Department was "unruffled" and minimized the importance of the coup, just as it had attached no significance in the 1960s to Noor's Marxist reputation when he was hired. Afghanistan is the linchpin of the Soviet design to undermine Iran and take control of the Strait of Hormuz and the Persian Gulf littoral whence western Europe draws 70 percent of its oil, Japan 90 percent, Israel and South Africa almost all, and the United States about 10 percent.

36

All these instances of Soviet and Chinese Communist expansion have been greatly aided by a formula that has been disastrous to the Free World. The KGB and its formidable Peking counterpart have directed their efforts toward the successes of world Communism. We must concede that they have been resourceful and skillful. But the degree of our vigilance and resistance is often the determining factor in producing the outcome.

Where we have not been vigilant, and where in some cases American agents joined the Communist effort, the Communists have won. Where alert intelligence and resolute action prevailed, Soviet aggression was thwarted. The formula is clear. Unless we have good intelligence, strong internal security and good information sources, such as would be provided by the congressional committees and appropriate executive agencies, we can expect further expansion of Communist strength over the dwindling areas of the Free World.

5

The KGB on Your Long-Distance Calls

TOO OFTEN WE equate the work of the KGB, the Soviet security agency, with that of our Central Intelligence Agency. The Disinformation Desk of the KGB would not have it otherwise.

Both the KGB and its military subsidiary, the GRU, are charged with gathering intelligence. So is the CIA, but there the resemblance ceases.

The KGB's primary purpose is the suppression of the Russian people. Most of its activities are directed against internal dissent, against disloyalty to the ruling class. Since Russia and its satellites are police states, every manifestation of thought and speech is carefully supervised.

The KGB scrutinizes every act and pronouncement of every government official, at home or abroad, at a civilian post or on a military or secret service assignment.

The KGB is the main force that keeps the Soviet Union monolithic. It is the chief instrument of suppression, the slave master of the Gulag Archipelago, the force that thwarts the natural human craving for freedom.

The KGB is also a primary action agency of the Soviet Union. It engineers assassinations and acts of terror. It keeps watch on the Communist parties and their front organizations in all countries. Its Division of Disinformation spews out false reports to be credulously accepted and spread by the media in the non-Communist world.

Among other tasks, the KGB is charged with penetrating all departments of foreign governments and such private organizations abroad as foundations, media, churches, labor unions, educational institutions—in fact, every significant structural element in the societies that it considers worthwhile to infiltrate.

John Barron's authoritative study is the most comprehensive analysis of this enormous and protean organization available. It represents six years of research by its author in conjunction with the worldwide resources of the *Reader's Digest* and the cooperation of U.S. intelligence agencies. In addition to chronicling major episodes of espionage and counterespionage, sabotage, terror, and subversion by the Soviet secret police, it examines the organizational structure and function of the KGB in detail.

The power of the KGB in the Soviet government is illustrated by the elevation of its chief, Yuri V. Andropov, to the Politburo in 1973. Barron concluded that three of the seventeen Politburo members were KGB men and that the chairman of the Council for the Affairs of the Russian Orthodox Church, Major General Georgi Karpov, was also a KGB official.[1] While controlling the Russian Orthodox Church, the KGB also supervises the anti-religious and atheist propaganda activities of the regime. Barron describes KGB infiltration of Christian churches in the Communist world and also in the West. There are even KGB instructional centers for agents who are to become Buddhist monks.

The United Nations is obviously heavily infiltrated. The KGB textbook, *The Practice of Recruiting Americans in the U.S.A. and Third Countries*,[2] stresses the usefulness of U.N. organizations as cover. Barron lists eighteen U.N. officials who have been exposed or arrested for offenses ranging from espionage to kidnapping. During 1963–1973, the personal advisor to U.N. Secretary General U Thant was both an intimate friend of the Burmese diplomat and a KGB officer. His name was

[1] John Barron, *KGB* (Pleasantville, N.Y.: Reader's Digest Press, 1974).
[2] *ibid.*, p. 18ff.

Viktor Lessiovsky. The most important under secretary in the U.N., the man charged with political, military, and Security Council affairs, has always been a Soviet official.

The KGB regularly plants microphones in U.S. diplomatic and other missions in Soviet-controlled territory. One defector told U.S. intelligence the location of forty-four microphones built into the walls of the U.S. embassy in Moscow in 1952.

On June 23, 1975, the *Chicago Tribune*'s Washington bureau chief, Jim Squires, reported that the National Security Agency, while secretly tuning in on a massive Soviet KGB eavesdropping operation, overheard the private telephone calls of U.S. citizens, including government and business leaders and members of Congress. These conversations, carrying governmental and business secrets, were being computerized, plucked out of the air as it were by giant Soviet computers.

The disclosure prompted investigations by both the White House and a congressional committee to determine how much information was gathered and what if anything was being done to stop it.

The grim significance of this Soviet interception of telephone calls, while not generally known, disturbed the intelligence community. The Rockefeller Commission report on national security dealt briefly with Soviet electronic surveillance, but it was heavily censored for national security reasons by the White House.

However, details of the Soviet espionage capability have been made known to congressional committees. One congressman said: "Apparently we were being spied on by the Russians, and our own intelligence agencies knew about it and didn't tell us. What we must determine is how that information was being used by our own people and why they didn't stop the flow immediately."[3]

White House and intelligence spokesmen claimed that publishing details of Soviet electronic spying would harm national security by giving the Soviets insight into U.S. counterintelli-

[3]*New York Times*, July 10, 1977, p. 34. Copyright © 1977 by The New York Times Company. Reprinted by permission.

gence capabilities. One high-ranking U. S. intelligence official, however, retorted that the Soviets already know what the U.S. monitoring capacity is. The scope of Soviet monitoring at the time was placed at hundreds of thousands, perhaps millions, of interceptions.

In a report to President Ford by John M. Eger, acting director of the Office of Telecommunications Policy, the point was made that monitoring of this sort jeopardizes not only national security, but private and business communications as well.

A few months later, in November 1975, Thomas C. Reed, director of telecommunications in the office of the secretary of defense, stated that interception of long-distance phone calls "is a simple and straightforward matter for the underworld organizations, blackmailers, terrorists, or a foreign power."[4] Modern computer technology makes the interceptive techniques simple and precise.

In June 1977, former Vice President Nelson A. Rockefeller warned in a speech that the Russians can and do invade the privacy of U.S. citizens by listening to telephone conversations within the United States and throughout the world. Then he was quoted as saying, "Electronic intrusion in the business and private lives of American citizens is not only possible but it is being done. Information so recorded can be stored and analyzed from computer technology for myriads of usages that are deeply disturbing."[5]

On Sunday, July 10, 1977, more than two years after the *Chicago Tribune* broke its story, the *New York Times* reported in a feature front-page article that extensive efforts were being made to thwart the massive Soviet interception of our telephone communications.

This story reported that microwave telephone service was particularly vulnerable to the KGB interception and monitoring of telephone calls.

Microwave transmission, a system that now handles more than two-thirds of all domestic long-distance calls, was vulnera-

[4]*ibid.*
[5]*ibid.*

ble to massive high speed computers plucking out the conversations from ultra-high frequency radio signals.

A key weapon in this new espionage is the computer. We have made an effort to determine whether the computers engaged in this work were manufactured and produced in the United States. Most of the Soviet computer systems are. But according to the intelligence sources, the Russians pick up domestic American calls from their Washington embassy, from the United Nations offices in New York, from Soviet vacation residences on Long Island and in Maryland, and from a residence in the Riverdale section of the Bronx. The Russians are also believed to have listening posts at trade consulates in San Francisco and Chicago.

It certainly seems surprising that, more than two years after the disclosure made by the *Chicago Tribune* in June 1975, no means have been found to thwart the interceptions. I have learned, however, that the Ford administration decided not to disclose this widespread monitoring at the behest of Secretary of State Henry A. Kissinger, who opposed the disclosure of the Soviet eavesdropping because it might harm relations and block the policy of détente. Vice President Rockefeller, who learned of the problem while heading the commission that investigated illegal activities of the Central Intelligence Agency, argued forcefully for open discussion of the danger for fear that the Republicans might be accused of a cover-up.

Clearly this monitoring by the KGB represents a grave danger not only to the security of the nation but to the safety of confidential economic and business exchanges. It has been reported by the *New York Times* that such "plucked out" telephone conversations aided the Soviet Union in the wheat deals of 1973 that benefited Moscow and caused an inflationary surge in our economy.[6]

In trying to determine why the White House and two administrations endeavored to keep this Soviet interception a secret, I discovered some strange policies.

The policy of the Carter administration seems to permit the

[6]*ibid.*

USSR to use at least five stations to engage in monitoring, while the FBI and the CIA must obtain court orders to monitor the phones of the Soviet Embassy, or any suspected foreign agent of Moscow, Peking, Havana, or other hostile powers.

It is believed that the United States conducts a similar operation in Moscow and that for this reason secrecy is maintained concerning the KGB effort.

While the U.S. allegedly has conducted similar operations in Moscow for some time, the Soviet Union resorted to jamming the American effort by microwave radiation beams during the Carter administration. President Carter characteristically prohibited jamming the Soviet interceptors.

Paul Scott, the Washington columnist, reported on July 18, 1977, the contents of a confidential U.S. intelligence community memorandum on Soviet telecommunications espionage:

> Suppressed by then Secretary of State Henry Kissinger on the grounds the publication would inflame U.S.-Soviet relations, the memorandum also links the KGB operations in the U.S. with a Soviet monitoring base in Cuba and Fidel Castro's intelligence operations at the U.N.
>
> The Russians, who have set up an advanced military operational base in Cuba, have established an electronic microwave complex there capable of intercepting communications from U.S. satellites, according to U.S. intelligence experts.
>
> The Cuban complex is linked by microwave to the five major electronic spy and espionage bases that the Russians have set up at (1) the Soviet embassy in Washington, D.C., (2) the Russian offices at the United Nations, (3) the Soviet consulate in Chicago, (4) the Soviet consulate in San Francisco, and (5) the Soviet spy-recreation farm in nearby Maryland.
>
> As long as these Soviet monitoring and espionage bases are permitted to operate on American soil, this

nation's entire communications system is vulnerable to the nation's number one enemy.

Since the present U.S. leadership has lost the will to protect this nation's vital communications and the privacy of its citizens, only an aroused American public can clean up this security scandal. Each of us must demand that our representatives in Congress act to neutralize these Soviet spy and espionage bases now operating on American soil. The first step is for our government to begin jamming these Soviet installations.[7]

To protect the privacy of telephone communications against either commercial or KGB espionage, confidential phone calls are increasingly being encoded automatically. I have learned that IBM has developed a system which meets the fundamental conditions for communications safety. It will take a lifetime for an eavesdropper to decode the communications even if (a) he has decoding machinery as sophisticated as the encoder and (b) he has an unlimited volume of material to feed into his decoding system. Lower-priced electronic encoders are being moved from research and development into production by competing American companies. These will reportedly be within the means of small to middle-sized U.S. corporations.

On the remedial side, Senator Patrick Moynihan (D-NY) has introduced a bill to expel diplomats who engage in electronic surveillance in the United States. The Senator gave as his reason "the curious, even eerie unwillingness of the United States government to take steps to prevent the Soviet government from intercepting telephone calls made by economic leaders, stockbrokers and government officials." President Carter rejoined by saying that he would not interpret eavesdropping by the USSR or other embassies "to be an act of aggression."[8]

[7]Syndicated July 18, 1977.
[8]*New York Times*, July 28, 1977, p. A-20. Copyright © 1977 by The New York Times Company. Reprinted by permission.

6

Components of Internal Security

THERE ARE MANY organizational elements in national security. Most of them have been dismantled or are being disintegrated under relentless pressures.

The most well-known of these organizations are the Central Intelligence Agency, the Federal Bureau of Investigation, and the Committees of Congress, known as the Senate Internal Security Subcommittee and the House Internal Security Subcommittee. Then there are the Intelligence Section of the Defense Department and the intelligence divisions of each of the services: army, navy, air force, marines, and coast guard. In addition there were an Internal Security Division of the Department of Justice and the Subversive Activities Control Board.

Furthermore, some of the states established legislative committees that undertook the work of internal security. And the law enforcement agencies, particularly those in the large cities, have necessarily had to maintain the machinery of internal security. They are generally called the counterintelligence divisions of the police departments.

I stress the operations of the United States Senate Internal Security Subcommittee because I was its counsel for a long period of its existence, beginning in 1951. It had its counterpart in the House committee which was known as the House Un-American Activities Committee and, just be-

45

fore its demise, the House Internal Security Committee.

Very few people seem to understand the nature of these Committees or why they are necessary.

It must be remembered that they are legislative, not prosecuting agencies. There are three elements in the legislative process: fact-finding, deliberation and debate, and finally the passage, amending, or rescinding of laws.

The congressional Committees on security were primarily fact-finding bodies. Fact-finding is the most important element in the legislative process. Unless a legislature knows the truth about the subject matter of proposed legislation, the laws that it passes will fail in their purpose.

Currently there is a threat to our internal security. That fact is indisputable. Therefore, Congress must know the dimensions and nature of that threat. Knowing does not necessarily lead to action against the threat. But to maintain—as those people who not only advocated the abolition of the Committees, but worked to destroy them, have done—that there should be no fact-finding in this area is irrational. Not knowing the truth can serve no good end.

Even if the Committees were to find that no real threat existed and therefore recommended the amendment or repeal of existing statutes, they would serve a purpose. But today needed laws and safeguards are being struck down on the basis of emotional recommendations that coincide with the propaganda being spread by those who are the targets of the laws and safeguards under attack.

The congressional Committees had constitutional powers that executive agencies lacked. They had the power to subpoena witnesses and custodians of records and other evidence. Failure to comply could bring on a contempt citation which the Committees had the power to enforce.

The Committees had the power to compel testimony. Refusal to testify, not justified by the Bill of Rights, could form the basis of a contempt decree.

But above all, the Committees could publish their findings with privilege—that is, without fear of libel.

The nihilists often said that the work the Committees performed could be done by the FBI. (Now, having ravaged the Committees, they have turned their full fury against the FBI and are claiming that its internal security operations are unnecessary.) The assertion that the FBI can do the work of the congressional Committees is demonstrably false because neither the FBI nor other executive agencies can issue subpoenas, compel testimony, or cite for contempt. Legally, anybody can refuse to respond to an inquiry by the FBI.

Even more important, the FBI cannot publish the results of its investigations. It can merely turn over its findings of fact to executive agencies without recommendation for action. Thus, the educational benefit of the congressional Committees can be enormous, a benefit that other intelligence agencies cannot produce. If the United States should be unfortunate enough to have an attorney general who was lukewarm in his feelings toward internal security, then FBI reports covering major threats to the security of the United States could simply be pigeonholed or shoved under the rug. This sort of thing has happened in the past and can happen again in the future. When congressional Committees function in the internal security area, the American people can be alerted to such dangers.

On the Senate side, internal security was handled by a subcommittee of the Senate Judiciary Committee. Thus if any legislation was introduced bearing on subversion, enemy propaganda, terrorism, or other matters related to internal security, it would be referred directly to the Judiciary Committee, which would pass it on to one of its subcommittees.

The House Committee on Un-American Activities was a standing committee of the House. Its successor was a subcommittee of the House Judiciary Committee.

Because of the broad powers it possessed, the Senate Internal Security Subcommittee voluntarily established rules that were designed to prevent the publication of irresponsible charges or misinformation that could ruin a person's reputation.

Before any inquiry was undertaken, the chairman or in some cases the chief counsel would define the scope of that inquiry. This prevented the launching of fishing expeditions. The inquiry so defined had to be related to the legislative process.

The institution of the executive session, which adversaries tried to label "Star Chamber proceedings," was a safeguard to insure responsibility. A witness first testified in executive or closed session for a variety of reasons, primary among them the fact that his testimony had to be evaluated. To give any witness, unassessed or uncorroborated, a platform to put into the public record evidence that could be damaging to another's reputation would be an act of irresponsibility.

To give a practical application: If the Subcommittee were to learn that a particular individual was a possible source of evidence bearing on the inquiry, the chairman would be asked to issue him a subpoena. The summoned individual would be advised of his rights, would be allowed counsel should he choose to be so represented, and would be heard in executive or secret session.

All the constitutional safeguards contained in the Bill of Rights were accorded him, particularly his rights under the First and Fifth Amendments.

If he believed that an answer by him could prove to be even a link in a chain of evidence that could lead to his conviction for a crime, he could legally invoke his privilege under the Fifth Amendment of the Constitution. If, however, an admission could not conceivably so incriminate him, he could not justifiably invoke Fifth Amendment privilege.

After the executive session was held, the testimony and the evidence adduced were evaluated by the Subcommittee and staff. If that testimony and evidence were judged responsible, credible, verified, and relevant to the inquiry, an open session would be scheduled. The witness' testimony would then go into the public record to inform the Congress (and, incidentally, the people of the United States).

Before doing this, however, certain safeguards first had to be met. If a person was named in the testimony in an incriminating or dangerous manner—such as calling him a Communist or ex-Communist—that person would be subpoenaed and given an opportunity to deny or qualify the previous testimony before

48

the latter would be made public. If the person elected to invoke Fifth or First Amendment privilege, that fact would be appended to the public testimony. If he issued a denial, that denial would be recorded and the party so named would be given an opportunity to testify for the record.

7

How the Congressional Committees Were Destroyed

THE UNITED STATES government has the right and duty to protect its people. This is set forth clearly in the preamble of the Constitution which declares that the government was created to "establish justice, insure domestic tranquility, and provide for the common defense."

This obligation has been reiterated and reaffirmed in hundreds of judicial decisions and legislative enactments, stretching over the two centuries of our national existence.

The United States is threatened today by a force that makes little concealment of its intent to destroy our country and our institutions and to subjugate our people. This threat takes many forms, ranging from potential direct military attack to subversion, to acts of terror, to espionage, and to undermining the morale of the United States by the dissemination of false and seditious propaganda.

It seems incredible that I must begin this chapter by setting forth a proposition as elementary as the right of the United States to defend its security. Yet this precept is widely challenged even as I write these lines.

Back in the 1950s when there was an awareness of the Communist threat in the United States, both the executive branch of the government and the Congress created institutions to protect the security of the nation. The Committees of Congress were able to operate freely and an enormous amount of information bearing on the Soviet conspiracy, not only against the United States but against other countries, was put into the public domain. This information served as a tremendous educational force. The American people were alerted to the fact that the United States was targeted by the Communists for destruction.

In a long series of decisions, the courts have clearly endorsed the legality and propriety of these efforts by the executive branch and the Congress to defend the United States. In the case of *Barsky* v. *United States,* that was made clear when the Court said:

> The prime function of governments, in the American concept, is to preserve and protect the rights of the people. The Congress is part of the government thus established for this purpose.
>
> This existing machinery of government has power to inquire into threats to itself . . . for the basic reason that, having been established by the people as an instrumentality for the protection of the rights of the people, it has an obligation to its creators to preserve itself. . . .
>
> We think that inquiry into threats to the existing form of government . . . is a power of Congress under its prime obligation to protect for the people that machinery of which it is a part. . . . It would be sheer folly as a matter of governmental policy to refrain from inquiry into potential threats to its existence or security.[1]

The case of *United States* v. *Josephson* was even more explicit in its conclusion:

> One need only recall the activities of the so-called fifth column in various countries both before and

[1]*Barsky* v. *United States,* 167 F (2) 241

during the late war [i.e., World War II] to realize that the United States should be alert to discover and deal with the seeds of revolution within itself. And if there be any doubts on this score of the power and duty of the Government and Congress to do so, they may be resolved when it is remembered that one of the very purposes of the Constitution itself was to protect the country against danger from within as well as from without.[2]

In its 1955 report, after lengthy hearings on procedural rules for investigating committees of the Senate, the United States Senate Committee on Rules and Administration said:

Committees of Congress must function in a world of realities. . . . The global Communist apparatus is neither a study group nor a debating society. It is an engine of destruction. Cunningly fashioned, its component parts are artfully disguised when disguise carries advantage. It is no answer to its challenge to say that the beliefs and associations of its members or suspected members are "private" and thus beyond the scope of legitimate inquiry by Congress. . . . Congress has a legitimate function to perform in this field—that of informing itself and the public of the nature and extent of Communist penetration into our free institutions.

It is noteworthy that all during the period when the Committees of Congress were able to operate freely, when the Subversive Activities Control Board held some hearings in its particular jurisdiction, and when the Internal Security Division of the Department of Justice proceeded to prosecute lawbreakers, not only did the nation experience a relative calm within its borders, but world Communism was successfully contained.

Our secretary of state at the time was John Foster Dulles, a

[2] *United States* v. *Josephson* 165 F (2) 82

52

statesman who forged a foreign policy directed toward the extension of human liberty and the containment of world Communism. However, John Foster Dulles died in 1959. Then one by one those senators who had been most courageous in supporting the work of internal security died or retired, and they were seldom replaced by men of comparable determination. Sensing this, the Communist forces within the United States moved in for a campaign to destroy the entire internal security system.

Actually, the Communists had begun their organized assault on American security much earlier. Let me quote from a letter by the Security and Intelligence Fund released in June 1977. Before doing so, I should explain that the fund was organized by a group of dedicated and prominent Americans who were appalled to find that the Justice Department under the Carter administration was not only liquidating its activities against subversives, but was actually launching criminal action against dedicated FBI agents whose "crime" was that they had resorted to electronic surveillance against revolutionary terrorist organizations.[3]

[3]The Security and Intelligence Fund includes among its sponsors and members:
The Honorable Robert B. Anderson, former secretary of the navy and of the treasury
Admiral G. W. Anderson, former chief of naval operations and chairman of the President's Foreign Intelligence Advisory Board
Ambassador Shelby Cullom Davis, former United States ambassador to Switzerland
Ambassador Loy W. Henderson, former deputy under-secretary of state
Rear Admiral (ret.) R. H. Hillenkoetter, former director of the CIA
Ambassador William Kintner, former United States ambassador to Thailand
Charles J. V. Murphy, former senior editor of *Fortune* magazine
Senator George L. Murphy, president, American Cause
Lieutenant General W. W. Quinn, United States Army (ret.), former director of the Defense Intelligence Agency
Colonel G. R. Weinbrenner, United States Air Force (ret.), former commander, Foreign Technology Division
James Angleton, former chief of counterintelligence of the CIA

In this letter, the fund stated: Since 1948 the Communists have been running a campaign to defame and discredit U.S. departments and intelligence agencies responsible for national security. Their main targets have been the FBI and the CIA.

In the early 1960s our intelligence community obtained full details of this plan.

Congressman C. Melvin Price, now chairman of the House Armed Services Committee, put a summary of this secret plan into the *Congressional Record* on September 28, 1965. (page 25391) This showed that a central purpose of the Disinformation Department of the KGB was to "destroy the confidence of the Congress and the American public in U.S. personnel and agencies engaged in anti-Communist and Cold War activity."

In 1951 the U.S. Communist Party set up a front called the Emergency Civil Liberties Committee (so cited by the House Committee on Un-American Activities).

The ECLC devised "OPERATION ABOLITION" to campaign for the elimination of intelligence activities like: (1) the House Committee on Internal Security; (2) the Senate Internal Security Subcommittee; (3) the internal security committees in state legislatures; (4) state and city police files on subversives; (5) the Subversive Activities Control Board; (6) the Internal Security Division of the Department of Justice; (7) the counterintelligence functions of the CIA; and (8) the internal security functions of the FBI.

All of the above have been abolished except for the FBI and CIA.

Ambassador Elbridge Durbrow, retired career diplomat
Brigadier General Robert C. Richardson III, United States Air Force (ret.)

But the FBI and CIA had been so badly shattered that they no longer have adequate internal security or counterintelligence capabilities.

So much for the beginnings of this Moscow-directed effort to tear down our internal ramparts against Communist subversion. Let us return now to the 1960s.

Careful study of the radical press of the time and particularly of the *Daily Worker* reveals the strategy of attack. The plan called first for the dismantling of the Subversive Activities Control Board. The Internal Security Division of the Justice Department was marked for emasculation. Attacks on the counterintelligence departments of the nation's police forces began to mushroom.

The attack persisted and was intensified during the 1960s. Naturally, the onset of the Vietnam War was grist for its mill. Many years before, General MacArthur had warned the United States not to get embroiled in a war on the Asian mainland because this was the sort of war we could not win and because it would create war weariness in the hearts of the American people. Nevertheless, we sank deeper and deeper into the Vietnam quagmire.

Conflict over Vietnam provided an atmosphere that was most propitious for the people who wanted to destroy American internal security. They persisted with their campaign all during the long and sanguinary 1960s.

As we came into the 1970s, those people began to enjoy conspicuous success. The Subversive Activities Control Board had been the first to go—the Justice Department sent it no cases to adjudicate. Then came the Internal Security Division of the Department of Justice. More and more, the attacks concentrated on the counterintelligence agencies of state and city police, which had amassed over the years invaluable files on revolutionaries, subversives, terrorists, and potential political assassins. The attack also began to turn against the Committees of Congress themselves.

Every year a small minority in the House invariably moved to abolish what was then called the House Committee on Un-

American Activities. During the 1960s the average vote for dismantlement of the Committee was a mere 27. Then came the 1970s and the momentum we have already described began to make itself felt. In 1970, 307 votes were cast to continue the Committee, 52 against. By now the Committee had been given a new title, the House Committee on Internal Security, and had been downgraded from a standing committee of the House to a subordinate component of the House Judiciary Committee.

In 1971 the vote was 298 to 75 for continuance. The following year, there were 303 yeas and 102 nays. This was about the peak strength achieved by the enemies of internal security. In 1973 the tally was 289 to 101. In 1974 247 voted to continue the Committee, 86 were opposed, and, in a new development, 99 abstained.

For the story of how the Committee was finally destroyed, let me quote Frank McNamara, a dedicated public servant who was a senior staff member of the House Committee, and who served between 1970 and 1973 as executive secretary and chief clerk of the Subversive Activities Control Board:

> A chance to accomplish their objective by other means developed in 1973 when the House decided that reorganization of its committee structure was called for. Rep. Richard Bolling (D-Mo), a Committee foe, was appointed chairman of the ten-man select committee to hold hearings and submit a reorganization plan. Its proposed plan, as expected, called for abolition of the Committee and transfer of its jurisdiction to the Judiciary Committee.

> Did its hearings actually justify this recommendation? Not at all, though its record was ostensibly impressive, and most people therefore concluded that it must have had a very solid foundation for its proposal. It had held thirty-seven days of hearings in which sixty-five members of the House (including Speaker Albert and Minority Leader Ford), six key staff aides (staff directors and general counsel), and

twenty-eight representatives of national organizations testified. In addition, forty-six panelists, professors of government and political science from top-ranking universities, and Ph.D.'s from prestigious foundations and research centers, took part in panel discussions and submitted working papers.

How many of these 145 contributors to its deliberations recommended abolition of the Committee and transfer of its duties to Judiciary? Exactly five: four House members—Frenzel of Minnesota, Koch of New York, George Brown of California, and Drinan of Massachusetts—and Ralph Nader! (Bella Abzug of New York, Lucy Benson of the League of Women Voters, and Yale's Professor Thomas I. Emerson, speaking for the National Committee Against Repressive Legislation, wanted it abolished with no transfer of jurisdiction.)

So the Bolling Committee's recommendation represented the view of one-sixteenth of the House members who testified and one-third of one percent of all who participated in its proceedings.

The overall Bolling proposal sparked so much opposition that it later came up with a new one, recommending internal security's transfer to the Government Operations Committee (in response to an Ichord plea) and the abolition of three other committees.

Eventually three different plans were submitted to a House vote on October 2, 1974, each one calling for abolition of the Committee and transfer of its function to another. All were defeated in a straight, stand-up-and-be-counted vote—246 to 164.

The left-liberal clique had been defeated, but not for long. They laid their next plan well, taking full advantage of the fact that they now had what they never had before—a colleague, Philip Burton of California, as chairman of the Democratic Caucus.

The caucus met, as usual before the opening of each new Congress, in early January 1975. Burton, aided by the party's old left-liberals and the great majority of its new, young "reform" members, rammed through the caucus by a voice vote (no tally) several changes in House Rules, including one that eliminated the Internal Security Committee and supposedly transferred its jurisdiction to the Judiciary Committee.

When the new Congress convened on January 14, these new Rules were put before the House for vote a few minutes after the session opened—and under a procedure permitting no amendments. Republicans did not even know what the proposed changes were until they were read on the floor. There was no chance for adequate debate, much less time to prepare for it.

Every member had to vote for the Rules as they were, or put himself or herself in the position of opposing all Rules and thus preventing the House from acting on anything until a new set of Rules could be proposed, debated, and approved. Even so, 172 members, Democrats as well as Republicans, opposed the new Rules being voted on as they were. . . . However, a vote was taken and the Rules were adopted, 259–150.

Thus, by railroading and sleight of hand, the Internal Security Committee opposition won the day. The "transfer to the Judiciary" wording of the new Rules was completely phony. It provided only that the "property" (including invaluable files, collected over a period of forty-five years) of the Internal Security Committee would be transferred to the Judiciary Committee and that an undetermined number of the

Committee staff members would also be transferred (for some indeterminate period) to the Judiciary Committee, with their salaries paid out of House, not Judiciary Committee, funds. It was clear that, with Judiciary's subcommittees chaired overwhelmingly by leftists and liberals, it would never undertake any investigation of Communism or other subversive and revolutionary activities. (As of November 1975, most Internal Security Committee staff members had been fired, no investigations undertaken, and no Judiciary subcommittee formed to investigate subversion, while a special Judiciary subcommittee was still wrestling with the question of what to do with those voluminous and dangerous—to subversives—files.)

The House had a beautiful opportunity to correct the situation on March 21, 1975, when the appropriation for the Judiciary Committee was brought up on the floor. More than $1,800,000 was requested (about four times what the Internal Security Committee normally received), without a single word indicating it would do anything about internal security.

Rep. John Ashbrook (R-Ohio) introduced a resolution to increase its appropriation by $300,000, all of it to be earmarked for internal security work. He pointed out that the Judiciary Committee had done nothing to implement the "transfer" rule and that when he had talked to knowledgeable people about the matter, they sort of winked and said, "Well, we might study this thing for a year or so."[4]

Ashbrook's resolution was defeated, 206–169. The House had made its position clear.

After the House Internal Security Committee was rendered

[4] *The Case for Internal Security.* A.C.U. Educational Research Institute, 1975.

inoperative, the Senate Internal Security Subcommittee was targeted for eclipse. At the outset its funds were increasingly challenged and then reduced in size. Finally in 1977 it was merged with the Criminal Activities Subcommittee of the Senate Judiciary Committee where it is now virtually dormant.

Guidelines were issued by Republican and Democratic attorneys general restricting the FBI. Vast reorganizations were undertaken, supposedly to eliminate past abuses on the part of the FBI and CIA, but actually of a sort that would predictably cripple these two remaining strongholds of the nation's security. Drastic reorganization was coupled with the selective elimination of senior officials who had distinguished themselves in effective anti-Communist operations, with a drum-roll of adverse publicity on alleged illegal and tyrannical FBI and CIA acts designed to cast these agencies into public disrepute, with crippling surveillance and interrogation by a swarm of congressional committees, and with the issuance of guidelines that would make both intelligence and counterintelligence work extremely difficult.

8

The Wreckage of the FBI

ONLY A FEW years ago, the FBI was regarded as the outstanding law enforcement agency in the world. Under its veteran director, J. Edgar Hoover, it had acquired an international reputation for integrity, for dedication to duty, for public service, and for impartial enforcement of the laws of the land. The work of the FBI in destroying the gang terror and Prohibition Era lawlessness of the 1920s and 1930s was matched by its prompt and effective eradication of Nazi espionage nests in World War II and its invaluable activities in bringing Communist spies, subversives, and terrorists to justice in the 1950s, 1960s, and 1970s.

The FBI man was popularly regarded as an example for young Americans. He combined courage, decency, respect for law, integrity, and dedication to country.

In the course of a few brief years, all this has changed. Orchestrated by the Communist Party, which feared the FBI more than any other agency of the government, confused people in influential positions, launched a campaign against the FBI to achieve three purposes:[1]

---

[1] While the media carry the tag lines of "extensive abuses of J. Edgar Hoover's FBI," pinpointing these is difficult. The Department of Justice, rather inexplicably, conducted a two-year investigation into these alleged abuses and the most serious finding was that over almost a

61

(1) To smear the organization in the public mind and, in particular, to heap abuse on the head of its creator, J. Edgar Hoover, at a time when Hoover was dead and no longer able to defend himself.

(2) To make the American people completely change their view of the organization. Instead of portraying FBI men as outstanding Americans, they were to be depicted as abusers of personal rights. Instead of public servants dedicated to the defense of their country, they were to be considered reactionaries and intruders on personal liberty.

(3) On this tide of evil propaganda, the Carter administration proceeded to shatter the FBI as a rampart of American internal security. It did this by indicting its senior officials or subjecting them to other forms of unbearable harassment. It tied up the agency much as Lemuel Gulliver was bound by the Lilliputians. Mickey-Mouse "guidelines," begun by Attorney General Levi, and unworkable procedural requirements, coupled with the almost total eradication of the internal security divisions of the Bureau, completed the great task of making America safe for those ideologically committed to her destruction.

When the Associated Press reported on June 6, 1977, that the number of domestic security cases under investigation by the FBI had been slashed from 4,868 to 214, this was not enough to satisfy Representative Don Edwards, the California Democrat who chaired the House Civil Rights Committee. Edwards said that he planned quickly to prepare a bill "that would limit the Bureau to criminal investigations."

---

half-century of service some FBI agents had constructed a fishpond in the director's yard.

The most cited abuse of Hoover was his "harassment" of Martin Luther King, the civil rights leader. The surveillance of Dr. King, however, was ordered not by Hoover, but by Attorney General Robert Kennedy who was moved to action by specific evidence.

When the Senate Intelligence Committee looked into this particular abuse, the FBI submitted to that panel a 55-page memorandum that set forth the reasons for the surveillance. Not only did the Committee quash the memorandum but the Southern Christian Leadership obtained a federal court injunction sealing off the evidence from access to any other congressional committee or government agency.

Any such limitation would make the country helpless against terrorist attacks by such political revolutionary organizations as the Weathermen and the Puerto Rican FALN. If the FBI and local police are prevented from infiltrating these organizations and gathering information about their methods, membership, and plans *before* they commit new bomb outrages and murders, it will be powerless to protect the country against them.

FBI investigation of the Weathermen has led to the iniquitous prosecution of Special Agent John Kearney who headed this probe. The Weathermen are a terrorist offshoot of the Communist Party. A few years ago they blew up a house in New York City, killing three of their own members who had not yet acquired proficiency in handling explosives. More recently they bombed a State Department office and various defense installations in California and engaged in scores of other acts of terror and violence. In March 1971, J. Edgar Hoover testified that the FBI had sketches and photographs of 158 of the Weathermen activists and that "over 1,544 individuals adhered to the extremist strategy of the Weathermen."

One would think that any decent American would wish the Weathermen to be kept under surveillance and would consider FBI agents who carried out this hazardous duty worthy of the thanks of a grateful nation. In the opinion of Attorney General Griffin Bell, however, these FBI officials are more deserving of criminal prosecution.

One who bears a major responsibility for the emasculation of the FBI and the dismantling of American internal security is Vice President Walter Mondale. Addressing the American Bar Association in Chicago on August 9, 1977, Mondale said that President Carter would submit what he called "legislative charters" for "citizen protection" to the Congress. This would prevent the CIA from espionage directed against American citizens (even when these Americans were believed to be linked with international spy rings). The FBI would be severely restricted in the investigation of "political organizations" in the name of "domestic security."

After his address, the Vice President told reporters he believed warrants should be issued only on evidence of a crime, not on the basis of an act harmful to national security. What this apparently means is that the FBI and other agencies are to be barred from collecting evidence and files against known terrorists until they are linked to a specific crime, and that the FBI will be barred from taking such precautions against known revolutionary and terrorist organizations until an organization itself, as distinct from some of its members, is tied in to a specific crime.

This interpretation creates a sanctuary for Communist organizations and terrorist bands in the planning of espionage, hijacking, sabotage, and even presidential (and, let us add, vice-presidential) assassination.

The havoc that has been inflicted on the FBI is clearly and eloquently described in a letter dated December 12, 1977, written to raise money for the legal defense of FBI official John Kearney. I am allowed to quote from the letter, but not to identify its author. Since the letter tells the whole story, I shall reproduce it here in full:

> I know I speak on behalf of all my fellow agents in the FBI, and our counterparts in the other national intelligence and law-enforcement agencies, when I express my deep appreciation for the tremendous work you are doing. Knowing that we have the support of the American people has helped enormously in maintaining our morale and our resolve to do our jobs. Successful continuation of your work becomes more important to us each day in maintaining our ability to protect American citizens from criminal elements at home and abroad.

> Much more is at stake than the best possible defense for John Kearney. In the last few years, a series of adverse developments has been hampering the morale and effectiveness of the FBI with grave risks to our country's security interests. I am writing to you *not* in my official capacity but rather as an

American citizen deeply concerned with what is happening. If you see fit to use any of this information, I ask that you keep my name and sources confidential.

A few examples of what is happening:

—In recent testimony before the Senate Subcommittee on Criminal Laws and Procedures, Stuart Knight, the chief of the Secret Service, admitted that there are now cities in the United States which the President is advised not to visit. The reason: the erosion of police intelligence as a result of leakages to the press and the laws on disclosure (notably the 1974 amendments to the Freedom of Information Act) has reached the point at which the actions of radical demonstrators and potential terrorists cannot be predicted.

—Security appraisal of government employees, even at sensitive levels, is now much reduced. The Civil Service Commission has dropped the formerly standard question put to would-be federal employees: "Are you, or have you ever been, a member of the Communist Party?"

—Over 120 present and former special agents have been called before grand juries for the same reason John Kearney has been indicted—because they took part in the Bureau's nationwide drive to track down terrorist Weathermen fugitives wanted for violent crimes against society.

—It has already cost the Special Agents' Legal Defense Committee most of the roughly $300,000 it has been able to raise from past and present FBI personnel to provide these agents with legal counsel. None has been indicted yet, except Kearney. But if formal charges grow out of any of these proceedings, there will be urgent need for additional large sums to pay trial costs.

—There are any number of FBI agents and officials (as well as their counterparts in the CIA, DIA, Secret Service, and other intelligence and law enforcement agencies) who are targets of a rash of *civil* suits filed by groups and individuals, both criminal and radical Communist, as part of the efforts to undercut U.S. intelligence operations. Damage claims run into the millions. Legislation has been introduced to provide defendants in such cases with immunity from damage judgments. This is running into stiff opposition from the ADA, ACLU, Common Cause, and similar groups, as well as some members of Congress.

The worry caused by these suits and by the criminal grand jury proceedings has instilled an attitude of excessive caution in the ranks of the FBI and all other intelligence and security agencies. We cannot be expected to pursue our assignments as vigorously as in the past if we are faced with possible criminal charges or huge damage judgments that will put us and our families in debt for years to come.

Stringent new guidelines for FBI domestic security investigations, imposed by Attorney General Levi in April 1976 and still in effect, strip the Bureau of the intelligence function the courts have said it has a *duty* to carry out, cripple its ability to make adequate use of informants, wiretaps, and mail covers, and fail to provide it with the authority to take affirmative action "to prevent . . . threats to life or property."

These guidelines are so unrealistic that they confer virtual immunity from investigation on Communist fronts and many revolutionary-terrorist groups. Even the Communist Party (which the Supreme Court has found is controlled by Moscow) is immune.

A shocking reduction in FBI investigation of domestic subversion has resulted from the imposition of these guidelines and recent policy changes. FBI Director Clarence Kelley revealed in September 1976 that its internal security investigations had then dropped from 21,414 in mid-1973 to only 626 (78 organizations and 548 individuals)—an amazing ninety-seven percent cut.

That number has dropped even more, according to a recent GAO report, to a mere 17 organizations and 130 individuals in the entire nation. GAO also reports that only 143 special agents are now assigned to domestic security work, compared to 788 in 1975, and that the Bureau today has only 100 informants compared to the 1,100 it employed two years ago.

Obviously, the FBI is collecting no information at all on numerous organizations and individuals that clearly fall into the subversive or terrorist category. A friend, now retired, who held the top intelligence post in the Bureau a few years ago, recently told me that the FBI, once acclaimed as the most efficient investigative body in the world, has been reduced to a "paper tiger."

The FBI cannot function efficiently alone. It must have supplemental information from varied domestic and foreign sources. In the past it had received great quantities of needed information from the CIA and other agencies which operate abroad, from state and local police, from banks, corporations, utilities, etc. Now this vital free flow of information is drying up, in part because of two laws passed by Congress —the Freedom of Information Act, which gives individuals and groups the right to obtain information about themselves held by government agencies; and the Privacy Act, which bars the government from releasing information on anyone without his consent.

Police and other local and state investigative agencies are withholding information from the FBI, fearful that their informants and sources will be compromised through disclosures compelled by Freedom of Information Act requests filed with the FBI. The reverse is also true. The FBI is not giving police and other local law-enforcement agencies information they need for fear of violating the Privacy Act. Other agencies with important security and intelligence law-enforcement functions are also victims of the information gap caused by these laws—the Secret Service, the Drug Enforcement Administration, and the Bureau of Alcohol, Tobacco, and Firearms, to name just a few.

Only subversives and criminals are winners in this game!

The FBI received 15,658 Freedom of Information Act (FOIA) requests in fiscal year 1977, an average of over seventy per working day. It costs Washington headquarters $9.1 million to handle them. Today, 379 headquarters employees, including 54 special agents, are tied up in full-time work on such requests (field offices in all parts of the country handle their own requests at added costs in dollars and personnel). Earlier this year over two hundred agents had to be brought in from field offices for a period of five months to help eliminate the backlog.

Hundreds of thousands of pages from Bureau investigative files have been released to criminals, Communists, and other subversives because of the FOIA. By careful analysis of their contents (and deletions) these elements can sometimes deduce the identity of informants and learn how, by switching their operational procedures, they can avoid or frustrate FBI surveillance.

They also use the documents to instigate press attacks on the FBI. In the thousands of documents they receive, there is evidence of effective FBI operations that would win praise from most Americans. By selectively releasing only certain of them, however, they know that they can provoke reporters of a certain type into writing accounts critical of the Bureau. Thus, they win two ways.

In 1970 the American Civil Liberties Union, which three years earlier had decided to reopen its doors to Communist Party members, launched a nationwide drive to destroy all domestic intelligence-gathering agencies. A key feature of its campaign was legal harassment. Four years later a top ACLU official was able to gloat over the fact that it, the National Lawyers' Guild, and similar groups had instituted about seventy-five lawsuits against the FBI, CIA, NSA, and numerous local and state police forces.

The destruction of vital police intelligence files has been one result of the combined ACLU, Communist, and "liberal" anti-intelligence assault. It has taken place in New York, Los Angeles, Washington, D.C., Baltimore, and Houston, to name just a few of the cities affected. New York City destroyed eighty percent of its police intelligence files relating to "public security matters" in 1973, including information on Puerto Rican extremist elements. When the Puerto Rican terrorist FALN exploded a bomb in Fraunces Tavern in early 1975, killing four bystanders and injuring over fifty, the police were unable to obtain any leads on the guilty. That crime remains unsolved to this day. The same is true of the series of FALN New York bombings of last summer which killed one man and injured scores.

There have been similar cases of needless injury, loss of life, and large-scale property destruction in other cities—largely because of intelligence file destruction, the imposition of unduly restrictive guidelines on police intelligence gathering, and, in some cases, the elimination of intelligence units. The FBI is severely affected because, in addition to the FOIA problem, the police simply don't have, and are not collecting, the intelligence they were able to pass on to the Bureau in the past.

Friendly foreign intelligence services are no longer giving the CIA as much information as they once did (some are not giving any) and the Agency is finding it more difficult to recruit individual foreign agents abroad—because of irresponsible congressional and media investigations, leaks and exposures of its secrets, and the Freedom of Information Act.

Morale is down for the same reasons, and also because of the shabby treatment given former Director Richard Helms and CIA Director Turner's decision to fire about nine hundred officers with years of experience in its clandestine service. All this affects FBI morale and effectiveness, as it does the CIA's, because the Agency does not have the quantity or quality of information about threats from abroad that it once had to pass on to the Bureau.

A nationwide *Campaign to Stop Government Spying* is now under way. Its object: to end *all* intelligence gathering within the U.S., to halt all covert operations abroad, and to compel detailed disclosure of the budgets of all intelligence agencies. Headquartered in Washington and chaired by Morton Halperin, the Campaign to Stop Government Spying lists forty-five member organizations, about thirty-three "cooperating" groups, and nineteen locally active affiliates in major cities, plus organized units at a dozen universities and individual contacts at a score more. It would not present so grave a problem if all its support groups were cited Communist fronts (as the National Lawyers' Guild and National Emergency Civil Liberties Committee are), or openly radical-revolutionary (like the Black Panther Party). Unfortunately, however, the ADA, ACLU, American Baptist Churches USA, Catholic Peace Fellowship, National Jesuit Social Apostolate, units of the Disciples of Christ, and Friends of the Earth are also included on its roster, providing at least semi-respectable cover for the organization's objectively evil and subversive aims.

A majority of experts predicts "an eventual increase in terrorist activity and an escalation of its intensity"—that was the finding of the Task Force on Disorders and Terrorism. It is confirmed by CIA and State Department studies which also indicate an even greater danger that foreign terrorists may attempt operations in this country.

The FBI has a duty to protect the security of our country and our people. Today it is seriously hampered in fulfilling this duty through the drying up of its sources, the cut in agents assigned to security work, the constant press criticism, grand jury probes and civil suits, and the restrictions imposed by new legislation and weak judicial interpretation of such legislation. When weighing all of this, you can understand the great importance of your Citizens' Legal Defense Fund toward maintaining the morale and confidence of the Bureau and all of those who serve in it.

The Fund cannot solve all the Bureau's problems. Too much has to be done in many other areas. But it is a ray of hope in a gloomy FBI world. It is a sign that the American people care, that they are intelligently concerned, that they want to help men who face serious financial problems today only because they have devoted their lives to protecting the country. For this we thank you.

To conclude the story: When the Senate Internal Security Subcommittee held hearings on September 18, 1975 on the National Drive Against Law Enforcement and Intelligence Agencies, it learned that the Baltimore police intelligence squad had been forced to destroy all its files on so-called "activist" groups. In a move toward what the mayor of Los Angeles described as "positive social change," the police intelligence unit destroyed almost two million entries in their files.

When the Hanafis gang of terrorists put Washington, D.C. under a state of siege in 1977 by holding hostages in the Anti-Defamation League Building, District police were almost immobilized because civil rights groups had succeeded in having all the files concerning the terrorists destroyed.

When the president of the United States travels within the country, the Secret Service relies on FBI files and the files of the intelligence units of the cities which he visits. Most people do not realize this. If enemies of American internal security have their way, the Secret Service may find it virtually impossible to prevent future tragedies comparable to Lee Harvey Oswald's assassination of President Kennedy.

9

Communist Party U.S.A.

THE JUSTICE DEPARTMENT indicted John J. Kearney, FBI Supervisor in New York, for tapping telephones and opening mail of contacts of the Weathermen. When it became apparent that the case would fail, Attorney General Griffin Bell announced that the Kearney indictment was a "mistake," but then he proceeded to indict the former Acting Director of the Bureau L. Patrick Gray, former Chief of Counterintelligence Edward Miller, and former Acting Associate Director W. Mark Felt. They were to be tried not in New York, but in Washington, D.C., where juries are more inclined to convict defendants identified with security.

The case against Kearney rested on wiretapping and unlawful mail openings that were not authorized. When evidence began to unfold that indicated they were authorized, the charge against Gray and his assistants was changed to "conspiring to injure and oppress citizens of the United States," i.e. contacts of the Weathermen.

These indictments, as we have shown, have greatly depressed the morale of the FBI. Moreover, they put into focus the ominous inversion of values that has imperceptibly been occurring over the last two decades.

A major emphasis of governmental activity has changed from thwarting subversion to prosecuting security forces for overzealous pursuit of these purposes. As a result there is a tendency to overlook the fount and the wellspring of the Weathermen, the Communist Party USA.

> In the spring of 1977 letters from radical activists
> appeared in the media contending that the FBI
> should not infiltrate and investigate "any lawful po-
> litical group." The writers contended that Congress
> must enact legislation that would prohibit the FBI
> from infiltrating lawful political groups on the
> grounds that they may commit a crime. They also
> contended that the FBI be limited to criminal inves-
> tigations.

Several months later (September 19, 1977) Senators Edward Kennedy and Frank Church urged Senator Birch Bayh, chairman of the Senate Intelligence Committee, which is charged with writing a new charter of the FBI, to restrict the Bureau to investigations of criminal activities. Senator Kennedy described the surveillance and monitoring of the Communists, the Socialist Workers' Party, and their fronts as intrusions on "lawful political activity."

All of this becomes ominous when one realizes that with the organization of the new Congress in 1979, Senator Kennedy became chairman of the Senate Judiciary Committee, which has jurisdiction over internal security, and that Senator Church became chairman of the Senate Foreign Relations Committee.

In other words, the Communists would have to commit a crime such as espionage, terror, hijacking, or sabotage before they could come under the scrutiny of the FBI.

This development overlooks the many, many crimes that never were committed because the FBI, being forewarned by informants or by surveillance, prevented their occurrence. It also, in effect, would give the Communists and their allies a sanctuary from which to carry on their revolutionary propaganda and subversion.

A dispatch appeared in the *New York Times* on August 14, 1977, which revealed that the Justice Department was moving

74

to reduce the FBI budget in 1979 to 516 million dollars, thirteen million *less* than the budget for 1978.

A consideration in their reductions is the fact that the Federal Bureau of Investigation now has 375 agents working full-time to comply with requests for file information under the Freedom of Information Act, with 200 more brought in from the districts, all at a cost of twelve million dollars.

This is a reflection of the campaign against the intelligence role of the Federal Bureau of Investigation.

A concerted campaign is being waged against even keeping files on so-called "domestic" political groups. And the principal "domestic" political group is the Communist Party USA.

The Communist Party USA is a complete instrument of the Soviet Union. Volumes of evidence have been adduced proving that relationship. When Leonid Brezhnev visited President Richard M. Nixon in Washington in 1973, he actually visited Gus Hall, the Party's chairman.

American Communist Party leaders visit Moscow and other Communist capitals regularly and become privy to Soviet and Chinese Communist secrets.

The CPUSA plays a chameleon role. During the period August 1939 to June 22, 1941, when the USSR and Nazi Germany were allies, the apparatus in the United States sabotaged and undermined our efforts to aid our allies. Upon the nullification of the Stalin-Hitler Pact, it did an about-face and enthusiastically supported our war efforts.

At the present time the Party itself, not taking into account its terrorist offshoots and its espionage functions, is assuming the role of a legitimate political party. This role may change tomorrow. Its members are for the most part United States citizens.

Thus technically this is a domestic political group. To contend, as do Morton Halperin and Jerry Berman and a goodly number of political observers, that the Communist Party should not be the subject of scrutiny by the FBI is suicidal.

When Senator Pat McCarran, chairman of the Internal Security Subcommittee, opened the Subcommittee hearings on the Institute of Pacific Relations, he said:

It is virtually impossible to define fully and accurately, in the abstract, the components of disloyalty or subversion. The inner currents of the human mind are at best difficult to gauge. Motives are often so obscure that sometimes one does not fully comprehend his own impelling urges, and may completely misjudge the motives of an associate. Successful conspirators usually are consummate dissemblers; and thus the acts of such persons are often shrouded in the darkness of stealth, accompanied by acts of misdirection, or clouded by ambiguity of meaning. The measurement of men's motives, the assessment of the strands of thought and the elements of pressure which may have influenced another's behavior, is not a task to be sought. And yet if we are to do our full part to save our country and our way of life from subversion and erosion, we must make the effort. But we must withhold our judgment in all respects until the proper time. We must first make the record, so that the facts will be known.

In such an investigation as this, where a possible conspiracy is being examined, very often the only evidence obtainable derives from persons who once participated in the conspiracy. Only eyes that witnessed the deeds, and ears that heard the words of intrigue can attest thereto. Thus, ex-Communists and agents of the Government who posed as Communists often are the only sources of evidence of what transpired behind doors closed to the non-Communist world. Government agencies do not readily yield up their concealed agents. Fortunately, it is possible to verify the loyalty of an ex-Communist, in large part, by the very extent of his willingness to give full and frank testimony against the Communist Party. Many ex-Communists have labored loyally and valiantly to expose the intrigues of their former associates. They often have no illusions about the Communist Party and its purposes, and have developed antibodies against further infection.

"Once a Communist, always a Communist" has become, in effect, a Communist slogan; but no one who professes to comprehend the significance of transgression and repentance, of wrongdoing and contrition, can subscribe to such a shibboleth. These facts must be borne in mind as, later in these hearings, the testimony of ex-Communists is used to supplement the evidence found in the files.

If anyone doubts the present tactical posture of the Communist Party under "détente," let me quote Gus Hall, chairman of the Party, speaking before the Young Workers' Liberation League in Chicago in February 1970:

In the movement there has been some discussion about the use of guns and the willingness to use guns. I agree with those who say it is a tactical question. Like all tactical questions, it must be measured by how it affects masses in struggle.

At this stage of struggle, what would be the result of such a tactical slogan? What would be the effect on the masses? Would it get a response from the people? I don't think so.

Would it be a tactic that would alienate those who are moving into the struggle? I think it would.

In an explosive period like this, this reality could change and so tactics would change. But for all those reasons it is not a correct tactical concept for today's reality. It would not advance the struggle.

Not only must the FBI penetrate the Communist Party to keep informed, but it must keep files on its members and with persons who collaborate with that political force, allied as it is to the USSR.

Moreover, if the Senate Internal Security Subcommittee had kept no files, it could not have issued its very informative report on the Weathermen.

In September 1975, even while the anti-intelligence lobby was attacking the agencies for keeping files, charging them with violating rights of citizens, the campaign took a perverse twist.

During that period there was a rash of assassination attempts. These very same critics began to criticize the FBI for not keeping files on such characters as Squeaky Fromme and Sara Jane Moore, who had fired shots at then President Ford. They turned out to be wielders of firearms directed at the president, but before their entrance onto the stage of high drama, they were like scores of thousands of others—incipient, potential, or suspect subversives.

This demonstrates clearly that the campaign was not really directed against the keeping of files but against the Bureau itself.

The charges against the agencies for keeping files are balderdash. If agents gather facts they must be either recorded or else committed to memory. The necessary act of recording is the creation of a file, and when it is indexed it becomes personalized. Requiring an operative to commit the results of his investigation to memory is patently absurd. Everyone has to keep files. Every homeowner, every businessman, every utility company, every credit company, and even the newspapers which are sniping at the intelligence agencies keep files. The newspapers call them morgues, and they are used by every venomous investigative reporter who wishes, for some ulterior purpose or pure sensationalism, to calumniate or defame some political enemy.

When you read the accounts of how Patty Hearst was apprehended, you realize how mischievous has been the campaign against "files" and intelligence techniques generally.

The FBI had information that Miss Hearst had spent some time in a farmhouse, allegedly aided by a former athletic director of a prestigious college. When they searched the farmhouse they found fingerprints of Wendy Yoshimura, a familiar figure on the Berkeley radical scene and a member of the Venceremos Brigade.

The FBI had violated the latter's civil liberties to the extent of keeping a file on her and had recorded her fingerprints. They also learned that a Volkswagen that visited the farmhouse was sold to one Kathleen Soliah who, according to those deplorable files, was merely "friendly" with some SLA members. The FBI pursued its course of violating citizens' rights and put a surveillance on the Soliah mailbox. This surveillance revealed that mail was being picked up and brought to two addresses, one of which proved to be the hideout of Patty Hearst and Wendy Yoshimura.

And yet the criticism of the FBI has been that they did not act fast enough in capturing Miss Hearst. Just suppose they had no files with which to work!

One corollary of the Hearst case was the re-emergence of the Venceremos Brigade.

Just a few years ago, the Senate Internal Security Subcommittee was endeavoring to call the attention of Congress to the danger posed to the nation by the practice of young men being sent to Cuba, with the help of the State Department, to cut sugar cane for Castro. These hearings brought out that some of these "youngsters" were being trained for future guerrilla warfare back in the United States.

Congress requited this effort by doing away with the House Internal Security Subcommittee and cutting in half the appropriation of the Senate Subcommittee.

Now the country is strewn with Wendy Yoshimuras and other time bombs who will be working irreparable damage in the years ahead.

We should not be deceived by how relatively few Communist Party members there are in the United States. Although small in number, the membership is an elite corps that directs its far-flung network of front organizations and collaborators in business, government, the media, labor unions, educational institutions, foundations, and even environmental and humane societies.

From time to time I come across a person occupying a high

and strategic position who I learned (when I labored in the field of internal security) was a Communist. All I can do is to let the FBI know about it. There are no committees of Congress interested in such information.

On the issue of small numbers, Henry Winston, a leading American Communist, wrote in *Political Affairs* (July-August 1977), the theoretical organ of the Communist Party USA:

> It is very interesting to note, comrades, that Lenin, in reference to the American and British Parties, speaks about a small Party with a correct policy and what it can accomplish. Let us keep in mind this quote from Lenin: "It is possible that even a small Party, the British or American Party for example, after it has thoroughly studied the course of political development and become acquainted with the life and customs of the non-Party masses, will at a favorable moment evoke a revolutionary situation. *Quite a small Party is sufficient to lead the masses. At certain times there is no necessity for big organizations. But to win, we must have the sympathy of the masses.*"

10

... And the Mice Will Play

WITH THE DESTRUCTION of internal security checks on U.S. government officials and employees, people began to gain employment in high posts of responsibility and power in the federal government who should have been ineligible on loyalty or security grounds.

In the Vietnam War, U.S. forces suffered 46,572 battle deaths and a total of 210,291 casualties. American officers and men were subjected by their North Vietnamese captors to obscene mistreatment, savage tortures, and hideous deaths.

The end of the struggle was that, for the first time in our history, the United States lost a war, and North Vietnam applied for a seat in the United Nations. As I wrote in a letter to the *New York Times*, her admission was a violation of the U.N. Charter since she was an aggressor nation. Nevertheless, she was admitted and the United States failed to exercise its veto power.

For most Americans, this was a sad and shameful occasion —but not for all. Let me quote an account of the admission of the North Vietnamese to the U.N. by Pranay Gupte in the *New York Times* on September 26, 1977:

> With an explosion of emotion yesterday, Vietnam's new delegation to the United Nations was greeted by thousands of its American friends and supporters,

many of whom had opposed the United States involvement in Indochina. In songs and speeches they suggested that a new, more harmonious era between the two countries was about to begin.

"Your presence here finally puts the past behind us," Cora Weiss, a long-time antiwar activist, said to the Vietnamese at a ceremony at the Beacon Theater, Broadway and 74th Street. Her reference seemed to be as much to the end of the Vietnam War as to the recent admission of that nation to the United Nations—admission that the United States had opposed several times.

As she spoke, dozens of supporters of what was once the Saigon government stood in the rain outside the theater and chanted slogans accusing the Vietnamese government in Hanoi of ignoring human rights. Occasionally a sharp argument would break out between the demonstrators and passers-by, and at one point it even looked as though there might be a fistfight. There were no arrests, although policemen watched warily.

Mrs. Weiss was repeatedly cheered during her speech, but the applause was loudest when she called on the Carter administration to provide financial assistance for the reconstruction of Vietnam.

She looked down from the dais at members of the Vietnamese delegation. She smiled; they smiled back.

"Welcome, welcome in the name of the American people," Mrs. Weiss shouted.

The audience of about 2,500 rose to its feet, roared, and clapped for many minutes.

As the cheering continued, Mrs. Weiss beckoned to the Vietnamese, four of whom walked up to the stage and, with their hands clasped above their heads, acknowledged the applause of the crowd, which had been invited by Friendshipment, a coalition of peace and religious groups in this country, with which Mrs. Weiss is affiliated.

One of the Vietnamese, Ngo Dien, the Deputy Foreign Minister of Press and Information, then stepped to the microphone and read a speech, a substantial portion of which was an attack on United States "imperialists."

"From such a long distance the American imperialists send half a million troops to wage a bloody colonial war," he said in English. "Yet no enmity exists between the Vietnamese and American people."

Heavy applause interrupted him.

Mr. Dien motioned for quiet, then continued: "How can we accept that those who dropped fifty million tons of bombs on Vietnam not contribute to the healing of war wounds?" There was more applause.

"Long live the friendship between the Vietnamese and the American people!" Mr. Dien declared.

The crowd once again rose to its feet and cheered.

Among those who applauded was Ramsey Clark, the former United States Attorney General. "I'm very happy to see Vietnam finally in the United Nations, where they [sic] belong," he said.

The man next to him nodded. He was Sam Brown, the former antiwar activist, now an official in the Carter administration.

"I am deeply moved," he said. "It's difficult to describe my feelings—what can you say when the kinds of things that fifteen years of your life were wrapped up in are suddenly before you?"

"I believe we ought to aid the Vietnamese in their reconstruction," Mr. Brown said, adding that he hoped President Carter could be persuaded similarly.

Then Pete Seeger sang a few songs, some from the days of the antiwar protests in which many of those in yesterday's audience had participated. Later there were hugs and kisses, much like at a class reunion.

"We've waited so long, so long for this day," said Evie Moore, who was among those present. There were tears in her eyes.[1]

Sam Brown, who was so "deeply moved" by being able to greet enemies of his country who had killed or maimed a quarter of a million Americans, had been chosen by President Carter to head ACTION, a government organization which includes the Peace Corps and various other organizations. These groups are supposedly composed of Americans who want to contribute from idealistic motives to the well-being of humanity, either at home or abroad.

In the hands of a responsible and qualified leader, ACTION could be an immense force for good in the world. In the hands of an enemy of the United States, it could be an instrument for the destruction of American institutions and ideals both at home and overseas. Mr. Brown's visible qualification for this strategic position was that he had been one of the main leaders of the great antiwar demonstrations which shook the United States in the 1960s and which were heavily infiltrated, and often controlled, by Communists and by dissident elements who wanted to see their country defeated on the battlefields of Vietnam. It seems odd that a President who

[1]Copyright © 1977 by The New York Times Company. Reprinted by permission.

stressed his career as a professional military man should appoint a person who first worked for his country's defeat in the Vietnam War and then emotionally embraced the butchers of his countrymen when we had lost it.

11

Decolonization, Disarmament, and Peaceful Coexistence

Trust us, comrades, for by 1985, as a consequence of what we are now achieving with détente, we will have achieved most of our objectives in Western Europe. We will have consolidated our position. We will have improved our economy. And a decisive shift in the correlation of forces will be such that, come 1985, we will be able to exert our will wherever we need to. We are achieving with détente what our predecessors have been unable to achieve using the mailed fist. . . . We have been able to accomplish more in a short time with détente than was done for years pursuing a confrontation policy with NATO.

Leonid Brezhnev[1]

In Soviet strategic thinking, the three primary weapons of global conquest in the second half of the twentieth century are decolonization, disarmament, and peaceful coexistence.

Immediately after World War II, the West was placed under tremendous pressure to give full and immediate independence to far-flung colonies that had provided it with geopolitical power, indispensable natural resources, and potential military manpower. Western rule, on the whole, had developed huge

[1] *Washington Post,* Feb. 12, 1977

regions of Asia and Africa toward more modern societies with emergent professional, educated, and middle classes, due process of law, representative government, individual freedom, and well-administered law enforcement and social services.

When the components of these empires were suddenly cast adrift without adequate preparation, they landed in political vacuums. These vacuums have often been swiftly filled by native revolutionaries, indoctrinated in Communism and generally controlled by the Soviet Union or, less often, by Communist China.

Thus the old colonialism, on the whole a constructive force for progress and civilization, has been replaced over enormous areas by a more aggressive, more coercive, and more authoritarian Soviet-dominated colonialism. Red vassal states have sprung up like mushrooms throughout Africa.

At the end of World War II, the United States had the greatest military establishment in the history of man. Not only did we have superiority in our navy, air force, and army, but we alone had the ultimate weapon—the atom bomb.

However, we began to disarm at once, and we did so at a precipitous rate. Between 1945 and 1950, U.S. army strength declined from over eight million men to fewer than one million men. Aggregate military forces were reduced from fourteen million in 1945 to 1.4 million in 1950.

The Russians did not disarm at anywhere near a comparable rate. Instead of turning toward peaceful pursuits, they waged a series of aggressions in Eastern Europe that caused us to pause in dismantling our military power.

Under the foreign policy of John Foster Dulles, with his doctrine of "massive retaliation" based on our nuclear weapons supremacy, we began to add ICBMs, Polaris submarines, and B-52s to our arsenal.

When the Hungarian Revolution erupted in November 1956 and the Hungarians appealed vainly to the U.S. for military assistance, we had a 100-to-1 nuclear supremacy over the Soviets.

In 1959, Khrushchev's Soviet Union was ringed by U.S. bases

in Allied countries. He recognized that our strategic air force and navy could utterly destroy the Soviet Union's economy, its military forces, and its power to wage aggressive war.

Under these conditions of decisive military inferiority, he proposed on November 18, 1959 total mutual disarmament to the U.N. General Assembly. He suggested that over a period of four years all states should divest themselves of all means of waging war.

The American reaction came soon. We proceeded to disarm.

Walt W. Rostow and Jerome Weisner, advisors to the newly-elected President, John F. Kennedy, went to Moscow in late 1960 and returned with disarmament plans. Bilateral talks ensued in Washington from June 19 to June 30, 1961, in Moscow from July 17 to 29, and in New York from September 6 to 19. By September 20, 1961, we had actually arrived with Valerian Zorin, the Soviet delegate to the U.N., at eight agreed-upon principles of disarmament. They included:

• Disbanding of armed forces, dismantling of military establishments, including bases, and cessation of the production of armaments, as well as their liquidation or conversion to peaceful uses.

• Elimination of all stockpiles of nuclear, chemical, bacteriological, and other weapons of mass destruction and cessation of the production of such weapons.

• Elimination of all means of delivery of weapons of mass destruction.

• Abolition of the groups and institutions designed to organize the military effort of nations, cessation of military training, and closing of all military training institutions.

• Discontinuance of military expenditures.

On September 25, 1961, the U.S. proposed to the United Nations Disarmament Committee a "Program for General and Complete Disarmament." We envisaged three stages of disarmament and provided for United Nations "committees of experts" to direct them and verify compliance. No mention was made of how verification was to take place. As the military establishments and armaments of the nations declined, the authority and power of the U.N. Peace Force and the "International Disarmament Organization" were to grow. This extraordinary document concluded:

> States would retain only those forces, non-nuclear armaments, and establishments required for the purpose of maintaining internal order; they would also support and provide agreed manpower for a U.N. Peace Force. . . .
>
> The manufacture of armaments would be prohibited except for those of agreed types and quantities to be used by the U.N. Peace Force and those required to maintain internal order. . . .
>
> The peace-keeping capabilities of the United Nations would be sufficiently strong and the obligations of all states under such arrangements sufficiently far-reaching as to assure peace and the just settlement of differences in a disarmed world.

Thus our own planners began to move toward creation of a world force under the United Nations which would, in effect, rule the world. In his speech at American University on June 10, 1963, President Kennedy defined our primary long-term goal at the Geneva negotiations as "general and complete disarmament." The President supported transformation of the United Nations into a world government: "a genuine world security system—a system capable of resolving disputes on the basis of law, of insuring the security of the large and the small, and of creating the conditions under which arms can finally be abolished."

The President went on to formulate our arms policy as such "that it becomes in the Communists' interest to agree on a genuine peace." He said that he intended to avoid confrontations, military or diplomatic, which might hinder the progress of disarmament.

Robert S. McNamara became our secretary of defense, and during the almost eight years of his tenure the United States adopted no new weapons systems. On the contrary, we began actively to dismantle our existing ones. By the late summer of 1963, our B-47 fleet had been cut in half; other military aircraft we simply did not replace, allowing age and wear to take their heavy toll. We stopped development of new missiles, such as the Skybolt and the Nike-Zeus, and dismantled existing missile bases all over Europe.

During this period, the government secretly financed "think factories" where university professors received grants to propagate the official line on disarmament. Books and studies were published calculated to mold "mature" and "informed" public opinion.

Dr. Morton H. Halperin energetically promoted unilateral United States disarmament. On October 6, 1961, he suggested in a paper ("A Proposal for a Ban on the Use of Nuclear Weapons") that the United States should disarm even if the Russians did not. In this study for the Institute of Defense Analysis, a think factory that had substantial foundation support, Halperin wrote: "It might be stressed that inspection was not absolutely necessary," and he added that "the United States might, in fact, want to invite the Soviets to design the inspection procedures if they seem interested in them." A decade later, the White House ordered Halperin's telephone bugged to see whether he was betraying official secrets.

Dr. Lincoln P. Bloomfield, formerly with the State Department Disarmament Staff and then with the Arms Control Project at the Center for International Studies at MIT, was also active in promoting world government through disarmament. In a paper entitled "In a War Effectively Controlled by the United Nations" (March 10, 1962), Dr. Bloomfield asked: "And how can the American people be conditioned to accept the State Department plan to eliminate national armies and replace them with a U.N. police force?" He answered that if the world were taken to "the brink" through a series of "unnerving trips," it could be accomplished.

A new approach evolved. Instead of superiority, "mutual deterrence" became the prevailing policy of our planners. It was said that the Russians were building their nuclear arsenal out of a sense of insecurity and that this insecurity was the cause

90

of the arms race. Therefore, we should allow them to reach "parity" with us, and because of this insecurity, a little more than "parity" could be tolerated.

When President Nixon came to power, under the guiding hand of Secretary of State Henry Kissinger "sufficiency" replaced "parity." We allowed the Russians to achieve significant superiority in ICBMs and decisive superiority in nuclear throw-weight.

Meanwhile the Russians moved on to achieve a first-strike capability. They boasted, contrary to theoreticians who contended that no one can win a nuclear war, that they could win a nuclear encounter *and survive.*

The disarmament drive seems irresistible. As the United States prepared for a third strategic arms limitation conference, President Carter decided to abandon unilaterally the production of the B-1 bomber that was to replace our aging B-52s, without asking for any Soviet concession in return. Long-range bombers, nuclear-powered submarines, and intercontinental ballistic missiles comprised the triad that was considered essential for successful defense of the nation in the event of a nuclear war. The amputation of one leg of this triad undermined the entire defense structure of the country.

The President declared that he would rely on the cruise missile borne by the B-52s instead. This decision was made despite the fact that the USSR was proceeding vigorously with the production of its near counterparts to the B-1, the Backfire* or Tupolev bomber and the Sukhoy attack plane, both of which could destroy Western Europe. If based in Cuba they could destroy United States cities as well.

This decision was made, even though it was known that the cruise missile was to be a highly debated pawn in the forthcoming Strategic Arms Limitation Talks where the Soviets would demand that it be sharply limited.

Opponents of the decision to halt the production of the B-1 recalled that Secretary McNamara had eliminated the

*At the end of 1978 the USSR had 150 Backfires and was building at a rate of 26 a year.

B-70 in the early 1960s when that planned replacement of the B-52s was in development, saying that he would rely on the Skybolt missile to extend the life of the then aging bombers. Shortly thereafter, McNamara killed the Skybolt even though Great Britain, which was to share that missile, protested strongly.

Jane's All the World's Aircraft declared in its 1977–78 edition that President Carter's decision to scrap the B-1 would bring about a Western defeat if a general nuclear war were to break out.

Jane's editor John W. R. Taylor, in an unusually biting commentary for that generally dispassionate and authoritative London annual, wrote that the B-1 decision may endanger the military balance that had prevented war between the two major powers for more than a generation.

Soviet leaders "must be surprised beyond belief that the U.S. President has disposed of the B-1 without asking any Soviet concession in return," Taylor wrote. "If our planet is subjected one day to the unimaginable horrors of a third world war, 1977 might be recorded as the year in which the seeds of defeat for the Western powers were sown."

That is strong language for an objective journal that commands the world's respect.

Taylor went on to minimize the effectiveness of the cruise missile. While it is a formidable weapon, it moves slower than the speed of sound and is incapable of jamming enemy defense radar.

Taylor further asserted that the United States need not have proceeded with the production of its estimated full fleet of 244 B-1s. "Even 100 B-1s would have compelled the Soviet Union to expend huge sums of money and immense effort in developing, producing, and maintaining defenses against air attack," he stated.[2]

The London report also pointed out that the United States was delaying replacement of its interceptors and other aircraft

[2]John W. R. Taylor, editor, *Jane's All the World's Aircraft 1977-1978* (New York: Franklin Watts Inc., 1977), p. 61.

while the USSR had given its squadrons a five hundred percent increase both in radius of action and in weapons load.

The same week of the *Jane's* publication (December 7, 1977), Paul Scott wrote that the Carter administration had abandoned the policy, in force since before the Cuban missile crisis of 1962, of overflying Castro's defense installations. The reason given to the House Committee on Appropriations by high State and Defense Department officials proved to be fatalistic rather than reassuring: "Since the build-up of intercontinental ballistic missiles in the Soviet Union has been very substantial since the time of the Cuban missile crisis, a few more ballistic missiles based in Cuba would be nowhere near as important as they were in 1962 when the Soviet Union had few ICBMs."

Paul Scott continued:

> Although administration officials refuse to discuss it, the Russians now have operating from Cuba *more* long-range bombers than they did during the Cuban missile crisis in 1962.
>
> These reconnaissance and nuclear-bomb-carrying bombers are now testing and trying to disrupt air defenses located on the eastern and southern coasts of the U.S. while photographing and mapping U.S. military installations and warships.
>
> As reported in an earlier column, their long-range objective is to develop a plan to neutralize the radar system designed to detect and alert U.S. defense forces to enemy aircraft and low flying cruise missiles launched from offshore submarines.
>
> Since the ending of the intelligence overflights makes it almost impossible for the U.S. to know exactly what now goes on at the Soviet bases in Cuba, the official position given the [Appropriations] Committee is that because of the ICBM build-up in Russia, the presence of Soviet missiles in Cuba, if there are any, is really not important.

Equally disturbing is the failure of Defense and State Department officials in their briefings of the lawmakers to mention the number (from 17 to 24) of Soviet bombers now stationed in and operating from Cuba.

Operating from *inside* the U.S. defense perimeter for the Western Hemisphere, these bombers have the capability of destroying one-third of the nation's industrial capacity and killing up to seventy million Americans in a surprise attack. Not even the Japanese at Pearl Harbor had this power to cripple the U.S.

Also completely ignored in these briefings is the fact that the Russians have gradually turned the strategic Caribbean island into an advance "offensive" military base for the purpose of expanding Soviet political and military influence throughout the world.

In light of these developments, it appears to be an appropriate time to ask ourselves: If this advance Soviet base can be used to support the immense military involvement of between 30,000 and 50,000 Soviet trained and equipped Cubans in Angola, Ethiopia, Mozambique, and no fewer than eight other African states, will it eventually be used against the Panama Canal and even to blackmail the U.S.?

Lieutenant General Daniel O. Graham, former head of the Defense Intelligence Agency, warned that "the Soviets have surpassed—or are surpassing us."[3]

Clare Boothe Luce, former United States ambassador to Italy and a former congresswoman, pointed to overwhelming Soviet superiority in ground forces: "The Soviets now have 168 ground divisions; we have 19. They have 45,000 tanks; we have 10,000.

[3] *Washington Report*, February 1977 (American Security Council).

94

Moreover, they have been building up this superiority in conventional weapons with incredible speed and single-minded determination since they signed the détente agreement."[4]

Peaceful coexistence, which we call "détente," is the third of the Soviet weapons of political warfare and conquest.

While the United States generally labels the relationship that exists between it and the Soviet Union "détente," theoreticians of the latter refer to it as "peaceful coexistence."

In my *Disarmament, Weapon of Conquest* (Bookmailer, 1963), I wrote as follows concerning peaceful coexistence:

> Khrushchev's peaceful coexistence is not a mystery. It is defined in the Communist Manifesto of 1960, in the draft platform of the Communist Party of the Soviet Union of 1961, the most authoritative Soviet source, and in official Soviet journals as a means to achieve world-wide victory. The Communist Manifesto of 1960 referred to it as an "intensification" of the world struggle. Assurances were given that "peaceful coexistence" does not mean, of course, "peace" in the class struggle between socialism and capitalism or reconciliation of the Communist with the bourgeois ideology. Peaceful coexistence means not only the existence of states with different social systems, but also a definite form of world-wide class struggle between socialism and capitalism.
>
> Khrushchev assured the comrades in 1961 that it involved "no compromise" in Soviet principles, but was, instead, an "intensification" of the world struggle.

Spokesmen for the USSR tend not to use the word "détente." They insist that it is inaccurate. They prefer "peaceful coexistence" or the Russian word *razryadka.* They define the latter

[4] *Washington Report*, March 1977.

as "the state of international relations resulting from the observance of the principles of peaceful coexistence."

This disagreement about terminology may seem academic, but it is not. The Soviet government is concerned with making absolutely clear to the Communist world and to its legions of supporters precisely what the new policy does and does not imply.

Soviet World Outlook, an authoritative publication of the Center for Advanced International Studies at the University of Miami, summed up the Soviet attitude toward détente in its January 15, 1976, issue. The article quoted *Pravda* (November 27, 1975) as stating that use of the word "détente" has "caused a certain confusion in the minds of American philistines. Americans do not properly understand it, and sometimes even associate it subconsciously with the word *entente* (understanding) or even *entente cordiale* (meeting of minds). . . ."

The Soviet journal *Za Rubezhom* echoed the same view. It pointed out that peaceful coexistence does not imply seeking the "preservation of the status quo," because such a world would be "as petrified and lifeless as a lunar landscape, a world without social cataclysms and storms, where imperialism could continue unhindered its tyranny in the areas remaining in its sphere of influence."[5]

Soviet publications characterize the condition of détente, as understood by the West, as "illusory," "dead," "bankrupt," and ignoring the "real" world of class struggle.

To avoid these confusions, the Soviets suggest that the United States and the West substitute the phrase "peaceful coexistence," which has been defined with "exhaustive clarity" in official Soviet documents and speeches by Soviet leaders.

Thus, Brezhnev declared that peaceful coexistence must be based on the premise that "the world outlook and class aims of socialism and capitalism are opposed and irreconcilable."[6] As the Soviet theoretical journal *Kommunist* asserts, peaceful co-

[5]*Soviet World Outlook*, vol. I, no. 1 (Jan. 15, 1976, Center for Advanced International Studies, University of Miami), pp. 2-3.
[6]*ibid.*

existence must be viewed as "a specific form of the class struggle in the international arena." Its purpose is to "assure favorable conditions for the world-wide victory of socialism."[7]

In the Soviet view, peaceful coexistence applies only to the relationships between states. It consists solely of agreements to avoid nuclear war or confrontations that might lead to nuclear war.

Peaceful coexistence, according to the Soviets, does not signify any moderation, but rather an intensification of competition and struggle in the economic, political, military-readiness, psychological, and ideological fields. However, the Soviets insist that intensified struggle can only be in one direction.

While Moscow reserves the right to do all it can to upset the socio-political order in any country of the West, including the U.S., it violently denounces as a revival of "Cold War anti-Communism" any thought of Western penetration of the Soviet Union through such means as intellectual exchanges, economic contacts, "building bridges," and dissemination of "convergence" theories.

Furthermore, the Soviets insist that peaceful coexistence means that the West is unilaterally restrained from "exporting counterrevolution," i.e., from opposing and resisting revolutionary and national liberation movements in the capitalist countries and the Third World.

Peaceful coexistence, as the Soviets explain it, does not even mean the avoidance of war. Peaceful coexistence aims only at avoiding war between the major powers and the Soviet Union. It does not preclude war by or on behalf of revolutionary and national liberation movements or "progressive" states in their struggles against what the Soviets call "imperialist aggression, oppression, and exploitation," nor does it preclude support of such wars by the USSR and other socialist states. Indeed, since 1971, Soviet authorities have increasingly characterized support of the global revolutionary and national liberation struggle as one of the main duties of the Soviet armed forces. It is in these terms that Moscow has justified its acts of aggression

[7]*ibid.*

and conquest in Angola, the Horn of Africa, and elsewhere.

The Soviets understand peaceful coexistence as a one-way street. As they see it, peaceful coexistence gives them the moral right to intervene in any country, anywhere in the world, to suppress human rights, to eradicate representative government, to abolish due process of law, and to transform the countries which they subvert, invade, or ravish into appendages of Moscow. In this manner, they propose to continue extending the domination of Moscow over larger and larger sections of the earth. The transformation of once-independent societies into satellites of the concentration camp known as the Soviet Union is described in Soviet propaganda in terms of such noble concepts as "liberation," but the reality is, of course, the opposite of the theoretical formulation.

Peaceful coexistence, according to the Soviets, precludes the United States, Japan, or any other country from resisting, from taking up arms in the cause of freedom, and from seeking to defend or assist in the defense of free nations threatened by the Soviet juggernaut.

This is an instance of the Communist use of double-talk, popularized by the late George Orwell in his caustic novels *Animal Farm* and *1984*, where the purpose of speech is to conceal the truth, and the purpose of language is to make black appear white, to make war seem to be peace, to make slavery take on the guise of freedom.

The Soviet concept of peaceful coexistence is a heads-I-win, tails-you-lose philosophy of politics. They are free to commit any and every kind of aggression. We in the West are not free to reply in kind. As Anatole France once wrote: "That is an evil animal: it defends itself when it is attacked."

Not only did the lure of détente cause the disregard of internal security, but it extended far into the realm of strategic East-West trade. Here is a column I wrote on this aspect of détente in February 1978:

> An accounting has yet to be made of the results of Henry Kissinger's many "initiatives" in foreign policy. When this ultimate tally is recorded, his efforts

to establish "economic détente" with the USSR should be highlighted.

The American Council for World Freedom has just released a study on strategic trade compiled by Miles M. Costick and several academic and military specialists. This study sets forth, with stunning specifics, the ominous consequences to the security of the United States of Kissinger's eight-year plan "to spin a web of vested interest" between us and the USSR by giving the latter access to almost limitless American technology. He rationalized this by saying: "Over time, trade and investment may leaven the autarkic tendencies of the Soviet system. . . ."

At the same time Kissinger negotiated SALT I which limited the U.S. to a three-to-two inferiority in missile launchers on the premise that we had qualitative superiority and the ability to put multiple warheads on our launches (MIRV).

His "economic détente," however, was responsible for the USSR's closing the qualitative gap in almost all military and strategic areas.

Here are only some of the technological exports, approved and even encouraged by the State Department, to the USSR:

1. 164 Centalign-B machines and accompanying technology that produce precision miniature ball bearings that enabled the USSR to close the MIRV gap by deploying 7100 MIRVS.

2. The KAMAZ-Kama River integrated heavy-duty truck plant in the USSR that apparently exceeds anything here in the U.S. This plant will have an annual production of 250,000 ten-ton multiple axis trucks, more than the capacity of the entire U.S. heavy duty truck industry. This is equipped with one of the largest industrial computer systems in the

world, provided by the IBM Corporation. It will produce 350,000 diesel engines per year even though KAMAZ will have the capacity to produce tanks, military scout cars, rocket launchers, and trucks for military transport. It was approved by Commerce and State as "non-strategic."

3. Extensive computer technology (where the USSR is inferior) that has been used in the advancement of Soviet military technology in missiles, aircraft, tanks, helicopters, surveillance systems, ABM defense systems, and submarines.

4. Twelve fifty-one-thousand-pound-thrust CF-6 jet aircraft engines, the most powerful in the world, for their cargo jets. These engines will enable the USSR to develop a new generation of manned bombers capable of carrying blockbusters against our cities.

By way of compounding this suicidal gesture we allowed much of this to be acquired on credit. Today the USSR and its allies owe the West more than sixty billion dollars—and this is now escalating. Even this deficit can be an asset to world Communism. It gives the Soviet bloc leverage, for, by threatening to default, it can cause economic and fiscal upheaval in Western financial circles.

The study also sets forth extensive evidence that the USSR is using and is planning to use this technology for military purposes against the U.S.A. and the West.

I entitled this column: "Seeding Our Own Destruction."
I have recently come upon an exchange that I believe epitomizes the mood of which I write.
At the beginning of this chapter I quoted a speech in which Leonid Brezhnev predicted that by 1985 world Communism would "be able to exert our will wherever we need to."
The *Washington Post* has a monopoly on the morning news-

paper field in the nation's capital. Every senator, congressman, and government official is exposed to its editorial viewpoint.

For that reason I compared the reaction of Murray Baron, president of Accuracy in Media, to the comments of Phil Geyelin, editor of the editorial page of the *Post*, at the annual meeting of stockholders of the Washington Post Company on May 11, 1977.

When Accuracy in Media criticized the *Post* for playing down the significance of the secret papers found in the briefcase of the slain Chilean exile Orlando Letelier, revealing that he had been not the quixotic romanticist who had been eulogized by Washington officialdom and some Catholic prelates, but a paid agent of Fidel Castro, the following comment was made by Geyelin:

> The first thing to point out—it is really necessary, I think—is that AIM is not interested in accuracy. It is interested in the media only as a means of putting forth its own particular view on a very narrow range of issues. *It is a perfectly respectable view. It's a minority view. The issues are very narrow.* We never hear from Reed Irvine about welfare reform or civil liberties or the energy crisis. *We only hear about a narrow range of national security questions, mostly having to do with the threat of international Communism.* He has one view. *It's a very extreme view.* His organization has one view. We think we cover it adequately, given the amount of evidence there is to support it and the number of people who hold it. And I think that the Letelier case is a very good example.

Then Murray Baron, President of AIM, told Mr. Geyelin that any effort to portray AIM as being reflective of a narrow view would fail. He pointed out that its National Advisory Board included some very notable civil libertarians and conventional liberals. He himself had been a founder of the ADA and the Liberal Party, and he had served for years as a trustee of Freedom House. "I always assume," Mr. Baron said, "that it is

101

quite consistent with conventional liberalism to be anti-communist, anti-fascist, and anti-racist."

But, most important for the issue I raise here, Mr. Baron noted that Mr. Geyelin had described anti-Communism as a narrow issue. He observed that the heads of the seven nations who had just met in London thought that it was more than a narrow issue. He said that AIM was supported by those who had joined together because they thought there was a constitutional imbalance in America that could not be corrected.

AIM, he said, was one component of a growing awareness that the only way to curb excesses of the media in a free society is to use the resources, techniques, and philosophies of the media, criticizing them when this was justified. He said he personally was concerned about the "Finlandization" of the media that was already taking place in Italy and Western Europe (referring to deferential treatment of Communism). Mr. Baron concluded: "Mr. Geyelin, don't ever define anti-Communism as a narrow issue."

Here then is a concrete example of the influences putting Washington into a somnolent mood while Soviet imperialism roars on to its avowed goal.

Some years earlier, in July 1961, Senator William Fulbright, then chairman of the powerful Senate Foreign Relations Committee, sent a secret memorandum to the president and secretary of defense, requesting the cancellation of a 1958 White House directive which called for making use of "military personnel and facilities to arouse the public to the menace of the Cold War."

The senator declared, "Fundamentally, it is believed that the American people have little, if any, need to be alerted to the menace of the Cold War." He stated that there are "dangers involved in education and propaganda activities by the military, directed at the public. . . ." Specifically, he went on to say that the menace of the Cold War as described in these activities "has great appeal to the public," and therefore the "principal problem for [administration] leadership will be, if it is not already, to restrain the desire of the people to hit the Communists with everything we've got. . . ."

The late Rear Admiral Chester Ward, an expert on naval affairs and international law, answered the Fulbright memorandum and coined the term "no-win strategy." Here is the gist of Admiral Ward's article answering Senator Fulbright as it appeared in the *Washington Report* of the American Security Council of September 1977.

The extreme danger of the muzzling of military strategists becomes clear when we examine plans of the pacifists who are exerting ever greater influence on U.S. strategy.

The really serious drive for disarmament is, of course, vigorously sponsored by pacifists. However, they are also moving on a much more sophisticated and devious alternate plan. This alternate pacifist program for U.S. foreign and military policy is short, simple—and deadly. It has three principal points:
1. Adopt as the primary national objective "peace," instead of the preservation of American freedom.
2. Adopt a "no-win" national strategy.
3. Develop a military posture deliberately weaker than the Soviets'—for all types of war.

The pacifists believe that the overriding national objective of the United States must be the avoidance of war. They believe, also, that such a great end as avoidance of war justifies the means to accomplish it. Thus they can justify restraining us from "hitting the Communists with everything we've got" by the simple expedient of making sure in advance that everything we will have to hit the Communists with will be so relatively inferior to what the Communists have to hit us with that it will be obviously stupid and suicidal to "lash out at the enemy."

Such a plan sounds incredible to most Americans. It must be remembered, however, that it has many features which would make it tremendously appealing to those who consider that avoidance of war is the most important objective in the world—and is the only thing that can save the world. It appears to them to be the best possible insurance against nuclear war. The Soviets will not need to start one. The United States will not dare risk one—let alone start one.

Furthermore, the sophisticated pacifist plan described above is really quite close to what will result if a coalition of nuclear-pacifists (they are not Communists) who have membership in elite groups of policy advisors in Washington are able to continue their influence on national strategy.

The basis of the nuclear-pacifist theory of strategy is that there is serious risk of war if we even threaten credibly to resist Communist demands by resort to military power. They fear that so long as the United States has sufficient military power to have a rational chance of success in either actually using it or threatening to use it, we may be tempted to do so.

To eliminate this temptation (and thereby the risk of war) they plan a military posture tailored to the strategy of "minimum deterrence," not capable of winning a war should deterrence fail. Our power is to be so clearly inferior to the Soviet power that it would be manifest suicide to oppose Communist expansion by anything stronger than the sort of words we have used regarding Laos, Cuba, and Berlin.

Thus it is that the elite groups which so largely influence foreign and military policy—the scientist-pacifists, the internationalist-pacifists, the disengagement-pacifists, the nuclear-pacifists—all support the underlying theme of the Fulbright memorandum. The American people must be deprived of all sources of information that could interpret to them the real meaning of strategic and foreign policy theories which the elite groups seek to sell to the president or to push through in lower echelons.

This is the true reason that pacifists believe the anti-Communist military must be gagged; this is why civilian groups which can't be gagged (such as the ASC) must be discredited if they otherwise speak with authority in the fields of foreign policy and national strategy.

Putting it in even simpler terms, the pacifists would prefer to make the currently false alternative "Better Red than dead" into our only actual choice. As it stands now, we still have one additional choice—if we are strong enough militarily, we don't have to be either Red or dead. . . .

Our national strategy is in danger of shifting to the cheapest and most dangerous of the five recognized national strategies, that of "minimum deterrence." It relies on the assumed deterrent effect of presumably being able to destroy Russian cities in retaliation if they should launch a massive attack on this country. It provides no effective defense for this country —let alone for our major allies. It is a "no-win" strategy. We no longer appear to have a strategy of "win, strike-second," the only non-suicidal strategy for a nation pledged as we are never to strike first.

We are shifting dangerously away from the concept stated by General Nathan Twining, then the retiring chairman of the Joint Chiefs of Staff, in September 1960: "The American capability for decisive, war-winning response to any attack must be kept sure whatever the costs. It is the only reliable guarantee of peace. Forces that cannot win will not deter."

The United States has been a powerful force in encouraging decolonization, and we have adopted, almost totally, peaceful

105

coexistence or détente, dropping the latter by name only for a few months during the Republican primaries when Ronald Reagan pierced the sophistry of our unilateral concessions to the Russians and to the Chinese Communists.

As a result of our adoption of détente, the political climate in the United States is most conducive to a softness and indifference to the geopolitical and military nuclear whirlwinds that, in fact, are raging. While he was secretary of state, Dr. Henry Kissinger forbade any exposure of Communist treachery by any government agency that he controlled directly or indirectly. The Republican administration was indifferent to and even discouraged any exposure by the Committees of Congress of Communist influence in the nation or beyond. Its China policy in particular validated and gave great credibility to the Chinese Communist sympathizers in academia and in the media who have been promoting the cause of Peking for decades while that force has been waging its aggressions.

The Communist agents and propagandists and their fellow travelers who have been discredited by congressional hearings, and by their clear identification with Communist aggressions in Eastern Europe, in China and Tibet, in Korea, and later in Vietnam, have been rehabilitated and are pouring out propaganda that is undermining and enervating the will and the resolution of the American people.

One of the most effective stratagems of the Communists is their fabrication of the epithet "McCarthyism." When I was Senate counsel in 1950 I had to trace the origin of that term. It originated in the *Daily Worker*.

Senator McCarthy came to Washington as a liberal Republican in January 1947. He did not become involved in the subversion issue until February 1950. At that time several security people, concerned with the Communist penetration of policymaking positions in the government, supplied him with information bearing on subversion.

He was quite inexperienced when he undertook a Lincoln Day dinner speech in Wheeling, West Virginia, and made some serious charges. Since there was no formal copy of the speech on Communists in the State Department, no one could say for certain what the Senator had charged.

But the Democratic leadership of the Senate, concerned that the issue could damage their 1952 campaign, elected to capitalize on what they thought were unprovable charges and then hoped to put the issue to rest.

The Tydings Subcommittee of the Senate Foreign Relations Committee was created, with Senator Millard Tydings of Maryland, considered electorally invulnerable, as chairman.

I served as counsel to the Republican members of that Subcommittee, B. B. Hickenlooper and Henry Cabot Lodge.

The Subcommittee attempted to whitewash the issue, but we were able to insert enough in the record to make our point that there was subversion in the State Department. The following exchange between the chairman and myself is an example of the bias of the Subcommittee:

> MR. MORRIS. May I say, Senator, that the first basic request that I made in commencing this investigation was for the books and records of Frederick Vanderbilt Field, inasmuch as there was evidence that his money was the heart of the Communist cell in the Institute of Pacific Relations. I maintain that that was necessary. It was basically necessary to start that kind of investigation.
>
> SENATOR TYDINGS. There isn't anything, Mr. Morris, that isn't pertinent, and we can keep on asking for things, and there is no doubt in the world that would be a good thing to get, and you could ask for 5,000 different things, but we are pretty far away from loyalty in the State Department when we get out in the Institute of Pacific Relations with our little force. We just haven't got it. . . .
>
> MR. MORRIS. Senator, may I mention just one case here?

SENATOR TYDINGS. Mr. Morris, we can mention cases from now until doomsday.

MR. MORRIS. It is in the record, Senator. May I just finish?

SENATOR TYDINGS. Of course you are not a member of the Committee. When we want counsel to speak, we will ask them, but I am going to let you speak. However, that is a matter for the Committee to decide.

SENATOR LODGE. I would like to hear what he has to say.

MR. MORRIS. There is the case of a man named Theodore Geiger. He has been an employee of the State Department. He is now one of Paul Hoffman's top assistants. He is doing work that is quasi-State Department in character. I have gone and gotten some witnesses together who will testify that he was a member of the same Communist Party unit as they were, and I think that we would be delinquent if in the face of this evidence that is now on the record. . . .

SENATOR TYDINGS. Why didn't you tell us this? Why did you wait until this hour to tell me?

MR. MORRIS. I am not waiting, Senator. One day Senator Green made me a witness and I put it all in the record.

SENATOR TYDINGS. You haven't told me about it. This is the first I have heard about it.

MR. MORRIS. Senator, I assume that you are aware of everything in the record.

SENATOR TYDINGS. No. There are some things in the record I haven't been able to read.

MR. MORRIS. Certainly Mr. Morgan knows it. I have mentioned it several times to him.

SENATOR GREEN. That wouldn't have anything to do with my motion.

SENATOR TYDINGS. Turn it over to the FBI or do something else with it. I would like to get a decision here. We don't want to waste this afternoon.

Also during this exchange, Senator Hickenlooper mentioned the twenty to thirty potential witnesses whom the minority had interviewed and who had pertinent testimony.

When Senator Lodge noticed that these statements had been deleted, he raised the point on the Senate floor with considerable feeling, and a special volume of fifteen pages was ordered printed by Senator Tydings as a supplement to the principal volume of testimony.

The following year, however, Senator Pat McCarran (D-Nev), long-time chairman of the Senate Judiciary Committee and a former chief justice of the Nevada Supreme Court, formed the Internal Security Subcommittee. I was a special counsel to the Subcommittee that probed the Institute of Pacific Relations and State Department policy on the Far East. Jay Sourwine was counsel to the full Judiciary Committee.

In the next two years, the Subcommittee went on to prove much more than Senator McCarthy ever charged.

The Senator conducted himself in a most correct and decorous manner in those two years. He refrained from commenting on the evidence as it unfolded and was rather modest when the unanimous conclusions of the Subcommittee, supported by the equally unanimous acceptance of the report by the full Judiciary Committee, composed of eight Democratic senators and seven Republican senators, came rolling out of the Government Printing Office in July 1952.

Later Senator McCarthy became chairman of the Government Operations Committee and undertook investigations into Communists in the government and related issues. The hearings became very controversial, and because the object of the inquiry was, for the most part, the Republican administration, his party was divided behind him and he lacked the political support to carry on.

His career effectively ended when he was censured by the Senate in 1955. The censure came, however, not on the two counts raised against him. Both of those failed. But his opponents then censured him for being contumacious toward the chairman of the Censure Committee.

I relate this summary because it limits the role of the late senator to a certain period of time and to certain investigations.

The Communist ploy of "McCarthyism" is sweeping. Any exposure of Soviet intrigue is so labeled. Any charge against a subversive, justified or not, is also so labeled. So successful has this stratagem been that successive administrations have discouraged inquiries into subversion, with their beneficial educational dividends, lest they encourage a revival of "McCarthyism."

In fact the whole period of 1950 to 1959, when Secretary of State John Foster Dulles died, has now become the "McCarthy Era." In so describing it, the scribes do not mean it as a complimentary appellation. It is used to discourage any effort to renew concern with Communist aggression or subversion in the government.

As I write this, Hollywood and the media are turning out films and articles deploring "blacklists" and "McCarthyism." Long are the sufferings and the estrangements experienced by so-called victims of witch hunts. Lillian Hellman, who was herself deeply involved, wrote a best seller on the subject entitled *Scoundrel Time.*

Joe McCarthy was not even in Washington when the House Un-American Activities Committee held its very effective hearings into the massive penetration of Hollywood. As for the "innocent victims," if a person is shown by responsible evidence to have been a member of the Communist Party and then cannot enter a denial in the record, he does not acquit himself in a fashion worthy of one who would, by his script writing, be in a position to mold the outlook of impressionable young people.

The Communists used the term to label any exposure of their

underground operations. In order to make the sobriquet detestable, every possible vilification is heaped on the late Senator Joseph R. McCarthy. The ploy has been eminently successful, and a ready following has been only too willing to join in the chorus.

The whole period of Communist containment is now broadly labeled the "McCarthy Era," and the work of the Senate Internal Security Subcommittee, of which I have been counsel, is loosely labeled "McCarthyism" even though the late Senator had no connection whatever with that body or its counterpart in the House of Representatives.

On February 6, 1977, the NBC television network put this whole issue in focus by running a three-hour so-called documentary entitled *Tailgunner Joe*. This is what I wrote of that dramatic offering in my column that week:

> I elected to watch NBC's "documentary" on the late Senator Joe McCarthy this week and came away from it greatly distressed and even alarmed at the ability of a powerful network to rewrite history— and to the detriment of our nation at that. The three-hour scenario was about as objective as a lynching. An episode in contemporary history that certainly had two sides was depicted with only one. There was no balance whatever, and there were outright distortions of truth.
>
> During three of the years, the history of which was rewritten in the telecast, I was a front-row spectator to the interesting spectacle that unrolled. I was asked by the Republican leadership in the Senate in 1950 to be counsel to the minority members on the Tydings Committee who had been selected to serve on that subcommittee of the Foreign Relations Committee that was created to investigate Senator McCarthy's charges.
>
> While it is true that Senator Tydings and the two other Democratic members of the Committee dis-

111

missed Senator McCarthy's charges, as NBC mockingly related, both Senator B. B. Hickenlooper and Senator Henry Cabot Lodge voiced such strong dissent that in the next session of Congress, Senator Pat McCarran, a Democrat and chairman of the powerful Senate Judiciary Committee, formed an Internal Security Subcommittee which explored the general area of the Tydings imbroglio.

As evidence of how distressing the NBC telecast was, let me cite just one case—that of Owen Lattimore. Whereas NBC reviled McCarthy for exposing Lattimore, the seven senators on the Judiciary Subcommittee—four Democrats and three Republicans—concluded after two years of hearings: "On the basis of these facts and others, including (but without limitation) Lattimore's editing of *Pacific Affairs*; his recommendations on policy to the State Department, coinciding as they do with Lawrence Rosinger's; his falsifications about his close association with Lauchlin Currie; his conference with the Soviet agent Rogoff, and the Soviet Embassy official Gokham; and his subservience to Soviet officials in Moscow in 1936, the Subcommittee can come to no other conclusion but that Lattimore was for some time, beginning in the middle 1930s, a conscious, articulate instrument of the Soviet conspiracy."

This conclusion, in a rare show of unanimity in Washington, was approved by all fifteen members of the full Judiciary Committee. Naturally this did not fit the NBC script, and not only was it eliminated from history, but the very opposite conclusion was drawn by the unobjective lady commentator in summing up.

Not only were the distortions of fact shocking, but the cruelty of the network was relentless in exaggerating all of the late Senator's weaknesses and totally obscuring his redeeming qualities, and in blackening the reputations of everyone associated with him. Mellow and kindly Dr. J. B. Matthews, for instance, was shamefully vilified without reference to his side of the controversy.

At the outset of this column, I wrote that I was distressed at the ability of a network to rewrite history, and I added "to the detriment of our nation at that." The Communists today have a ploy. It calls for relating all exposure of their subversion to "McCarthyism"—a term which they and Owen Lattimore coined in 1950. The second part of that ploy is to vilify and calumniate Joe McCarthy and everyone associated with him so that "McCarthyism" becomes a despicable epithet. "*Nihil nisi bonum de mortuis*" becomes "*Nihil nisi malum.*" ["Speak only good of the dead" becomes "Speak only evil."]

Meanwhile Communist subversion becomes more ominous and more menacing. There is no doubt that the United States is the prime target. FBI Director Clarence Kelley told the nation this week that subversion by Soviet and Chinese forces is growing and not waning, as NBC would have us believe.

But because of performances like the NBC telecast *Tailgunner Joe,* the political atmosphere of the country is becoming such that it is difficult to counter these noxious forces.

12

Castro Communism— An Engine of Conquest

MORE THAN TWENTY years ago, a Communist agent with a handful of disciples landed in the Sierra Maestra on the island of Cuba. He had shown his colors as a Communist clearly in 1948 and, to some discerning eyes, considerably before that. But he had friends.

One of these, Herbert Matthews of the *New York Times,* visited him in his island fortress and began to glamorize him as the Abraham Lincoln of Cuba. He had other friends in Moscow and the whole conglomerate soon went to work to bring him to power.

The first target was Batista, the Cuban dictator. The intricate machinery of Communist propaganda cleverly exploited the desires of a large part of the Cuban people for a democratically elected government. The Communists, many of the liberals, and perhaps the majority of the intellectuals converged on Batista. Clearly his days were numbered.

The American ambassador to Cuba, Earl E. T. Smith, like his predecessor, recognized Castro for what he was—at the very least a dangerous left-wing political leader whose democratic promises were cynical rhetoric. Though openly opposed and derided by some of his senior advisors in the Havana embassy and the chief of the CIA section, Smith stuck to his guns. In a desperate move, he tried to form a coalition with all anti-

Batista forces, except Castro, to take over the Cuban government.

The State Department, with William Arthur Wieland, director of the Caribbean Division, in charge of Cuban affairs and with confused—or even worse—superiors, insisted that we support Castro. Cooperating with an orchestra of gullible or leftist molders of American public opinion, they labored to bring the bearded leader to power and succeeded in due course in achieving their objective.

Ambassador Smith testified at length on these tragic events and their causation before the Senate Internal Security Subcommittee in August 1960 at the time that it was holding hearings on the Communist threat to the United States through the Caribbean. I believe that some of the things he said then are worth repeating:

> Fidel Castro landed on the south coast of Oriente in December 1956 with an expeditionary force of eighty-one men. Intercepted by Cuban gunboats and patrol planes, Castro and a handful of stragglers managed to ensconce themselves in the rugged 8,000-foot Sierra Maestra range.
>
> After the Matthews articles which followed an exclusive interview by the *Times* editorial writer in Castro's mountain hideout and which likened him to Abraham Lincoln, he was able to get followers and funds in Cuba and the United States. From that time on, arms, money, and soldiers of fortune abounded. Much of the American press began to picture Castro as a political Robin Hood.
>
> Also, because Batista was the dictator who unlawfully seized power, American people assumed that Castro must, on the other hand, represent liberty and democracy. The crusader role which the press and radio bestowed on the bearded rebel blinded people to the left-wing political philosophy with which even at that time he was already on record. . . .

115

I would say that Mr. Wieland and all those who had anything to do with Cuba had a close connection with Herbert Matthews.

I will go further than that. I will say that when I was ambassador, I was thoroughly aware of this and sometimes made the remark in my own embassy that Mr. Matthews was more familiar with the State Department thinking regarding Cuba than I was.

Directed to name the pro-Castro elements in the American embassy, Ambassador Smith reluctantly identified "the chief of the political section, John Topping, and the chief of the CIA section." He added that the No. 2 CIA man had actually met with pro-Castro officers in the Cuban navy who were plotting revolution against the established government and had apparently promised them American recognition if their revolt were successful.

The pro-Castro group succeeded. No sooner had he come to power than Castro began to show his fangs. He held kangaroo courts and sentenced thousands of innocent people to death or prison under ghastly conditions of confinement. He also proceeded to eliminate all those forces that would interfere with his transformation of Cuba into a Soviet state.

The gravamen of this chapter is that, through a failure in internal security, intelligence, and policy, a Communist dictator seized power in an island ninety miles from Florida and proceeded to use that Soviet base to conquer far-flung sections of the globe through both internal subversion and armed invasion.

In establishing a Soviet military base just off our shores, Castro blasted the Monroe Doctrine into oblivion. It was replaced by the Brezhnev Doctrine which carved out Cuba as a Soviet sphere of influence and defied any power to tamper with it.

Despite all this, Castro has always had and still has his friends in the State Department. When he was establishing a missile base in Cuba in 1962 that directly threatened the major cities of the United States with obliteration, State Department officials first denied the evidence of the missile build-up, then tried to turn away mounting public concern by contending that the Soviet armament was "defensive."

A beguiled President Kennedy was finally awakened to the nature of the threat. The missile crisis that ensued was proclaimed by the administration as an "eyeball-to-eyeball" confrontation in which the United States had both emerged victorious and preserved the peace of the world.

The reality was otherwise. Khrushchev got everything he wanted—a guarantee against invasion of Cuba and the dismantling of U.S. missile bases in Turkey and Italy. In a letter to Fidel Castro, the Soviet dictator wrote:

> . . . we have secured the existence of a Socialist Cuba for at least another two years while Kennedy is in the White House. And we have reason to believe that Kennedy will be elected for a second term. . . . And six years from now the balance of power in the world will probably have shifted—and shifted in our favor, in favor of Socialism.

Khrushchev added: "The Caribbean crisis was a triumph of Soviet foreign policy and a personal triumph in my own career. . . . We achieved, I would say, a spectacular success without having to fire a single shot."[1]

There was never any inspection on our part or on the part of any responsible agency to verify that the missiles had actually been withdrawn. U Thant, the secretary general of the United Nations, encouraged Castro to resist any attempt at inspection.

Of course, the Soviet Government did not keep faith or abide by its agreement to keep offensive missiles out of Cuba.

In September 1970, according to the memoirs of President Nixon's chief of staff, H. R. Haldeman, it was discovered—and confirmed by reconnaissance—that the Russians were building a nuclear naval base on Cuba. The strategic pur-

[1]*Khrushchev Remembers* (New York: Little, Brown, 1970), p. 508.

pose of this was diabolical. The Arctic approaches to the American heartland were protected by the highly efficient Ballistic Missile Early Warning System (BMEWS) which could detect incoming Soviet assault missiles in time for massive American nuclear retaliation. The Soviet nuclear construction at Cienfuegos was designed, according to Haldeman, to enable the Kremlin to knock out all twenty-one American nuclear defense command headquarters from the unprotected Caribbean side. Once this was accomplished, the Soviets could launch their main devastating nuclear assault over the Arctic approaches, confident that no American official or officer would remain alive with the authority to order a retaliatory counterattack by our triangular system of nuclear weaponry.

In his eager quest for détente, President Nixon withheld these ominous facts from the American people, facts which would have revealed the perfidy of the Kremlin in glaring colors. The Soviet ambassador, Anatoly Dobrynin, was warned that the Soviet Union must either dismantle the Cienfuegos nuclear base or face a second missile crisis.

On March 27, 1978, Robert Moss, a British journalist known internationally as an expert on Communism, wrote in the *Daily Telegraph* that U.S. aerial surveillance showed that the Cubans were building a pen for nuclear submarines at Cienfuegos. Citing Western military observers whom he did not identify by name, Moss concluded: "There is a strong suspicion that Soviet strategic missiles have already been smuggled back to Cuba."

The Defense Department denied the report.

American internal security delinquency concerning Castro has spawned a new and far-flung Communist aggression and violation of human rights. Let us look at the toll.

Ever since the consolidation of Red power in Cuba, Castro has maintained a complete police state equipped with torture chambers and slave labor camps comparable to the worst such institutions in the USSR and in Communist China. On May 31, 1977, as reported in the *New York Times,* President Carter stated that he was concerned about the fact that there were

118

between 15,000 and 20,000 political prisoners in Cuba.[2] This apparatus of repression and network of bondage was installed under the guidance of Soviet military advisors and KGB overlords.

The Cuban terror and despotism has apologists in the highest circles of the administration. President Carter's ambassador to the United Nations, Andrew Young, characterized the Cuban invasion force which conquered Angola for the Communist minority in that country as an element which had brought "a certain stability and order" to the former Portuguese possession. This is the moral equivalent of asserting that Adolf Hitler brought "a certain stability and order" to Poland.

Ambassador Young has consistently supported pro-Communist causes and the national interests of the Soviet Union. When asked: "Would you support the destruction of Western civilization if you were convinced that the rest of the world would thereby be liberated?"[3] Young replied, "I probably would." Young, moreover, told his colleagues in the Black Caucus of Congress that he had accepted the post of ambassador to the U.N. solely because "Carter agreed to support a policy of using all means necessary to overturn the white-ruled governments of Rhodesia and South Africa."[4]

While Young was praising the Cuban invaders of Angola as a stabilizing force, Castro's vice president, Carlos Rafael Rodríguez, was telling a BBC correspondent in Havana: "We are revolutionaries, we are Communists, and we hope that some day the entire world will be Communist."

And on the day that the United States Senate, in a mood of irresponsible isolationism, voted to bar any assistance to the anti-Castro forces in Angola, the chief theoretician of the Soviet government, Mikhail Suslov, told the Cuban Communist Party Congress in Havana: "The revolutionary-liberation

[2]The gruesome mistreatment and torture of Cuban political prisoners is reported in *Of Human Rights,* Georgetown University, Box 648 East Campus, Washington, D.C. 20057.

[3]The verb "liberate" means "Communize" in Marxist-Leninist jargon.

[4]*Herald of Freedom,* March 11, 1977, XXXI:4.

movement now as never before is linked into a unified global whole. The Cuban revolution has placed an indelible imprint on the development of the whole liberation process in Latin America."

But the malignancy is not confined to Cuba. Operating from a firm Soviet bastion, Castro is now extending Communist conquests in Latin America and across Africa.

The Cuban dictator supplies the police and military advisors, intelligence and secret police professionals, and technical experts needed to organize and train the 20,000-man Jamaican police force under the pro-Communist Jamaican prime minister, Michael Manley. In 1977, when Manley was proceeding as rapidly as circumstances permitted to silence his liberal opponents and establish a Castro-style regime, Rosalynn Carter paid an official visit to Jamaica, heaped praises on the Manley regime for its far-reaching "social reforms," and humbly observed that the United States had much to learn from these Jamaican experiments.

Working in concert with Panamanian dictator Omar Torrijos, Castro agents under the direction of Major Manuel Piñeiro Losada, a high official of the Cuban secret police (DGI), have been advising and guiding the special Panamanian forces that plan to take over control of the Canal Zone.

Senator Jesse Helms (R-NC) has warned the President and the State Department about the subversive military activities of Castro agents and Chilean Red expatriates in the regime of Peru.

Ever since 1969, the Cuban General Directorate of Intelligence (DGI) has organized Venceremos Brigades, consisting of some 3,000 young Americans who went to Cuba, were exposed to Communist propaganda and, if found promising, were trained as professional revolutionary agents.

A classified FBI report, prepared in August 1976, was made public a year later in connection with Department of Justice charges against FBI agents for opening the mail of the terrorist Weathermen's contacts.

The report revealed that the most promising elements among the young Americans in the Venceremos Brigades were selected for special advanced revolutionary training and for training in weapons use and terrorist techniques and tactics by Cuban military officers.

Those who wished were given training in guerrilla warfare techniques, including the use of arms and explosives. The report described the number so trained as "very limited." An objective of the DGI in setting up the Venceremos Brigade, according to the report, "is the recruitment of individuals who are politically oriented and who someday may obtain a position, elective or appointive, somewhere in the U.S. government which would provide the Cuban government with access to political, economic and military intelligence."

The FBI report further brought out that Cuban and North Vietnamese officials were influencing radical antiwar strategy in meetings held abroad.

It also revealed that Cuban intelligence officers were communicating with the underground members of the Weathermen from the Cuban UN mission and the Cuban embassy in Canada.

After those trained in guerrilla warfare and in military techniques of terror completed their indoctrination in Cuba, they were sent back to the United States to carry on acts of sabotage, but more importantly to establish a base from which to strike, should world conditions dictate an open attack on the United States.

The power failure of July 1977 revealed U.S. vulnerability to sabotage. Power grids, the long exposed Alaskan pipeline, the nuclear power plants—all these are potential targets of terror.

Castro's greatest contribution to Soviet world conquest has been his expeditionary forces in Africa.

Their first great success was the conquest of Angola for the Communist minority in that country, an operation made possible by the blind isolationism of a majority in the U.S. Senate which had no warning from the State Department about what was transpiring.

The paralysis of American nerve in the Angola crisis aroused the indignation even of political leaders whose illusions about the alleged liberalization of the Soviet Union are notorious.

Speaking before the Palm Beach Round Table on March 22, 1978, former Presidential Advisor W. Averell Harriman said: "I decry what is being done to intelligence today. . . . Our first line of defense is the CIA."

Having conquered Angola for the Kremlin, Castro moved the bulk of his expeditionary force into Ethiopia. Serving as a spearhead in more than full division strength and equipped with the most modern Soviet weapons, the Castro forces and the raw and badly trained Ethiopian army swept the Ogaden clear of its Somali defenders. Immediately after victory the Communist conquerors of the territory proceeded, according to newspaper reports based on refugee and survivor accounts, to exterminate all Ogaden inhabitants who had given aid to, or sympathized with, Somalia.

This operation in the Horn of Africa followed Fidel Castro's tour of the Communist and pro-Communist states of the Dark Continent: Libya, Somalia, Ethiopia, Mozambique, Angola, Congo-Brazzaville, Algeria, Uganda, and Guinea. He left behind or planted secret agents, technical advisors, and military cadres.

The crushing defeat of the Somalian forces in the spring of 1978 gave Marxist-Leninist states domination over the Horn of Africa. Strategically they were in a position to close the Red Sea in cooperation with the Communist Republic of South Yemen, with a vital naval base at Aden and the strategic island of Socotra on the Asian side of that waterway. The Soviet Union would be able to erect a major naval base from which it could dominate the Indian Ocean and close the vital sea lanes that bring Persian Gulf oil to Western Europe and the United States.

In conjunction with Mozambique, a former Portuguese possession which also succumbed to Communist conquest, Soviet and Cuban forces threatened to forestall any peaceful creation of a democratic multiracial state in Rhodesia (Zimbabwe) and to provide the military base for an eventual invasion of South Africa.

The use of tens of thousands of Communist troops for this massive military operation, designed to conquer sub-Saharan

122

Africa and in particular the only modern industrial state on the African continent, served two purposes.

(1) Since the Cuban forces are to a large extent black or racially mixed, they are less unacceptable to Africans than Russian troops would be.

(2) In the unlikely event that the Carter administration would be induced or compelled to defend American interests in Africa, the Soviet Union could avoid a direct confrontation. It could inform either state that it had no means of controlling Cuban actions or that it would use its best efforts to persuade Fidel Castro toward a more moderate course.

13

Soviet Espionage

ESPIONAGE IS A distinct and principal Soviet industry. This must be so, because the Soviet Union, alone
of all the great powers, regards itself as being in a
continuous and chronic state of covert warfare with
the whole world outside the borders of the Communist empire. And conspiratorial techniques are natural to a regime that seized power and maintains
power by conspiratorial methods. Soviet espionage
has reaped a rich harvest by such methods, especially against friendly and unsuspecting countries.
Vladimir Petrov, MVD defector from the USSR[1]

When Swedish Air Force Colonel Stig Eric Wennerström was
revealed in 1963 to be a Soviet espionage agent, the AP reported:

Stockholm, Sweden, July 14, 1963 (AP). Sweden's
armed forces have embarked on a massive program
to close the defense gap caused by the betrayal of
military secrets to the Soviet Union by Air Force
Colonel Stig Erik Wennerström.

[1]Vladimir M. Petrov, *Empire of Fear* (New York: Praeger, 1957), p.
268.

124

There is an atmosphere of almost wartime urgency at the Defense Ministry.

Lights burn far into the night as army, navy, and air force officers grapple with the task of repairing the probable loss of Sweden's entire defense strategy to the Russians.

Officers have been recalled from vacation and redeployment of army, navy, and air force units may already be under way.

Security services are working day and night to investigate other possible leaks in the military establishment or the government.

Everyone—the government, opposition parties, defense staffs, and the newspapers—agrees that Wennerström crippled Sweden. The tall, suave airman diplomat has confessed that he gave military secrets to the Russians for fifteen years.

And during that period he had access to Sweden's entire defense strategy. Defense sites and strengths? Military codes? Key mobilization and communication plans? Wennerström knew all about these and more. He knew a lot about the North Atlantic Treaty Organization's defense plans and weapons. He visited NATO military installations. He was in frequent contact with Danish and Norwegian military men. He was friendly with many top Western diplomats here.

The armed forces are reported to be acting on the assumption that Wennerström "gave away Sweden" and that the Russians now know all about its plans to repel a possible Soviet attack.

Stockholm's influential *Expression*—the largest newspaper in Scandinavia—referred to "a time of acute crisis for our defense" and said editorially:

"The Wennerström spying has in essential parts knocked out the Swedish defense. About this all reports agree. Hectic measures are being taken to repair, if possible, the damage caused.

"The armed forces face an immensely complicated and costly task. Fortifications, headquarters and battle stations, hangars, ship tunnels, repair shops, and storage depots have been built into granite accommodations at top-secret locations. Newspapers have reported there are five hundred of these.

"Two deep tunnels have been carved out of a mountain to accommodate destroyers, submarines, and other naval units. Plans have called for the entire navy to be provided with tunnels. These installations cannot be moved even though their locations may now be precisely located by the Russians. Must new ones be built?

"Military expenditures now take about one-fifth of Sweden's national budget. According to some estimates, it now must spend the equivalent of hundreds of millions of dollars more, and quickly, to repair the damage of the loss of defense secrets. Newspapers predict taxes will be substantially increased to pay the cost.

"Informed sources say Sweden probably will face vastly increased military research costs as a result of the Wennerström case. Although Sweden is neutral and not a member of NATO, the Western powers for some time have quietly passed on to the Swedish armed forces important technical data on defense matters. They also sold weapons to Sweden. The view here is that the West probably will halt such aid in view of uncertainty about Sweden's security system."[2]

[2]Reprinted with permission of The Associated Press.

Wennerström also "gave the Russians data about American weaponry while serving as an attaché in Washington," according to John Barron's authoritative *KGB* (p. 189). The Swedish traitor was sentenced to life imprisonment.

Another report on Soviet espionage came, ironically enough, from Cyrus Eaton, an aged retired industrialist and devoted friend and supporter of international Communist causes.

Eaton visited Hanoi for ten days in 1969 while the United States was at war with North Vietnam. On his return, he gave a local newspaper a revealing interview, which was picked up by the UPI on July 4, 1971:

> The leaders of North Vietnam had advance knowledge of virtually every major American move in Indochina, including the incursions into Cambodia and Laos, according to industrialist Cyrus S. Eaton.
>
> In a copyrighted interview with the *Sunday Lorain Journal*, Eaton, 87, said Communist leaders in Hanoi and Moscow had no surprises in reading accounts of the recently published secret Pentagon documents.
>
> Eaton, a confidant of world Communist leaders, said the North Vietnamese had the "most complete" information on secret United States plans within hours of their formulation. . . .
>
> He said he was told in visits with Premier Pham Van Dong and the head of state Ton Doc Thang that the U.S. was planning to invade Cambodia, then Laos.
>
> Five months later, in May 1970, the Cambodian invasion began. The Laos incursion occurred in February of this year.[3]

[3]"Reds Knew Everything, Eaton Says" (*Washington Post*, July 3, 1971). Reprinted with permission of United Press International.

Eaton revealed that the head of North Vietnamese intelligence had shown him the contents of secret cables stolen from the Saigon U.S. embassy and from American military headquarters in Vietnam. He revealed that he had been in close touch with the North Vietnamese Communist leaders ever since.

The UPI dispatch continued:

> Eaton said the Hanoi government knew that the U.S. planned to bomb North Vietnam before it happened, that the U.S. had discussed contingency plans to use nuclear weapons in Vietnam if the Red Chinese entered the war, and that former President Lyndon B. Johnson planned to escalate the war even though he was publicly saying he would not send Americans to die in Vietnam.

Cyrus Eaton established these close and cosy contacts with the enemy at a time when thousands of young Americans were fighting and dying in Vietnam. He was in continuous contact with the leaders of a government at war with the United States. He was so trusted that they showed him American secrets that their Communist agents had stolen.

In a speech to the Lawyers' Association of Kansas City on February 9, 1977, former FBI Director Clarence M. Kelley described the battle against espionage in these terms:

> In the last two years the number of Soviet officials alone has increased twenty percent.
>
> The People's Republic of China also has appreciably increased its official presence in the United States.
>
> In addition, since 1973, the number of Soviets entering the United States under special exchange agreements, such as students and scientists, has more than doubled—more than 5,000 visit each year. There has been a concurrent increase in the number

of Eastern European officials and visitors coming to the United States.

Our experience has shown us that a substantial number of these Soviet-bloc and Chinese officials are directly connected with their intelligence services.

Their targets are virtually all-encompassing, including our political, economic, agricultural, military, and scientific and technical resources.

It's no secret that we constantly endeavor first to *identify* and then to *neutralize* these intelligence operatives, as well as to penetrate hostile intelligence services.

By necessity, our successes are seldom publicized. Occasionally there are arrests but they are rare, because an arrest is often the least desirable action. Spies, after all, are replaceable. And once an intelligence agent is identified, he can be monitored to determine who sent him, his contacts and objectives. Patience usually pays off.

But occasionally there *are* arrests. *For example, last month we arrested a Soviet immigrant in New Jersey for espionage.* He was charged with attempting to obtain a classified, sensitive document relating to a satellite communications project at the RCA Space Center at Princeton. The document allegedly was to be delivered to the second secretary of the Soviet mission to the United Nations. The Soviet was named as a co-conspirator.

Also, last month we arrested a California man for espionage. He had a top secret security clearance. He was charged with passing classified information concerning the work of a military contractor to a colleague who sold it to Soviet agents. A science attaché to the Soviet embassy in Mexico was named as a co-conspirator.

One highly publicized case was a classic illustration of the determined efforts of hostile intelligence services to penetrate the United States policy- and decision-making process.

A native-born U.S. citizen allegedly cooperated for years with an East German intelligence organization, undoubtedly under Soviet control. He allegedly maintained clandestine contact with his East Berlin principals and allegedly received training, assignments, and money in return for information.

Congressman Paul Findley of Illinois disclosed in the *Congressional Record* of April 8, 1976, how this individual was recommended and was considered for a sensitive foreign policy position on Capitol Hill in 1975.

While complimenting the FBI, the Congressman characterized the experience as a sobering reminder that the real world is one of spies, intrigue, and double-dealing. He said: "It swept aside any illusions that Communist governments closely allied with the Soviet Union have dropped their undercover work in this era of détente."

So, from time to time, these cases surface into public view, but for the most part counterintelligence investigations are silent and unseen.

14

The Senate Committee and the Alger Hiss Case

THE ALGER HISS perjury-espionage case was incontestably the most profound criminal trial of our century. It was also the most dramatic, protracted, and philosophically significant confrontation between the forces of global Communism and those of Western civilization that the world has yet seen.

In all its reverberations and labyrinthine complications, the case stretched across the enormous time-span of more than a third of a century. It began a few days after the conclusion of the Stalin-Hitler pact which unleashed World War II on suffering mankind. At that time, August 1939, Isaac Don Levine, a journalist and writer of international distinction, brought Whittaker Chambers, who had emerged from the Soviet underground and secretly defected from the cause he served, to see Assistant Secretary of State Adolf Berle about a matter of grave national importance. What Chambers revealed to Berle was the existence of a secret cell of Soviet agents strategically placed in the most sensitive areas of the government. One of the men he named was Alger Hiss. Chambers and Levine asked Berle to bring the matter to the personal attention of President Roosevelt. He did so, but Roosevelt, for reasons which remain obscure, shrugged the whole matter off.

I knew Whittaker well, and as a naval intelligence officer I reported to my superiors that he had told me that Hiss was a secret Communist.

The next act of the drama occurred at the end of World War II when Igor Guzenko, a terrified code clerk working for the office of the Soviet military attaché in Ottawa, took his wife and small child with him in a desperate flight for freedom. In 1945, Guzenko turned over to the Canadian Royal Mounted Police more than a hundred documents which disclosed the main outlines of a vast Soviet espionage network directed against Russia's wartime allies. These documents named "an assistant secretary to the [American] Secretary of State's Department" as a Soviet spy.

The case exploded in a series of confrontations between Alger Hiss and Whittaker Chambers, then an editor of Time Inc., before the House Committee on Un-American Activities. Alger Hiss was indicted for perjury in connection with his espionage activities. His first trial resulted in a hung jury, 8 to 4 for conviction; the second in a guilty verdict. He was sentenced to five years imprisonment and served forty-four months at Lewisburg Penitentiary.

Parenthetically, I would like to point out that the reason Hiss was indicted for perjury, rather than for his real and far more heinous offense of espionage, was that the statute of limitations had lapsed on the latter offense. Chambers had defected from the Communist conspiracy shortly before the outbreak of World War II. Had there been evidence that Hiss had continued his spying activities for the Soviet Union after Pearl Harbor, he could have been tried for espionage. Spying in wartime was a capital offense at the time, and there is no statute of limitations on crimes carrying the death penalty.

Hiss has spent the decades since his release from prison vociferously asserting his innocence, and inspiring gullible Establishment writers and others to write tendentious articles and books to prove that he was a victim of hysteria, injustice, and "McCarthyism."

For all intents and purposes, the curtain closed on the Hiss case with the publication in 1978 of the definitive study of the case by Professor Allen Weinstein of Smith College. Weinstein, who had approached the subject as a Hiss sympathizer and partisan, gradually became convinced that his protagonist was

132

guilty as charged and that Alger Hiss was "a victim of the facts."[1]

We in the Senate Internal Security Subcommittee were not primarily concerned with the Hiss case. However, when we conducted our inquiry into the Institute of Pacific Relations in the early 1950s, we encountered, without seeking it, extensive evidence that supported Whittaker Chambers' charges.

Listen to the testimony of Nathaniel Weyl, a respected writer and former government worker:

MR. MORRIS. Did you come to join a Communist cell in Washington?

MR. WEYL. I did.

MR. MORRIS. Who induced you to join a Communist cell, Mr. Weyl?

MR. WEYL. A man named Harold Ware.

MR. MORRIS. Mr. Weyl, would you tell us who were the members of that Harold Ware unit of the Communist Party?

MR. WEYL. Yes, Mr. Morris. I hope I will not omit any names because sometimes you remember the names very well but you can't remember them to recite in a series after nineteen years or so. Alger Hiss, of course, Lee Pressman, Charles Kramer, Henry Collins, John Abt.

MR. MORRIS. Was Nathan Witt a member of that?

MR. WEYL. Yes, he was.

MR. MORRIS. Was Victor Perlo?

MR. WEYL. Yes, he was.

MR. MORRIS. When you say Alger Hiss, Mr. Weyl, did you see. . . .

[1]Allen Weinstein, *Perjury* (New York: Alfred A. Knopf, 1978).

MR. WEYL. Excuse me. Still with this question, should we deal with that matter we discussed in executive session, or skip it?

MR. MORRIS. I think we will come to that, Mr. Weyl.

MR. WEYL. All right.

MR. MORRIS. Mr. Chairman, Mr. Weyl has indicated he left out one name which he has given in executive session.

SENATOR EASTLAND. I think he should supply it.

MR. MORRIS. He has supplied it.

SENATOR FERGUSON. I might say that I presided at that meeting, and the Committee has that name.

SENATOR EASTLAND. Is there any reason why he should not testify now as to the name?

SENATOR FERGUSON. I think so. I will explain it to the Chair.

SENATOR EASTLAND. That is all right.

MR. MORRIS. Mr. Weyl, when you say that Alger Hiss was a member of that unit, how do you know that Alger Hiss was a member of the Harold Ware cell of the Communist Party?

MR. WEYL. Well, I only know that, Mr. Morris, because I saw him there on, let us say, more than two occasions, because nobody was in that unit who was not a Communist Party member, and I saw him pay dues.

SENATOR FERGUSON. In the cell?

MR. WEYL. In the cell.

SENATOR FERGUSON. You sat with him, in other words, in the cell meeting?

MR. WEYL. Precisely.

SENATOR FERGUSON. On at least two occasions?

MR. WEYL. More than two occasions.

MR. MORRIS. Would you estimate the number of times, Mr. Weyl, that you saw Alger Hiss in closed Communist meetings of the Harold Ware cell of the Communist Party?

MR. WEYL. I am afraid I couldn't do that, Mr. Morris.

MR. MORRIS. Would it run as high as twenty?

MR. WEYL. Well, I think I have to repeat my answer for this reason: The lapse of time is eighteen years. I attached no particular importance to Mr. Hiss and would have no reason to remember the number of times he was present and the number of times he was absent.

MR. SOURWINE. You said that in the past tense—you "attached"?

MR. WEYL. Yes, attached.

MR. SOURWINE. No particular importance at that time?

MR. WEYL. Of course, subsequently it has assumed very great importance.

MR. MORRIS. Would you say it was more than five times, Mr. Weyl?

MR. WEYL. If I can answer this as a guess, I would say yes.

SENATOR FERGUSON. A guess would not do us any good. You do testify absolutely that it was more than two?

MR. WEYL. Yes.

MR. SOURWINE. He could not have attended a meeting of that cell once without being a Communist, could he, Mr. Weyl?

MR. WEYL. No, he could not, Mr. Sourwine.

SENATOR EASTLAND. You said you saw him pay dues. I think he has covered that.[2]

Then there is the testimony of Hede Massing and Elizabeth Bentley, both former Soviet operatives, who had knowledge of Hiss' involvement with the Soviet apparatus:

MR. MORRIS. Did you succeed in recruiting Noel Field into the Communist apparatus?

MRS. MASSING. Yes.

MR. MORRIS. How long did it take you?

MRS. MASSING. It took me about three quarters of a year and it was the typical work of a recruiter in meeting the object regularly, discussing with him principal issues, issues that he was particularly interested in, leading him toward my goal, namely to consent to be a member of my apparatus. I didn't put it in these words, of course. What I said was, in gist, that this was the thing we are up against, Fascism was the menace of the world and each one of us had to fight it, that he was in a very privileged position, that he could furnish us with documents and material to help in this fight. Though he was reluctant and he had great misgivings about handing me documents, he consented to do so.

[2] *Hearings to Investigate the Administration of the Internal Security Act and Other Security Laws of the Committee on the Judiciary of the United States Senate* (Washington: U.S. Goverment Printing Office, 1951), pp. 2795–2823; 2871–2876.

MR. MORRIS. Mrs. Massing, in this connection did you ever have an encounter with Alger Hiss in connection with Noel Field?

MRS. MASSING. Yes, I did.

MR. MORRIS. Will you explain that to the Committee, please?

MRS. MASSING. Yes, it is this encounter with Alger Hiss that forced me out of my seclusion, because I don't believe that ex-Communists tend to go out and talk about their experiences, and I recall so well that when Whittaker Chambers was very reluctant and low-voiced in his testimony, how well I understood him, because it is a very difficult and horrible thing to not only speak about one's own past deviations in sins but about other people's involvements.

When Noel Field and I had established a rapport to the extent that he was quite willing to help me, when I had also convinced him—and I would like to say this here—that he must not join the open Party because for a man of Noel Field's status and importance it would be very unwise and useless to join the open Party, and he had wanted to do so—when he had agreed to work with me, which was not something like black and white—I mean there were many ups and downs, he would say "Yes" today and "No" tomorrow, and he would say "Yes, I will only do so much; I am willing to give you verbal reports but I am not willing to show you any documents, and I don't have any documents to show"—I mean it is an involved process—one of his last reluctances or one of his last resistances toward me came up in this way:

I visited with him and his wife. As a matter of fact, I lived in their house. He said to me, "You know,

Hede, I thought the whole thing over and I have come to the conclusion that it is really quite ridiculous that I should work with you where I can work with an old friend of mine who works with me in the State Department and who is a man of my kind. Not that I mean to say I don't respect you but, you see, you are a foreigner and this man is an American and we see eye to eye on all principal issues, and you understand even technically it would be so much easier for me to work with this man." Well, this was, of course, quite a disappointment for me. I had invested very much labor and intensity to get this man. If you do a job like this you want to do a good job, as I think everybody wants to do a fairly good job, and I was an espionage agent and I tried to do a good job, and having to lose Noel Field would have been quite a shock. So I said, "Who is this man?" He said, "I don't think you know him. His name is Alger Hiss." I said, "Well, why don't you introduce me to him? I just don't believe he has any priority over you. In reality I believe you are much better off in my apparatus." Then I said to him, "Where does he work? Where does he really work? How do you know he is the right man?" He said, "I don't know. I don't know where you work either." Noel Field arranged this meeting with Alger Hiss.

MR. MORRIS. So you did meet Alger Hiss?

MRS. MASSING. I did meet Alger Hiss. This is a meeting that I have spoken so much about that I find it very difficult to speak about again.

My superior, Russian superior at that time, Boris, was quite distressed about this meeting because it was unorthodox and it had not gotten the O.K. from Moscow. You see, Noel Field immediately arranged this meeting. Such things are not done without an

O.K. from Moscow. But Boris said since it had been arranged I should go ahead and meet him.

I came to Washington and the meeting was at the Noel Field apartment, and though it was a long evening, I believe the only thing that interests us here is that the discussion between Hiss and me ran like this:

He said, "So you are this woman that is trying to get Noel Field away from me?" I said, "No, you are the man who is trying to get Noel Field away from me, because I have worked with Noel Field for quite some time." He said, "Well, where have you worked?" I said, "Look Alger"—you understand among Communists people call each other Hede and Alger and not Mr. Hiss and Mrs. Massing. "You know, Alger, you shouldn't ask that and I wouldn't ask that either." He laughed and said, "Well, we will see who is going to win." I think I said, "Well, you know I am a woman," being very coy, and in order to break up this rather unpleasant conversation, and at the end either he or I agreed that it would not be for us to decide on whoever would get Noel Field; after all, we were working for the same boss.

SENATOR FERGUSON. When you say "get," what do you mean?

MRS. MASSING. Get, meaning soliciting him into your own unit as a co-worker.

SENATOR FERGUSON. In the apparatus?

MRS. MASSING. In the apparatus.

SENATOR SMITH. What difference would that make so far as the objective is concerned?

MRS. MASSING. That really is competition. There are always similar apparatuses in one country. There is a Comintern apparatus, a Red-army apparatus, a military-intelligence apparatus, an NKVD apparatus; and none of them have terribly much to do, I am made to believe, and getting a man as an informant is a very great thing to achieve. It is real competition. I mean you have worked on this man, you want to fulfill your job, you want to finish your job. In reality, actually, as for information, it would not probably make a great difference.

SENATOR SMITH. It gave you different recognition in the Party by getting and holding the man?

MRS. MASSING. Why of course. For example, when I had achieved this and later on had achieved soliciting Laurence Duggan into my apparatus, I was given honor, I was recognized as a fine comrade.

SENATOR SMITH. That is what I thought you meant. I wanted to bring it out.

MR. MORRIS. You mentioned Laurence Duggan. Did you have the assignment of recruiting Laurence Duggan into the apparatus?

MRS. MASSING. Yes, after I had met him and had reported about him.[3]

Another important witness who testified before our Subcommittee was Elizabeth Bentley, who had served as courier for two espionage rings in Washington during World War II. Appearing before the Subcommittee on May 29, 1952, she had the following to say concerning Alger Hiss:

MR. MORRIS. Miss Bentley, I wonder if you can tell us what you know about Alger Hiss?

Mr. Chairman, we have had previous testimony showing that Alger Hiss was an advisor of the IPR [Institute of Pacific Relations], and a member of the

[3]*ibid.*, pp. 233–234.

board of trustees of the IPR. For that reason, we are going to ask Miss Bentley if she had any connections, indirect or direct, with Alger Hiss.

MISS BENTLEY. They were indirect ones, but to my mind conclusive ones. In 1944 I took on a group of people I called the Perlo group.

MR. MORRIS. Who is Perlo?

MISS BENTLEY. Victor Perlo is a gentleman that I understand was a quite brilliant statistician with the War Production Board. He is now out of the government. The last I heard of him, I think he is in the Jefferson School in New York.

One of the members of the group was a Mr. Harold Glasser, in the Treasury.

In the process of checking everyone's past, I found that Mr. Glasser had, at one time, been pulled out of that particular group and had been turned over to a person whom both Mr. Perlo and Mr. Charles Kramer refused to tell me who it was, except that he was working for the Russians, and later they broke down and told me it was Mr. Alger Hiss.

Of course, I immediately checked that with my Soviet superior, because it could have been somebody else's intelligence service, and could be dangerous. Word came back to me: "That is all right. Lay off the Hiss thing. He is one of ours, but don't bother about it anymore."

MR. MORRIS. And you did not bother about it?

MISS BENTLEY. No. When you were told by your superior to lay off, you laid off.

Miss Bentley also told us that there was a fourth spy ring operating in Washington concerning which she knew only that it existed.

141

MR. MORRIS: In other words there was still a third group that you knew of that existed at that time?

MISS BENTLEY: There was a third group that I knew of because of Mr. Hiss, and there was another group that was mentioned to me by my Soviet contact without identifying it further.

MR. MORRIS: There is still a fourth group?

MISS BENTLEY: Yes.

MR. MORRIS: And you know, as a matter of fact, that neither one of those two groups, as far as you know, has been exposed as of this date?

MISS BENTLEY: As far as I know, they haven't been exposed.[4]

This testimony was not admissible at the first Hiss trial. Nathaniel Weyl did not come forward until after the Korean war began. The testimony of Weyl, Massing and Bentley did not bear directly on the issue of perjury, namely Chambers' relationship with the defendant.

Hiss had held a long series of important positions. He testified with evident pride concerning his role at Yalta where the stage was set for the prodigious gains that Communism would make in Europe and Asia. It was also at Yalta that the iniquitous Operation Keelhaul was approved which caused more than a million Russian expatriates to be forcibly sent back to the Soviet Union to face the Gulag Archipelago or execution.

Under questioning, Hiss expounded on his impeccable career. In the *New York Review of Books*, Garry Wills wrote about this testimony with biting sarcasm in a review of *Perjury*, Weinstein's major work on the case:

> He was almost drearily correct. He specialized in innocence. He was innocent of failure—so he could

[4] *ibid.*, pp. 441–443.

not understand his father. He was innocent of doubt —so he could not understand his brother, Bosley. He was so innocent of psychic turmoil that his sister was in and out of mental institutions for several years without his being aware of her disturbance. He passed through the Thirties so innocent of ideology that he could later swear he met no Communists at all, or—if he did meet any—he could not recognize them. He was innocent of friendship except with the well placed, with patrons. He seemed to spring fully armed from the head of Chief Justice [*sic!*] Oliver Wendell Holmes. He became the perfect civil servant, a political Jeeves who knew his place and filled it perfectly.[5]

This drab, colorless bureaucrat became a power in the Department of State during and after World War II.

MR. MUNDT. Did you draft, or participate in drafting, parts of the Yalta Agreement?

MR. HISS. I think it is accurate and not immodest to say that I did so to some extent, yes.[6]

Hiss was an eminent organizer of American postwar planning. Here is the testimony of Dr. Edna Fluegel, one of his assistants, concerning his role in that area:

MR. MORRIS. In other words, you testify that, although he had been acting director prior to February 1945, he formally became the director of what was in effect the postwar planning division of the State Department?

[5]Garry Wills, "The Honor of Alger Hiss," *New York Review of Books,* April 20, 1978.
[6]Whittaker Chambers, *Witness* (New York: Random House, 1952), p. 551.

MISS FLUEGEL. That is right.

MR. MORRIS, Now, will you tell us about the nature of his duties in that role, Dr. Fluegel?

MISS FLUEGEL. Well, right before Dumbarton Oaks, when he first came, he immediately took a very active part. He was in charge of all of the arrangements. He was secretary to several of the top planning committees and attended Dumbarton Oaks in that capacity.

I suppose you would describe his job as pretty much the job of a secretary general plus personal advisor to the delegates.

MR. MORRIS. What documents or what material would be available to him in that role?

MISS FLUEGEL. Everything that existed.

MR. MORRIS. Everything in the entire department of the highest classification?

MISS FLUEGEL. Yes. At that particular time, you see, Postwar involved everything, economics, social, political.

SENATOR WATKINS. Do you know that of your own personal knowledge?

MISS FLUEGEL. Yes. You see, everything, every single decision—at that time, they had this top secretary's committee which was the final place where policy decisions were made, and it really operated then. So that every paper on every subject requiring top policy decision came to it, and Mr. Hiss was, ex officio, a member of that committee.

SENATOR WATKINS. And all that material was then available to him, as it was to the members of the committee?

MISS FLUEGEL. That is right. Do you want me to carry on?

MR. MORRIS. Yes.

MISS FLUEGEL. Following the Dumbarton Oaks Conference, he did, of course, participate in all of the meetings, discussing plannings for Yalta, since a major part of the Yalta Conference—as a matter of fact the reason for the Yalta Conference—was the failure to settle certain questions during the Dumbarton Oaks Conference.

Among other things, I think you probably remember that there was a stage during the Dumbarton Oaks Conference when it was touch and go as to whether the conference would continue. There was a great deal of correspondence between Mr. Roosevelt and Mr. Stalin.

MR. MORRIS. Would you tell us when the Dumbarton Oaks Conference was held?

MISS FLUEGEL. I would have to check the exact date. Roughly in August and running through September.

MR. MORRIS. August of 1944?

MISS FLUEGEL. That is right. It was held in two stages. The first stage in which Great Britain and the United States and the Soviet Union participated, and the second between the United States, Great Britain, and China, with the final session that brought all four together.[7]

Alger Hiss was secretary-general of the conference at San Francisco where the United Nations was founded. His conduct there aroused grave suspicions of his true purposes in the mind

[7] *Hearings* . . . p. 2838.

145

of Canadian Prime Minister Mackenzie King. Soviet Foreign Minister Andrei Gromyko had the happy thought that Alger Hiss would make a splendid secretary-general of the United Nations, but this proposal aroused no enthusiasm in the White House. In large part due to Hiss' activities, the Secretariat at the United Nations would, however, be riddled with Communists and Soviet agents.

The evidence of Hiss' disloyalty was mounting, and the time had come for him to get out of the government. He arranged to get himself considered for the prestigious post of president of the Carnegie Endowment. When John Foster Dulles, chairman of the Endowment's Board, questioned Hiss about reports that he was suspected of having Communist ties, Hiss dismissed these reports as mere rumors of no importance. Yet he had considered them important enough to ask Dean Acheson whether they would prevent his rising further in the State Department. When Acheson told him that they were a threat to his promotion, Hiss decided to get out. By lying to Dulles, he wangled the appointment of president of the Carnegie Endowment for World Peace.

The Hiss case, the Kim Philby story, and the Burgess-Maclean case are examples of the ability of Soviet operatives to penetrate the very highest councils of the government of the United States, betray national secrets, and pervert American policies in the interests of a foreign enemy.

Hiss was finally brought down by the courageous testimony of Whittaker Chambers, who decided to stand up to the ascent of Soviet power. Here is what Chambers had to say about that decision in his moving autobiography, *Witness*:

> For the moment had arrived when some man must be a witness, and so had the man. They had come together. The danger to the nation from Communism had now grown acute, both within its own house and abroad. Its existence was threatened and the nation did not know it. For the first time, the Committee's subpoena gave me an opportunity to tell what I knew about the danger, not for the special

information and purposes of this or that security agency, however important its work. I knew that the FBI, for example, could not initiate action against Communism. By law it could only gather information which the Justice Department might or might not act on, as it saw fit. . . . I now know a little more about what I was then completely ignorant of—the problems of prosecution, the nature of evidence, the difficulties of proof, the long labors of investigation. Then I only felt, like many others, that the Communist danger was being concealed from the nation. The Committee, in effect, challenged me to spell out that danger where all men could hear it. I, unfortunately, was the man who could speak.[8]

The sequel to the Hiss story is interesting.

In the 1970s Alger Hiss made a career of speaking to college audiences belonging to a generation that was ignorant of the facts about his life, depicting himself as a victim of "McCarthyism," Richard Nixon, the forces of reaction, and the obscurely motivated and wholly supposititious malice of Whittaker Chambers, and also of the FBI.

When he reached the age of seventy, Hiss obtained his readmission to the Massachusetts bar—the first convicted felon in the state's history to win that privilege.

But this 1975 Massachusetts decision was not the final chapter. Using the Freedom of Information Act, liberal history professor Allen Weinstein examined 30,000 pages of classified FBI files and thousands of pages of other Department of Justice material on the case, obtained oral evidence from over eighty persons, interviewed Hiss half a dozen times, traveled 125,000 miles, and worked on the project for over four years.

When *Perjury* appeared in 1978, *Time* reviewed the book at length in an article entitled: "HISS: A NEW BOOK FINDS HIM GUILTY AS CHARGED—On the basis of fresh evidence,

[8]Whittaker Chambers, *Witness* (New York: Random House, 1952), pp. 551–553.

147

a scholar concludes that he spied and lied." The review exploded Hiss' spurious contentions of innocence and cited from the book massive new evidence that pointed irrefutably to his guilt.

Weinstein interviewed forty people who had never previously given testimony or statements on the case. These included Jozef Peters, the powerful director of all the illegal work of the American Communist Party in the 1930s and 1940s; the widow of Chambers' espionage superior in 1931–34, a resident of Israel; the widow of Lincoln Steffens, and many others. The Czech historian Karel Kaplan was able to tell Weinstein that former State Department official and Communist agent Noel Field testified to the Communist Czechoslovak authorities before his death that Hiss was in the U.S. Communist underground in the 1930s. Kaplan had read the interrogation transcript.

The Weinstein book conscientiously demolished the entire structure of Hiss' plea that he had been framed. It provided irrefutable proof that he had betrayed the American people during two decades of public service and then lied to them for the next two decades.

Alfred Kazin reviewed the Weinstein book in the March 28, 1978, issue of *Esquire* and was also overwhelmed and convinced by the mountain of evidence. Even the *New York Review of Books* hailed the book as a conclusive demonstration of Hiss' guilt.

While a few stalwart diehards will no doubt continue to protest Hiss' innocence until the end of time, for all intents and purposes the books are closed. The Liberal Establishment has finally seen the true face of its counterfeit hero.

The overwhelming prejudice in favor of the Left, the assumption of so many intellectuals that socialist revolutionaries are of necessity idealistic and decent people, whereas their conservative opponents are materialistic and sordid, prevented many, probably most, liberals from seeing what was self-evident until every last item of evidence was in.

This is not true of everyone concerned. Shortly after Nathaniel Weyl's testimony that Alger Hiss had been in the same

Communist cell with him in the early 1930s, Weyl ran into Norman Thomas, the perennial presidential candidate of the Socialist Party and a man universally respected for his unquestioned integrity. As Weyl remembers the encounter, Thomas said to him in effect:

> What I find hardest to understand about the case, Nathaniel, is why so many of the liberals and New Dealers defend Alger Hiss. Why, he dragged every decent thing they believe in into the mud and slime of espionage. And in addition, he lied about it. You would think they would realize that he betrayed them and that they would be, not his defenders, but his most bitter enemies.

The Hiss case may have finally ended. If so, justice has been served. But the deterioration and dry rot continue. When Hiss predicted that he would be vindicated within his lifetime, what he meant was that the trends that I am writing about are becoming irresistible and that there is a strong prospect that a Soviet or crypto-Soviet viewpoint may become the dominant attitude in America. Those who doubt that possibility should reflect on the significance of the decision of the Carter administration to prosecute John J. Kearney, a loyal, responsible, and dedicated counterintelligence officer, for having used allegedly illegal surveillance methods to checkmate the terrorist activities of the Weathermen.

The attorney general who initiated the prosecution observed that "times have changed."

Indeed they have.

15

A Tale of Three Traitors—Philby, Burgess, and MacLean

THE AMOUNT OF damage that a handful of highly placed Soviet agents can inflict on the security, foreign policy, and military operations of the United States is illustrated by the case of three notorious British traitors: H.A.R. (Kim) Philby, Guy Francis Burgess and Donald Duart Maclean. These three upper-class Englishmen had much in common. Burgess and Maclean were Cambridge educated; Philby was an Oxford man. Their country had given them high honors and positions of power. They repaid it with treason.

Philby was the master. American intelligence operatives who knew him have said that he was privy to everything. During the crucial Korean War years, 1949–1951, Philby was liaison between MI-5, also known as the British Special Intelligence Service (SIS), and the Central Intelligence Agency, the FBI, the Royal Canadian Mounted Police, and a host of other agencies.

After his defection to Moscow, Philby wrote an autobiography, *My Silent War*, which has proved to be of considerable assistance to me in writing these pages. In his introduction, Philby states:

> In case doubt should still lurk in devious minds, a plain statement of the facts is perhaps called for. In early manhood I became an accredited member of

the Soviet Intelligence Service. I can claim to have been a Soviet intelligence officer for some thirty odd years.[1]

Philby was in Washington with access to American internal security secrets during what he calls "the era of Hiss, Coplon, Fuchs, Gold, Greenglass, and the brave Rosenbergs—not to mention others who are still nameless." The reference is to Soviet espionage agents of the period, two of whom (the Rosenbergs) were electrocuted, four of whom served prison terms for their crimes (Hiss, Fuchs, Gold, and Greenglass), and one of whom (Coplon) had her conviction overturned for technical reasons.

While Philby was liaison for all U.S. intelligence in Washington, his fellow Soviet agent, Burgess, headed the Far Eastern section of the British embassy in Washington, while their colleague in disloyalty, Maclean, was assigned first to the British embassy in Washington and then was returned to London to head the American department at the British Foreign Office.

At the same time, E. Herbert Norman, whose career will be discussed later, was the head of the American and Far Eastern desks of the Canadian Foreign Office.

Thus influential agents were ensconced in strategic positions which gave them comprehensive access to American military and security information and a clear view of American capabilities, strategic intentions, and policy directions during the crucial years when General Douglas MacArthur was bearing the brunt of resisting the North Korean invasion of South Korea and later containing the hundreds of thousands of Chinese Communist "volunteers" who swarmed across the Yalu River to destroy the American and South Korean armies.

General MacArthur wrote in his *Reminiscences*:

[1]H.A.R. Philby, *My Silent War* (New York: Grove Press, 1968). Reprinted by permission of Grove Press, Inc. Copryright © 1968 by Grove Press, Inc.

That there was some leak in intelligence was evident to everyone. Brig. Gen. Walton Walker continually complained to me that his operations were known to the enemy in advance through sources in Washington. I will always believe that if the United States had issued a warning to the effect that any entry of the Chinese Communists in force into Korea would be considered an act of international war against the United States, the Korean War would have terminated with our advance north. I feel that the Reds would have stayed on their side of the Yalu. Instead, information must have been relayed to them, assuring them that the Yalu bridges would continue to enjoy sanctuary and that their bases would be left intact. They knew they could swarm down across the Yalu River without having to worry about bombers hitting their Manchurian supply lines.[2]

An official leaflet by General Lin Piao published in China read:

"I would never have made the attack and risked my men and military reputation if I had not been assured that Washington would restrain General MacArthur from taking adequate retaliatory measures against my lines of supply and communication."[3]

A decision had been made, itself a military monstrosity, that General MacArthur would not be able to bomb the Yalu River bridges that the Chinese Communists used to cross into Korea. Clearly the Reds had been informed of this secret directive by their intelligence agents in Washington. This was November 1950 when Philby, Maclean, and Burgess were all at their vital posts.

[2]Douglas MacArthur, *Reminiscences* (New York: McGraw-Hill, 1964), p. 365ff. Copyright © 1964 Time Inc. All rights reserved.
[3]*ibid*, p. 375.

152

MacArthur wrote of the directives under which he operated:

I was even more worried by a series of directives
from Washington which were greatly decreasing the
potential of my air force. First I was forbidden "hot"
pursuit of enemy planes that attacked our own.
Manchuria and Siberia were sanctuaries of inviolate
protection for all enemy forces and for all enemy
purposes, no matter what depredations or assaults
might come from there. Then I was denied the right
to bomb the hydroelectric plants along the Yalu. The
order was broadened to include every plant in North
Korea which was capable of furnishing electric
power to Manchuria and Siberia. Most incomprehen-
sible of all was the refusal to let me bomb the important supply center at Racin, which was not in Manchuria or Siberia, but many miles from the border,
in northeast Korea. Racin was a depot to which the
Soviet Union forwarded supplies from Vladivostok
for the North Korean Army. I felt that step-by-step
my weapons were being taken away from me.

Despite the welter of restrictions placed upon me by
Washington, I felt there remained one weapon I
could use against massive Chinese intervention. I
ordered General Stratemeyer to employ ninety
B-29s on the following morning to destroy the Yalu
bridges and cut this easy line of communication between Manchuria and North Korea, over which
large armies of Chinese Reds could swarm. Up to
now I had avoided doing so because of the danger of
accidentally missing the targets and dropping bombs
in Manchuria, which had been forbidden.

An immediate dispatch came from Secretary Marshall countermanding my order and directing me "to
postpone all bombing of targets within five miles of
the Manchurian border." It seemed to me incredible
that protection should be extended to the enemy, not

153

only of the bridges which were the only means they had for moving their men and supplies across that wide natural river barrier into North Korea, but also for a five-mile-deep area on this side of the Yalu in which to establish a bridgehead. It would be impossible to exaggerate my astonishment, and I at once protested.

The head of the Far East Bomber Command, Major General Emmett (Rosey) O'Donnell, made the following estimate of the situation:

We were not allowed to violate Manchurian territory, and by violation of the territory I mean we were not allowed to fly over an inch of it. For instance, like most rivers, the Yalu has several pronounced bends before getting to the town of Antung, and the main bridges at Antung we had to attack in only one manner—in order not to violate Manchurian territory, and that was a course tangential to the southernmost bend of the river. As you draw a line from the southernmost bend of the river to the bridge, that is your course. These people on the other side of the river knew that and put up their batteries right along the line, and they peppered us right down the line all the way. We had to take it, of course, and couldn't fight back. In addition to that, they had their fighters come up alongside and join our formation about two miles to the lee and fly along at the same speed on the other side of the river while we were making our approach. And just before we got to bomb-away position, they would veer off to the north and climb up to about 30,000 feet and then make a frontal quarter attack on the bombers just about at the time of bomb-away in a turn. So they would be coming from Manchuria in a turn, swoop down, fire their cannons at the formation, and continue to turn back to sanctuary.

154

General MacArthur continued, "One of those bomber pilots, wounded unto death, the stump of an arm dangling by his side, gasped at me through the bubbles of blood he spat out: 'General, which side are Washington and the United Nations on?' It seared my very soul."[4]

All during the Korean War, President Chiang Kai-shek offered to make available 600,000 of his fresh and well-trained troops. General MacArthur mentions President Chiang's offers of cooperation many times in his memoirs.

The State Department and President Truman always overruled MacArthur's recommendation that Chinese Nationalist troops be used. The rationale was that it would antagonize the Chinese Communists and draw them into the war.

The spurious character of this reasoning became evident when the Chinese Communist armies swarmed across the Yalu River nonetheless and attacked MacArthur's forces in North Korea. The Chinese Reds joined battle when it suited their purpose. If anything, our appeasing tactics encouraged them to attack. When it seemed possible that MacArthur's advice would prevail, the Chinese Communists maintained substantial forces opposite Formosa. When MacArthur was overruled, these forces were released and moved to Manchuria and the region of the Yalu.

We learned nothing from this experience. During the Vietnam War when American forces were having a difficult time battling the North Vietnamese, President Johnson asked Chiang to send a division. Chiang replied that he would send not one but six divisions which would attack Hanoi, then largely undefended, from the north. They would have probably ended North Vietnamese resistance. But the suggestion horrified the State Department, which again alleged that any such action would bring the Chinese Communists into the fray.

I had the felicitous assignment of being liaison to General MacArthur when I served as counsel to the Senate Internal Security Subcommittee. I visited him half a dozen times at his suite at the Waldorf-Astoria and our conversations lasted for

[4]MacArthur, *Reminiscences*, p. 369.

many hours. The General confided many matters to me and amplified the material that he would publish in his *Reminiscences*.

One of his most fascinating disclosures during these sessions was that he had a written agreement with Senator Robert A. Taft that if Taft won the Republican nomination in 1952 and was elected, MacArthur would be his vice-president "plenipotentiary" in charge of both defense and American foreign policy.

I have often thought what a different world we would live in today if that had come to pass.

To continue with the sordid story of Philby's treachery, in 1950 the CIA planned to assist a force of Albanian emigrés in invading their country and restoring its freedom. Albania was isolated geographically from the Soviet Union following the partial defection of Marshal Tito of Yugoslavia, and intelligence reports indicated that the Albanian armed forces were a rabble. The operation seemed to have every prospect of success and would have served as the first great step in the liberation of the subjugated states of the Balkans and the Danube basin from the Soviet yoke.

Philby, however, was in on the planning. In his autobiography he boasts of the fact that he betrayed the gallant force of five hundred Albanian exiles to the enemy. When they crossed the Albanian border from Greece in April 1950, they were ambushed at their supposedly secret border crossings and cut to pieces by artillery, mortar, and machine gun fire. Two hundred died in the attempt; one hundred and twenty were captured and executed; a bare one hundred and eighty survivors straggled back.

The CIA immediately realized that one of the few key men who had been cognizant of the entire operation must be a traitor. Frank Wisner, the CIA official in charge of secret operations, had been completely hoodwinked by Philby and had characterized him to Allen Dulles as a "great fellow . . . a real friend." But James Angleton, who headed CIA counterintelligence, had distrusted Philby for years. He took his suspicions to Allen Dulles and to CIA Director Walter Bedell Smith. Angleton's suspicions were confirmed, but there was not enough evidence to put Philby on trial. The answer was obviously intensive and patient surveillance. Unfortunately, either the deputy director of intelligence (DDI) or somebody on his staff blundered and ordered that certain top secret matters be withheld from Philby. This ill-considered move alerted the master spy, and he was thus able to arrange for the instant defection of Burgess and Maclean, two weaker links in the espionage chain, both of whom promptly surfaced in Moscow as avowed Communist agents.

Philby achieved this with characteristic ingenuity. He ordered Maclean to speed along the Virginia highways at such excessive rates that he received three tickets in a single day. An outraged governor of Virginia protested to the State Department, charging Maclean with a flagrant breach of diplomatic privileges. The British ambassador "regretfully" notified Maclean that he had to leave Washington. Once he was out of the country, escape to the USSR was simple.

"Beetle" Smith, according to Leonard Mosley's excellent biography of the Dulles family, sent a strongly worded letter to the SIS declaring Philby *persona non grata* with the Agency. He added, in a private note to his old friend in London, General Kenneth Strong: "I hope the bastard gets his. I know a couple of Albanian tribesmen who would like to have half an hour apiece with him."[5]

Thus warned, the British Special Intelligence Service subjected Philby to what Mosley believes was a "merciless" grilling, but without decisive results. Philby remained unmolested and continued his activities as a Soviet spy for the next twelve years.

With unconcealed glee, Philby relates how years later, when he was the SIS intelligence officer for Turkey, he betrayed a Russian official who wished to defect. Philby learned that one Konstantin Volkov, vice-consul of the USSR embassy in Turkey, had identified himself to the British resident diplomat as a secret KGB agent and had stated that he wanted to defect.

[5]Leonard Mosley, *Dulles* (New York: Dial Press, 1978).

Volkov told the resident diplomat that there were three Soviet agents inside the British Foreign Office that he could identify. Philby's consternation can be imagined.

Fortunately for Philby, Volkov vetoed having his intention to defect communicated by radio in code. Philby took advantage of the opportunity this delay provided and held matters in suspended animation until he arrived in Ankara from London.

When Philby did arrive the following week and the British intermediary phoned the Soviet embassy to carry out the offer of asylum, he was curtly told that nobody by that name had ever been accredited to the USSR delegation. Volkov had been betrayed by Philby and sent home to the Soviet Union during the week.

British intelligence had, however, noted the unusual increase in the volume of communications between the KGB offices in London and Moscow and coincidentally between the Soviet embassy in Turkey and Moscow during that week. British suspicions were finally concentrating on Philby. The traitor fled, just in time, to Moscow.

I have written elsewhere in this volume that when I was an assistant counsel to the New York State Legislative Committee investigating the New York public school system for subversion, I caused a subpoena to be served on General Walter Krivitsky in Washington, D.C. Instead of responding to the subpoena, Krivitsky was found shot to death in a Washington hotel room. This occurred in 1940.

Philby writes in his book that Krivitsky had warned British intelligence that the head of Western European intelligence for the NKVD had recruited a young Englishman in the mid-1930s and that this man was operating in the British Foreign Office and on the periphery of intelligence.

As we know, the British failed to follow through on this information. Had we had the opportunity to explore the matter thoroughly with General Krivitsky, it is possible that Philby could have been caught, indicted, and imprisoned a quarter of a century before his flight to Moscow. To have done this would have saved the lives of valiant fighters for human freedom and possibly changed the course of history.

Philby's revelations about his methods are instructive. He boasts in his memoirs that he did his best espionage work not at his desk reading official papers, but circulating in the intelligence and diplomatic circles where he was usually accepted without suspicion. He wrote that a half hour with an informant is more important to a spy than official documents:

> The fact is that the Soviet Union is interested in a very wide range of Middle Eastern phenomena. Enjoying a wide margin of priority at the top of the list are the intentions of the United States and British governments in the area. For an assessment of such intentions, I was not too badly placed. One writer, discussing my case, commented on the fact that I seldom asked direct questions; I was the least curious of journalists. Of course! If you put direct questions on matters of substance to any American or British official, you are apt to get either an evasion or a whopping great lie. But in the course of general conversation, discussion, and argument, it is not impossible to get the drift of your interlocutor's thinking or to estimate with fair accuracy his standing in respect of policy decisions.

> It is difficult, though by no means impossible, for a journalist to obtain access to original documents. But these are often a snare and a delusion. Just because a document is a document, it has a glamor which tempts the reader to give it more weight than it deserves. This document from the United States embassy in Amman, for example: Is it a first draft, a second draft, or the finished memorandum? Was it written by an official of standing, or by some dogsbody with a bright idea? Was it written with serious intent or just to enhance the writer's reputation?

Even if it is unmistakably a direct instruction to the United States ambassador from the secretary of state dated last Tuesday, is it still valid today? In short, documentary intelligence, to be really valuable, must come as a steady stream, embellished with an awful lot of explanatory annotation. An hour's serious discussion with a trustworthy informant is often more valuable than any number of original documents. Of course, it is best to have both.[6]

How many Burgesses, Philbys, and Macleans are there coiled in strategic vantage points?

When Elizabeth Bentley, who ran two military intelligence rings in Washington, testified in the early 1950s, she identified as Communist agents the then assistant to the president of the United States, the assistant secretary of the treasury, the secretary of the International Monetary Fund, the head of the Postwar Planning Section of the State Department, and a score of others.

With the ramparts of our internal security torn down by complacency and smug illusions concerning Soviet intentions, do we have any reason to suppose that we are less effectively infiltrated today?

[6]Philby, *My Silent War*, p. 255. Reprinted by permission of Grove Press, Inc. Copyright © 1968 by Grove Press, Inc.

160

16

The Suicide of E. Herbert Norman

THE NORMAN CASE is closely related to those of Philby, Burgess, and MacLean. If those three provided the Soviet Union with information concerning secret U.S. foreign policy and internal security from the vantage points of the British Foreign Office and the British SIS, Norman was in a position to perform a similar service at the same time as a high official of the Canadian Foreign Office.

The salient difference between these cases is that the British trio escaped to Moscow to boast of their successful triumph, whereas Norman came to a tragic end.

E. Herbert Norman committed suicide in Cairo in 1957. Shortly before taking this step, he informed a close friend that he was destroying himself because he believed that the evidence against him would trigger a Canadian royal investigating commission, similar to the one which a decade earlier had unearthed the labyrinthine maze of Soviet espionage nets in the United States and Canada reported by defecting Soviet cipher clerk Igor Guzenko.

Norman stated, according to the same source, that if pressed, he would have to implicate between sixty and seventy American and Canadian citizens. This assertion seems to imply that he was in the process of disengaging himself from the Communist network and was experiencing remorse.

During the Korean War, Norman was chief of the Canadian

161

mission to SWAP, General MacArthur's headquarters in Tokyo. He strongly opposed General MacArthur's drive toward the Yalu. In 1951, when his name surfaced in the hearings of the Senate Internal Security Subcommittee, Norman headed the American and Far Eastern departments of the Canadian Foreign Office.

We discovered that Norman had extensive associations with the Institute of Pacific Relations, a prestigious academic front for Communist propaganda with interlocking connections with Soviet espionage. We received corroborative evidence that he was a member of the Communist Party.

The evidence on the latter point consisted of sworn testimony and a security memorandum which cited FBI, CIA, and Royal Canadian Mounted Police information. I should perhaps add at this point that the RCMP has responsibilities for the protection of Canadian internal security at the highest levels.

More recently, a sympathetic biography of Norman was published by Charles Taylor in a 1977 issue of *Anansi,* a Toronto publication. According to Taylor, Norman became close to John Cornford, the son of a prominent classicist who "left the Young Communist League to become a full-fledged Communist. Soon afterward, by his own account, Norman followed him into the Party." This was stated to have occurred in 1935.

Taylor added: "To this day there is no available evidence of how long Norman remained a member of the Communist Party."

The evidence that the Internal Security Subcommittee accumulated on the Norman case indicated that he remained a Communist for many years. Let us examine the story as contained in the official report of the Senate Internal Security Subcommittee on the case, eliminating numerous repetitions:

> During the spring of 1957 the Subcommittee was widely calumniated in connection with the case of E. Herbert Norman, a Canadian diplomat who committed suicide in Cairo on April 4. So widespread was this attack on the Committee that failure to include

mention of the matter in this report would be a der-
eliction.

The Committee regrets that accumulated events
make it impossible to preserve silence in deference
to the advent of death, which normally would cast a
protective veil over the events which preceded it. But
irresponsible persons have made totally false statements about the Norman case, creating widespread
mistaken impressions of the facts. The Committee
avoided controversy, and did not fight back. For the
Committee to remain silent on the subject in this
report, however, would be a newsworthy thing,
likely to give rise to more false and mistaken impressions.

The aftermath of Herbert Norman's suicide was
utilized to launch a major attack upon the Internal
Security Subcommittee, but an attack not limited to
the Internal Security Subcommittee or its staff.
Though the Subcommittee may have been intended
as the main target, this was in a very real sense an
attack upon the right of the Senate to exercise its
investigatory powers with respect to activities,
within the borders of the United States, in aid of the
world Communist conspiracy. The shrill, intemper-
ate, and in some cases actually vicious character of
this attack showed the emotionalism which under-
lay it. The Committee is of the opinion that this
emotionalism did not arise wholly from spontaneous
sympathy for the late E. Herbert Norman, but arose
in many instances from hatred of the Internal Security Subcommittee and what it stands for: hatred of
all investigating Committees which have Communism as their target; hatred, in fact, of anti-Communism itself.

The Committee feels, therefore, an inescapable duty
to report the facts of the Norman case.

First, the Subcommittee was interested in E. Herbert Norman, not because of his diplomatic position in Canada, but because we had evidence that he had been an active member of Communist units in New York City and Cambridge, Massachusetts and had participated in other Communist and pro-Communist activity in the United States, and with American Communists, over a period of more than fifteen years.

Second, the evidence to this effect was not hearsay, or innuendo, or baseless slanders, but authentic documents and eyewitness testimony under oath.

Third, despite the oft-repeated assertion that Canada long ago "cleared" Mr. Norman of these "charges" by means of a "double security check," none of the items of derogatory information in our record was ever specifically challenged, and in fact no representative of the Canadian Government has ever talked to the eyewitness who gave testimony before us that he knew Mr. Norman as a Communist.

Fourth, separately and in addition to the above, Herbert Norman, according to an FBI report, admitted having lied to the FBI in Cambridge, Massachusetts, in 1942.

In 1951, when the Internal Security Subcommittee commenced its hearings into the machinations of the Institute of Pacific Relations, as the first segment of our continuing study of Communist strategy and tactics, we began to accumulate evidence about the Communist conspiracy in the United States as it was operating to subvert our Far Eastern policy and to augment the power of Red China. It must be stressed that this was an inquiry into the identity and the movements of Communists operating in the United States. This investigation was based on sworn testimony of competent witnesses, and on the records and papers of the Institute itself; and it enabled the Subcommittee to make numerous findings and conclusions in aid of legislation.

During the IPR inquiry, the name of E. Herbert Norman came into the record thirty-six times without any effort by the Committee to pursue an investigation with respect to Mr. Norman. These references to Mr. Norman were entirely collateral to the main inquiry with respect to the activities of the IPR, and came about because the facts as the Committee uncovered them show substantial and continuing activity by Mr. Norman in connection with the activities of the IPR and its leading officials and directors. Early in 1957 Mr. Norman's name again crossed the path of the Internal Security Subcommittee in connection with an inquiry into faulty intelligence reports from the Far East by American diplomats more recently moved to the Middle East. Here is what the evidence shows:

Mr. Norman in 1937, while at Harvard University, was a member of one of the groups that the Communists were fostering in the furtherance of their organization on the campus.

Shigeto Tsuru, testifying under oath before the subcommittee, told us that Norman was a member of this group, and both Tsuru and the written record indicated that one contribution of Norman was a paper called "American Imperialism."

A year later our evidence indicated the same Mr. Norman was a member of a Communist group which was meeting near Columbia University in New York City.

It was reported in a security memorandum which has been fully identified in the executive record of our Subcommittee, but which has been identified publicly only as a United States government executive agency security report, that in February 1940 E. Herbert Norman, who was at that time attending Harvard, was a member of the Communist Party.

We next encountered the name of Norman in this same security report which read:

"When Shigeto Tsuru, Japanese instructor at Harvard, was apprehended for repatriation purposes in 1942, the FBI was approached by Norman who represented himself as an official on highly confidential business of the Canadian government in an effort to take custody of Tsuru's belongings.

"One main item of these belongings was a complete record of the Nye munitions investigations, largely prepared by Alger Hiss.

"Norman later admitted to the FBI agents in charge that his was only a personal interest and that he was not representing the Canadian government as stated."

Testimony taken from Mr. Tsuru confirmed this reference to the FBI, in that he testified Norman had acknowledged to him that he "pressed" to get these papers, which contained many Communist secrets.

The evidence in the IPR hearings, mainly from acknowledged written records of the Institute of Pacific Relations but partly from sworn testimony, relates to Herbert Norman's activities either in the United States or as reported in the papers of the IPR which were subpoenaed in the United States (such as Mr. Norman's designation while he was in Tokyo as a channel for transmission of "very secret messages" from one IPR character to another). This IPR activity and association on the part of Mr. Norman continued from the late 1930s until at least 1950—a span of more than fifteen years.

The inescapable conclusion from this record was that Mr. Norman was a Communist, that he had operated in the United States, and that this activity covered a long period of time.[1]

Norman's suicide was not only a personal tragedy (as all acts of self-destruction are), it was also a grave misfortune for the internal security of Canada and the United States. As a result, we may never know the identities of the sixty to seventy American and Canadian Communists and Soviet agents Norman believed he would be compelled to name under royal commission interrogation. We may never know how many of these people are still in office, whether any have risen to occupy key positions for the perversion of foreign policy or the transmission of secret information to the Soviet Union, what cells they belonged to, what has happened to these cells, and, if individual agents have retired, whether they have left successors behind them to continue their disloyal work.

[1] *Report of the Subcommittee to Investigate the Administration of the Internal Security Act and Other Security Laws to the Committee of the Judiciary of the United States Senate,* 1957, pp. 79–109.

17

Lee Harvey Oswald and the U-2

LEE HARVEY OSWALD triggered the greatest non-military crisis that the United States has ever experienced. The assassination of John Fitzgerald Kennedy convulsed the nation and sent political tables spinning. It renewed a dying Democratic Party and stopped short a growing resistance movement in the nation that threatened to sweep from power those forces which had, in the span of two years, permitted the Soviet build-up of missiles in Cuba, the overthrow of President Diem in South Vietnam, and other geopolitical retreats.

I was in Dallas when this terrible deed was accomplished. Dallas was then a city that was avant-garde in expressing indignation at the decline of the nation. Ted Dealey, the publisher of the *Dallas Morning News*, was a clear voice in rallying the people against the flaccid response of Washington in the face of the ruthlessness of Khrushchev and the boldness of Castro.

Chief County Judge Lew Sterret was the leading Democratic official in the city. He, too, was appalled at the trends he beheld.

Through a mutual friend, Judge Sterret asked me to arrange a meeting with Peter O'Donnell, the Republican chairman, and himself. At that luncheon meeting Sterret opined that the whole Democratic organization from the president to the county courthouse was about to be wiped out at the upcoming election and he did not intend that his long years of great service be ended by a political defeat brought on by the weakness of President Kennedy.

I report this as an indication of the mood that prevailed two or three days before the assassination.

Then the thunderclap struck, and Oswald's finger triggered a political revolution. Dallas was depicted as a city of "hate," and voices that had been raised against the retreats of our country were silenced and defamed. Ted Dealey lost control of his newspaper and his clear voice was stilled. Democrats swept the 1964 elections from the presidency to the county courthouse.

No one seemed to think it relevant that a Communist had done the killing. The Warren Commission Report was a whitewash in this respect. Under pressure from Lyndon Johnson to get its final report out in time to help him in the forthcoming November elections, the Warren Commission failed to check speculations that Oswald had come "into contact with Communist agents" while a marine in Japan. We now know that he did.

Although over one hundred men had served with Oswald in the marines and many of them would later tell author Edward Jay Epstein and a team of *Reader's Digest* researchers about the blatant pro-Communism of the future assassin and his evident hatred of his own country, the commission interrogated only one of them, a marine whose tour of duty had overlapped Oswald's for only a few months.

Later, a congressional committee was named and heavily financed to find out the truth behind the Kennedy assassination. To the date of this writing, it has done little or nothing to expose the self-evident Castro connection and Communist involvement of Oswald. Instead, resorting to lamentable standards of evidence and using double hearsay, it has attempted to smear Dallas businessmen in connection with the Kennedy assassination. The committee seemed, in 1977, to be taking guidance from Mark Lane, a writer who has been articulating the Communist rationalization of the crime for years.

We know that Oswald surrendered his United States citizenship and swore loyalty to the Soviet Union. We know that he

169

boasted of giving the Soviet authorities any and all military secrets he had managed to acquire. We know that he wrote to his brother from Moscow: "In the event of war I would kill any American who put a uniform on in defense of the American government—any American." As Epstein summarized it, Oswald "had put himself firmly under the control of his [Russian] hosts. He had defected, renounced his citizenship, compromised military secrets, and denounced his country and family."[1]

Even as a schoolboy, Oswald had parroted Communist propaganda. In the marines, he "railed against the American intervention in Korea," which he said had resulted in "one million useless deaths." He referred to his countrymen as "you Americans." He was called "Comrade Oswaldskovich" by fellow soldiers who despised and tormented him.

Although he was ridiculed for being scrawny and prissy and was called "Mrs. Oswald," he managed to get steady dates with a hostess at the Queen Bee bar, where dates cost from $60 to $100. (Oswald's monthly pay was $85, and he was, in the opinion of his fellow soldiers, not the sort of man who could get an attractive woman without paying for her.) An explanation of this apparent anomaly may well be that Oswald was already feeding valuable military information to his Russian masters. The Queen Bee hostesses were suspected by the Office of Naval Intelligence of serving as intelligence agents.

We also know that Oswald was permitted to marry a Russian woman, who was the niece of a lieutenant colonel in the MVD (Ministry of Internal Affairs), and to take her with him out of Russia. Foreigners are normally not allowed to take Soviet wives with them outside the USSR. The intelligence connections of Marina Oswald made it a virtual certainty that her husband was allowed to leave with her solely because he was a trusted Soviet agent.

One of the vital facts about Oswald that should have been

[1]Edward Jay Epstein, "Legend: The Secret World of Lee Harvey Oswald," *Reader's Digest,* March 1978. This and following material is taken from the engrossing condensation of *Legend,* the full text not being available at this writing.

thoroughly exposed, but was adroitly concealed until the publication of Edward Jay Epstein's findings, was the assassin's possible implication in the downing of the American spy-in-the-sky, the U-2. Readers will recall that the late Gary Powers, a U-2 pilot, was shot down over Soviet territory on May 1, 1960, and that Khrushchev used the ensuing furor as a pretext to torpedo a summit conference on world disarmament between President Eisenhower and himself.

Powers wrote in his book *Operation Overflight* as follows:

> The third bit of "evidence" poses far more questions than it answers. Yet it is, in its own way, by far the most intriguing. It concerns the possibility of the altitude of the U-2 having been betrayed.

> When the U-2's altitude is referred to as "secret," that term is qualified. In addition to those personally involved in U-2 flights, a number of others, by the nature of their duties, had access to this information. These included air-traffic controllers and at least some of the radar personnel at the bases where U-2s were stationed.

> In 1957 the U-2s were based in a new location, Atsugi, Japan. In September of that year a seventeen-year-old Marine Corps private was assigned to Marine Air Control Squadron No. 1 (MACS-1), based at Atsugi. MACS-1 was a radar unit whose duties included scouting for incoming foreign aircraft. Its equipment included height-finding radar. The private, a trained radar operator, had access to this equipment.

> He remained in Japan until November 1958, at which time he was returned to the United States and assigned to Marine Air Control Squadron No. 9 (MACS-9) at the Marine Corps Air Station at El Toro, California. El Toro was not a U-2 base, but U-2s frequently flew over this portion of southern Califor-

nia. At El Toro he had access not only to radar and radio codes but also to the new MPS 16 height-finding radar gear.

In September 1959, he obtained a "hardship discharge" from the U.S. Marine Corps.

The following month he defected to the Soviet Union.

On October 31 he appeared in the American embassy in Moscow to state his intention of renouncing his U.S. citizenship. According to Richard E. Snyder, the second secretary and senior consular official, and John A. McVickar, Snyder's assistant, who was also present, during the course of the conversation he mentioned that he had already offered to tell the Russians everything he knew about the Marine Corps and his specialty, radar operation. He also intimated that he might know something of "special interest."

His name was Lee Harvey Oswald.

Six months later my U-2 was shot down.[2]

Oswald's familiarity with MPS 16 height-finding radar gear and radar and radio codes (the latter were changed following his defection) are mentioned in the testimony of John E. Donovan, a former first lieutenant assigned to the same El Toro radar unit as Oswald, at the Warren Commission hearings. According to Donovan, Oswald "had access to the location of all bases in the west coast area, all radio frequencies for all squadrons, all tactical call signs, and the relative strength of all squadrons, number and type of aircraft in a squadron, who was the commanding officer, and the authentication code of entering and exiting the ADIZ, which stands for Air Defense Identifi-

[2]Gary Powers, *Operation Overflight* (New York: Holt, Rinehart & Winston, 1970).

172

cation Zone. He knew the range of our radar. He knew the range of our radio. And he knew the range of the surrounding units' radio and radar."[3]

Oswald's conversation with Snyder is mentioned at least three times in the Warren Commission's report:

"Oswald told him that he had already offered to tell a Soviet official what he had learned as a radar operator in the marines."[4]

"Oswald stated to Snyder that he had voluntarily told Soviet officials that he would make known to them all information concerning the Marine Corps and his specialty therein, radar operation, he possessed."[5]

"He stated that he had volunteered to give Soviet officials any information that he had concerning Marine Corps operations, and intimated that he might know something of special interest."

During the six months following the October 31, 1959, embassy meeting, there were only two overflights of the USSR. The one which occurred on April 9, 1960, was uneventful. The one which followed on May 1, 1960, wasn't.

Here the trail ends, except for one tantalizing lead, discovered during the research for this volume.

Among the Warren Commission documents in the National Archives in Washington, D.C., is one numbered 931, dated May 13, 1964, CIA national security classification secret.

In response to an inquiry, Mark G. Eckhoff, director of the Legislative, Judicial, and Diplomatic Records Division of the National Archives, in a letter dated October 13, 1969, stated: "Commission Document 931 is still classified and withheld from research."

[3] *Report of the Warren Commission on the Assassination of President Kennedy* (New York: McGraw-Hill, 1964), vol. 8, p. 298.
[4] *ibid.*, p. 618.
[5] *ibid.*, p. 665.

The title of Document 931 is "Oswald's Access to Information About the U-2."

To continue with the story as revealed in *Legend,* Oswald was assigned to MACS-1 at Atsugi marine base as an aviation electronics operator, and as Epstein relates:

> On the eastern part of the base, about four hundred yards from the marine hangars, was a complex of some twenty buildings, identified on several signs as the "Joint Technical Advisory Group." For these reasons, Atsugi remained a "closed" base, which meant that personnel on the base had to have cards showing their security clearance.[6]

We know that, according to Oswald's later confidential statement to a Dallas associate, he "had become involved with a small circle of Japanese Communists in Tokyo while in the marines."

Now let us consider this situation in relation to the overall U-2 picture. The U-2 was designed and put into production by a CIA team under Richard Bissell, Jr., and operational control of flights remained in the hands of the CIA. The first flight occurred in the summer of 1956, taking off from Wiesbaden, Germany, flying directly over Moscow and Leningrad, and returning via the Baltic. At peak operations, the CIA had three flight centers and U-2 detachments overseas: Wiesbaden; Adana, Turkey; and Atsugi near Tokyo.

The Russians became aware of the U-2 flights almost immediately, and they made a formal diplomatic protest within two months of the initial flight. There was no thought of heeding the protest, however, because the U-2 reconnaissance was such a spectacular success that the photographs brought back enabled experts to identify such details as the make of the cars in the Kremlin parking lot. Moreover, U.S. intelligence knew that Soviet missiles were at optimum efficiency in the 60,000–65,000 altitude range and believed that their highest potential range

[6]Epstein, *Reader's Digest*, March 1978.

was 81,000 feet. Nevertheless, as Mosley tells the story in *Dulles*, there was reason to fear that the Russians would ultimately design missiles with the capacity needed to bring down the U-2.

It was therefore of great importance for Soviet military intelligence to know U-2 flight altitudes and performance limitations. Obviously, Lee Harvey Oswald would not be given this information directly. As a radio man, however, he would hear requests for reports on weather conditions and wind velocity and direction at 90,000 feet. This would tell any half-competent intelligence analyst that the U-2 would be operating at that altitude. Moreover, as Epstein tells the story:

> At Atsugi, Oswald could have witnessed repeated takeoffs of Race Car, the still-supersecret U-2, and, from visual, radar, and radio observation, could have established its rate of climb, performance characteristics, and cruising altitude. With the proper guidance he might have been able to decipher elements of its radar-jamming equipment.[7]

I obtained document 931—or what was purported to be document 931—but it contained no evidence whatsoever that would justify the "secret" classification imposed upon it.

The Epstein book, however, brought out other revealing facts about the "erratic" Oswald.

For instance, while in Mexico City in September 1963, two months before the assassination, attempting to obtain a visa to return to the Soviet Union, he visited the Cuban embassy there. The ostensible reason for that stop was his wish to visit Havana on route to Moscow. When Oswald left the Cuban embassy, officials there cabled the KGB center in Moscow requesting guidance on the visa.

When Oswald returned to the Cuban embassy three days later, the visa official phoned the Soviet embassy once again. But before doing so, she asked Oswald to whom he had spoken.

[7]Epstein, *Reader's Digest*, March 1978.

Oswald replied: "Comrade Kostikov on September 28." It was suggested that he therefore speak to Kostikov again. He did so, ending the phone conversation by saying "I'll be right over," and hung up.

The significance of this is that Kostikov was a KGB officer of the Thirteenth Department that handled sabotage and assassinations in foreign countries.

After the conversation with Kostikov, moreover, Oswald abandoned his efforts to obtain a visa to Russia via Havana and took a bus to Texas.

Months earlier, according to the Epstein book, Oswald had attempted to assassinate retired General Edwin Walker in Dallas.

When he left his wife Marina for that attempt on April 10, Oswald gave her a note in Russian which instructed her what to do if he were apprehended: "Send the information on what happened to me to the embassy and include newspaper clippings (should there be anything about me in the newspapers)." As Epstein asserts, he was clearly referring to the Russian embassy which, he suggested in the note, "will come quickly to your assistance on learning everything."

This note, which reflected at least what Oswald thought his relationship to the USSR was, was kept by Marina after the assassination and not turned over to the FBI, the secret service, or the police. Only when a friend found it in a cookbook did she acknowledge it and that she knew of Oswald's attempt on Walker's life.

There are other intriguing details in the Epstein book that give credence to the late President Johnson's analysis of the assassination shortly before his death. In an interview he opined that John F. Kennedy was killed by Castro agents in retaliation for planned attempts on the life of the bearded dictator by the CIA.

18

The Shameful Case of Wilfred Burchett

OSTENSIBLY, WILFRED BURCHETT is an Australian journalist. The designation "journalist" implies, as a rule, a man whose profession is to report the news as objectively as he can, to let the facts speak for themselves, and to let the chips fall where they may.

The Senate Internal Security Subcommittee was able to take sworn testimony from former KGB operative Yuri Krotkov which depicted Burchett as a disgrace to his profession and a man guilty of unspeakable acts against his country and against the civilized world. Krotkov gave sworn testimony that Burchett was a KGB agent who had visited North Korean prisoner-of-war camps and pressured American POWs to confess to false germ warfare charges.

Australia, the nation to which Burchett owed and still owes allegiance, was part of the United Nations force repelling a North Korean invasion. Burchett was spreading the Kremlin-inspired lie that the United Nations forces were using germ warfare, and he was participating in the abuse of United Nations prisoners of war in Communist camps, while dutiful Australians were fighting and dying in the conflict.

On the grounds that he was a Communist agent, Burchett had been consistently denied a visa to visit the United States. The ban was rigorously enforced in part because of reports that he was implicated in the torture of American POWs.

The State Department lifted the ban on this alleged KGB

agent. By November 1977 he was touring the United States, speaking on college and high school campuses and busily spreading the propaganda fed to him by his Communist superiors.

The *New York Post,* which had come under the ownership of the Australian publisher Rupert Murdoch, ran a brilliant series of exposé articles on the Burchett case by reporter William Heffernan. The *Post* stated that the State Department had withheld vital security information and evidence that revealed Burchett's KGB role and his unspeakable actions against American and other United Nations prisoners of war.

Apparently these facts were suppressed to ensure Burchett's entry into the United States and his red carpet treatment in this country.

Mr. Heffernan's lead article, published in the *New York Post* on November 16, 1977, speaks for itself. Let me quote it:

> Communist newsman Wilfred Burchett, known to government officials here as a Soviet KGB agent who interrogated and tortured American POWs in Korea and Vietnam, is now making a speaking tour of this country with the help of the U.S. State Department, a *Post* investigation has found.
>
> Burchett, 66, an Australian, is listed by the U.S. Immigration Service as "ineligible" for a travel visa here because of his membership in the Communist Party.
>
> Last month, however, Burchett was granted a three-month waiver of that status at the request of high-ranking State Department officials after it was referred to State by the White House.
>
> The *Post* has learned, however, that these same State Department officials withheld information about Burchett's KGB activities from their Immigration counterparts.

They also failed to advise Immigration about Burchett's brutal interrogation of allied prisoners of war during the Korean and Vietnam wars.

The immigration official who approved the waiver, Ralph Kramer, deputy assistant commissioner for adjudications, told the *Post* in a recent Washington interview that the State Department never advised his office of Burchett's KGB status or his involvement in the torture and brainwashing of American POWs.

"If we had known that, you can be sure it would have been given heavy consideration," Kramer said. "I don't understand why that information was withheld."[1]

Faced with this evidence of his disloyal conduct, Burchett had the effrontery to retort that Krotkov, who had identified Burchett under oath as a paid KGB agent with whom he collaborated in Europe and in Moscow, had recanted that testimony.

Krotkov was living on the West Coast under an assumed name. Reporter Heffernan succeeded in obtaining his new address and phoned him. Krotkov stated that Burchett's assertion that he repudiated his charges was an unmitigated lie.

No cause is too odious for a certain type of prominent American intellectual whose main mental activity seems to consist of giving a veneer of respectability to foreign agents, including, of course, those who torture American prisoners of war. Accordingly, a Wilfred Burchett Support Committee was formed. Among its members were Noam Chomsky, David Dellinger, William Kunstler, Corliss Lamont, Cora Weiss, and Howard Zinn. If at some future date an American Hall of Infamy should somehow be established, these worthy people should be considered eligible for membership.

[1]Reprinted by Permission of the *New York Post*. Copyright © 1977, New York Post Corporation.

Having completed his mischief in Indochina and Korea, Burchett is now dedicating his unique skills and the funds he raised in the United States to destroying South Africa and Rhodesia.

19

The Mysterious Death of
Povl Bang-Jensen

POVL BANG-JENSEN was a Dane who worked at the United Nations and had stars in his eyes about what that organization could become "if it were in good hands." I met Povl at the New York Yacht Club with Ambassador Walter Anderson, formerly director of Naval Intelligence. Anderson brought us together because Bang-Jensen was secretary of the United Nations committee that was working with Hungarians who had fled to the West when Soviet tanks rolled into Budapest in the winter of 1956 and the Iron Curtain of police state repression again descended on the Hungarian people. My concern with this matter was that I was chief counsel to the Senate Internal Security Subcommittee which was hearing testimony from the Hungarian fugitives.

I became Povl's trusted advisor, and this relationship is the source of my story.

Povl was in a minority among United Nations officials because he was friendly toward the United States. Discerning that fact, our government gave him assignments which, I understand, he performed with dispatch.

The Hungarian revolution of 1956 and the ruthless Soviet repression of that popular uprising, followed by the occupation of the country by Red Army troops, caused deep revulsion even among veteran Soviet and Communist officials. Many wished to defect.

181

At the time, Povl was at U.N. headquarters in New York. Because of his reputation as a friend of the United States, he was approached on behalf of a group of Soviet and East European officials who wanted to defect and be granted asylum. They asked to be taken directly to President Eisenhower.

Realizing the impossibility of getting them to the president, Bang-Jensen proposed instead that they put their case in the hands of the top United Nations officials in the naive belief that receiving and protecting political defectors would be an appropriate role for the world body.

The dissidents were horrified. They replied: "Don't you know that Moscow controls the 38th floor?" (The 38th floor was the secretary-general's headquarters.)

Bang-Jensen was shocked and demanded proof. The incipient defectors showed him coded directives from Moscow which confirmed their charges.

Deeply shaken by this disclosure, Bang-Jensen urged that they go to CIA Director Allen Dulles with their information and their request for asylum. Povl agreed to make the necessary liaison.

For reasons that remain unclear, Bang-Jensen was kept waiting for months, as were the people he represented, and no appointment with Allen Dulles was ever made.

Against his better judgment, Bang-Jensen had told the top assistant to the U.S. ambassador to the United Nations the gist of the problem and had asked him to convey an urgent appeal for action to CIA Director Dulles. He also exacted a promise that the request of the Soviet and satellite officials to defect should not be put in writing.

It was put in writing, however, and it reached one of the three people who dominated the 38th floor. After this, Bang-Jensen was a marked man at the U.N.

The Senate Internal Security Subcommittee had taken testimony from survivors of, and fugitives from, the Soviet repression of Hungary. The witnesses were anonymous and wore surgical masks so that horrible reprisals could not be visited on their friends and relatives by the Soviet authorities and their Hungarian agents.

182

U.N. Secretary-General Dag Hammarskjöld demanded that Bang-Jensen reveal to him the real names and identities of the witnesses before the U.N. committee. Being an honorable and decent human being, Bang-Jensen naturally refused. Dag Hammarskjöld fired him.

Bang-Jensen fought doggedly for reinstatement. I spoke to him on many occasions during those days. Though he was being ground down by pressure, he once told me that he would never contemplate suicide. He made the same statement in a letter to his wife.

Yet one morning in November 1959, he was found in a lot near his home, shot in the head, with his own pistol beside him. I do not believe that he committed suicide, nor do I believe that General Walter Krivitsky, the defected chief of NKVD intelligence for Western Europe and the United States, committed suicide back in 1940 shortly after I had had a subpoena served on him.

Povl's widow, Helen Bang-Jensen, cast further light on this strange and tragic case in her testimony before the Senate Internal Security Subcommittee:

> MR. SOURWINE. Do you have any knowledge respecting an approach made to your husband by an individual member of the Soviet delegation to the United Nations or of the secretariat respecting the desire of one or more members of that delegation or of the secretariat to defect to the West?
>
> MRS. BANG-JENSEN. Yes, in a general way I do.
>
> MR. SOURWINE. This knowledge comes to you from communications made to you by your husband?
>
> MRS. BANG-JENSEN. Oral communication.
>
> MR. SOURWINE. Yes?
>
> MRS. BANG-JENSEN. Yes.
>
> MR. SOURWINE. You have no knowledge of it except what he told you?

MRS. BANG-JENSEN. Only what he told me, yes.

MR. SOURWINE. And what was it that he told you about this?

MRS. BANG-JENSEN. He told me that there were several members of the United Nations Secretariat who would like to defect. They were unwilling to do it through the normal channels because one of the bits of information which they told my husband was that there was infiltration in the security agencies of the U.S. government, in the CIA and in the State Department, and that they were unwilling to approach anyone in those particular organizations. They asked my husband if he would take this information for them to the president.

MR. SOURWINE. Of the United States?

MRS. BANG-JENSEN. Yes.

MR. SOURWINE. Now, by "infiltration," did you understand your husband to mean, or did he make it clear that he meant, Soviet infiltration?

MRS. BANG-JENSEN. Yes, and they were willing to bring some evidence of that, and also evidence of some control of the 38th floor, which is the administrative offices of the United Nations, by Russians, when they were given asylum.

MR. SOURWINE. To be sure I understand this, your husband was approached by a single member of the Soviet delegation or the UN Secretariat?

MRS. BANG-JENSEN. The information came from an individual speaking on behalf of several.

MR. SOURWINE. Yes. Do you know if the individual was, himself, one of the group who wished to defect?

MRS. BANG-JENSEN. Yes, yes.

184

MR. SOURWINE. The presumption would necessarily be that that was so.

MRS. BANG-JENSEN. It is more than a presumption. I know that.

MR. SOURWINE. Your husband said this to you?

MRS. BANG-JENSEN. Yes.

MR. SOURWINE. And this group of defectors, through the intermediary who approached your husband, said that they had information respecting Soviet infiltration of security in the United Nations. . . .

MRS. BANG-JENSEN. Yes. Not security in the United Nations, but the workings of the United Nations.

MR. SOURWINE. Respecting Soviet infiltration of the 38th floor, which you say is the administrative floor?

MRS. BANG-JENSEN. Yes.

MR. SOURWINE. And respecting Soviet infiltration of agencies of the government of the United States?

MRS. BANG-JENSEN. Yes.

MR. SOURWINE. Were those agencies specified?

MRS. BANG-JENSEN. I understood that they were the CIA and the State Department.

MR. SOURWINE. Your husband told you this?

MRS. BANG-JENSEN. Yes. And the reason for the reluctance of the men who wanted to defect, to defect through the normal channels, was because there was this infiltration.

MR. SOURWINE. They were afraid that their desire to defect would become Soviet knowledge before they had achieved safety and there would be reprisals?

185

MRS. BANG-JENSEN. Yes.

MR. SOURWINE. And they offered, through the intermediary who contacted your husband, to bring this information about this infiltration—bring it over and give it to the American authorities if their defection could be accomplished and they could be promised safety?

MRS. BANG-JENSEN. Yes. They did not give it to my husband. My husband's role was only that of an intermediary there.

MR. SOURWINE. He was only told they had such information.

MRS. BANG-JENSEN. Yes.

MR. SOURWINE. Not what it was?

MRS. BANG-JENSEN. No.

MR. SOURWINE. Not the nature of the infiltration?

MRS. BANG-JENSEN. No.

MR. SOURWINE. Did your husband assent to their desire to have a contact directly to the president of the United States?

MRS. BANG-JENSEN. No. He felt that that would be impractical and not the way to do it, and he gave the matter some thought and told them that he would try to find some way in which he could bring this information to the attention of the proper American authorities.

MR. SOURWINE. And did he find such a way?

MRS. BANG-JENSEN. He did.

MR. SOURWINE. Did he tell you about it?

MRS. BANG-JENSEN. Yes. He gave this information to a friend who was a member of the U.S. mission to the United Nations.

MR. SOURWINE. Who was this man?

MRS. BANG-JENSEN. It was Mr. James Barco.

MR. SOURWINE. B-a-r-c-o?

MRS. BANG-JENSEN. Yes.

MR. SOURWINE. What did Mr. Barco agree to do with this information, if you know?

MRS. BANG-JENSEN. My husband gave this information to Mr. Barco orally, in the middle of the delegates' lounge at the United Nations. He asked Mr. Barco to transmit it to the proper American authorities—with one restriction, and that was that this information was not to be put on paper in any form whatsoever.

MR. SOURWINE. Did Mr. Barco agree to this?

MRS. BANG-JENSEN. He did. He said that he would give this information to Mr. Lodge. He asked my husband to go with him later that day to give the information to Mr. Lodge.* My husband was reluctant to do it. He thought Mr. Barco could transmit the information himself, and he didn't.

MR. SOURWINE. Your husband told you all that?

MRS. BANG-JENSEN. Yes, he did.

MR. SOURWINE. Did he tell you that he was satisfied with Mr. Barco's proposal to give this information to Mr. Lodge?

*Henry Cabot Lodge, U.S. ambassador to the United Nations and head of the U.S. delegation.

MRS. BANG-JENSEN. Yes. He presumed Mr. Lodge, as a member of the Cabinet, would take it to the proper authorities.

MR. SOURWINE. As a member of the Cabinet?

MRS. BANG-JENSEN. Well, isn't he? I'm correct— I believe he is a member of the Cabinet. Isn't he?

MR. SOURWINE. I think the technical situation is that he is not a member of the Cabinet; he sits with them.

MRS. BANG-JENSEN. Attends Cabinet meetings. Excuse me. But, in effect, he is very close to it.

MR. SOURWINE. Do you know what Mr. Barco did with this information?

MRS. BANG-JENSEN. I did not know at the time. We have since heard that this information was put in a memorandum and transmitted to the State Department.

MR. SOURWINE. How did you hear this?

MRS. BANG-JENSEN. That we heard from journalists and from people in the United Nations. We did not hear it directly or from Mr. Barco.

MR. SOURWINE. Your husband heard this and told you about it?

MRS. BANG-JENSEN. Yes, he did. Yes.

MR. SOURWINE. Did the defectors in fact defect?

MRS. BANG-JENSEN. Pardon me?

MR. SOURWINE. Did these prospective defectors in fact defect?

MRS. BANG-JENSEN. No.

MR. SOURWINE. Do you know why not?

MRS. BANG-JENSEN. Well, I presume that this effort which they made came to nothing, so it was not possible for them.

MR. SOURWINE. Do you know what happened to them, or any of them?

MRS. BANG-JENSEN. I know that one went back to Russia, but I know no more than that about him.

MR. SOURWINE. Who was the one that went back to Russia?

MRS. BANG-JENSEN. I don't know his name.

MR. SOURWINE. But your husband told you that one had gone back to Russia?

MRS. BANG-JENSEN. Yes.

MR. SOURWINE. That indicates he knew the name of at least one of the defectors; did he not?

MRS. BANG-JENSEN. Of course he knew the name of the man with whom he had talked.

MR. SOURWINE. That was the man that went back to Russia?

MRS. BANG-JENSEN. I believe he also knew the names of the others, but he did not tell me the names, nor did I want to know.[1]

The Internal Security Subcommittee investigated the possibility that Bang-Jensen had not committed suicide, but had been murdered. The following statement by Peter S. Deryabin, a former member of the Soviet terror apparatus who defected to the West in 1954, sheds possible light on the problem:

[1] *The Bang-Jensen Case Report to the Subcommittee to Investigate the Administration of the Internal Security Act and Other Internal Security Laws of the Committee on the Judiciary,* United States Senate, September 14, 1961, pp. 27–30.

It is general knowledge among those who have worked in the ranks of the MVD that the MVD, when it undertakes the liquidation of political opponents, has certain techniques for simulating suicide and other techniques for inducing suicide. A convincing "suicide" may take a year or two to prepare. During this period, the subject's life is examined minutely in order to determine the methods most suitable to his personality and circumstances. Meanwhile, stories may be circulated to the press, if possible, and at the very least among his neighbors, that the subject is despondent. This prepares the ground for a plausible suicide story when the deed occurs.[2]

In 1959, when Bang-Jensen died, a plan was being pushed to grant extraordinary powers to the United Nations. State Department Document 7277 proposed that national armies be gradually disbanded and all military forces be turned over to an international peace force in three stages. The international peace force would, of course, be under U.N. control. The plan was actually submitted in the form of a treaty for the consideration of a seventeen-nation disarmament committee at Geneva. In fact, it was not until Lyndon Johnson was inaugurated in 1963 that the United States government decisively turned down this visionary plan.

If Bang-Jensen's information that the top United Nations leadership was directly controlled by the Soviet Union had been widely publicized, it might have killed the proposed U.N. Peace Force plan much earlier. Hence Moscow and the KGB had a strong motive to silence the Danish idealist.

[2] *The Bang-Jensen Case,* p. 62.

190

20

The People's Republic of China

I HAVE BEEN writing about the threat posed by the Soviet Union —its military and nuclear might and its dread KGB with incalculable potential for disinformation, political warfare, subversion, and terror.

Another force to be reckoned with is Communist China, now known as the People's Republic of China or even simply as China.

One of the myths that persist about China is that the United States aided the National Government of Chiang Kai-shek after World War II and thus alienated the Communists who, despite American assistance to their enemy, defeated a crumbling regime and drove it to its exile on Taiwan.

Actually, the very opposite is true. As the Senate Internal Security Subcommittee concluded without a dissenting voice, after long and exhaustive hearings of witnesses and participants, the U.S. State Department intervened in the Chinese civil conflict on the side of Mao's Communists and undermined our wartime ally, Chiang Kai-shek.

The following statement by Dr. Stanley Hornbeck, chief of the Division of Far Eastern Affairs and later assistant secretary of state, sums up the situation:

> It was then, in the year 1945—and not before then —that the government of the United States, first

191

having taken action inconsistent with tradition and commitment in regard to China, embarked upon what became a course of intervention in regard to the civil conflict, the conflict between the national government and the Communists, in China. It was then that words and actions of the government of the United States began to be expressive of an "against" and a "for" attitude; then and thereafter the government of the United States brought to bear pressures, pressures upon the national government, pressures which were not "against" the Communists, but were on their behalf, pressures not to the disadvantage of the Communists, but, in effect, to the disadvantage of the national government."[1]

The Subcommittee's verdict on the fall of China, which had the support of every senator on the full Senate Judiciary Committee, can be summarized as follows:

In April 1945, the Chinese Communist Party's Seventh National Congress, meeting in the fastnesses of Yenan in the northern area of China, resolved to set up an "independent" government for all of China. In June the Communist Party of the United States echoed this decision, one that meant all-out civil war with the Nationalist regime.

This decision was immediately carried forward by supposedly loyal and disinterested American officials and presidential advisors.

Owen Lattimore, who had been head of the Pacific Affairs Department of the Office of War Information, wrote a letter to President Truman on June 10, 1945, urging that American assistance to Nationalist China be stopped because the Chiang Kai-shek regime would use this military matériel to suppress its rivals. Lattimore followed this up with a visit to the White House on July 3 in which he urged that the United States support a coalition government in China. In this government

[1] *Institute of Pacific Relations, Report of the Committee on the Judiciary,* Eighty-Second Congress, pp. 202–3.

the real power in the coalition would be accorded to the Communists.

Lattimore also urged that top State Department officials whose background had been in Japanese affairs be eased out and replaced by men whose experience had been primarily in China. In practice this meant ousting conservatives and replacing them with radicals.

The Truman administration followed Lattimore's recommendations. The chief policy-makers in the Department of State in the Far East—Joseph Grew, Joseph W. Ballantine, and Eugene Dooman—were replaced. John Carter Vincent, an intimate of Lattimore, was made the new head of State's Far Eastern office.

On November 28, 1945, Vincent formally recommended that there be a coalition government in China. Moreover, he prepared a paper to be signed by Secretary of State James F. Byrnes on December 10, 1945, which became the official exposition of U.S. China policy. This document declared that the American purpose was to achieve "a strong, united, and democratic China," and it continued to the effect that to achieve that goal, it was essential that the "central" government of China and the various "dissident elements" show a willingness to compromise. According to the document, the government of Chiang Kai-shek must be broadened to include "representatives of . . . groups who are now without representation in the government of China," and the United States would exert its influence "in such a way as to encourage concessions by the central government, by the so-called [sic] Communists, and by the other factions." Clearly this was a call for intervention. Clearly, it implied that the Chinese Communists were not really Communists. It went on:

> The president has asked General Marshall to go to China . . . for the purpose of bringing to bear the influence of the United States. . . . Specifically General Marshall will endeavor to influence the Chinese government to call a national conference of representatives of the major political elements, to bring

about the unification of China and, concurrently, effect a cessation of hostilities, particularly in North China.[2]

General Marshall was being sent as a special representative of the president for "bringing to bear" upon the government of a sovereign country the influence of the United States toward achieving in that country objectives which the president and the secretary of state of the United States had decided were desirable.

At the end of 1945, when General Marshall left for China, the balance of power was with the Chinese Nationalists, and remained so until at least June 1946. Chiang's divisions were chasing the Communists northward and the prospect of victory by Nationalist China was at its highest. However, when General Marshall arrived in China, he undertook to bring about the coalition government which his directive demanded. And he began to bring pressure on Chiang in order to force his compliance.

General Marshall was empowered to grant a $500 million loan to China, but only on condition that the coalition government was set up. He proposed that the Chinese Nationalist army be reduced to fifty divisions and that ten Chinese Communist divisions be incorporated into it. He also instituted truce teams which stopped the advancing Nationalist forces and saved the Communists from total defeat.

When the coalition plan fell apart, all American military assistance to China ceased. Not only did we stop sending military supplies, but materials which had already been purchased by China were embargoed. The embargo continued for ten months.

According to testimony, General of the Armies Marshall told Admiral Cooke, who commanded the Seventh Fleet, that the United States had armed Chiang's forces, but was now engaged in disarming them.

Meanwhile, the Chinese Communist divisions, relieved of

[2]*ibid.* p. 201.

194

pressure from the Nationalist forces, went north to Manchuria where the Japanese Manchukuo army had surrendered to the Russians, who had been in the war for only two days after the atom bomb was dropped on Hiroshima. The Chinese Communists regrouped there, and the Russians trained them and equipped them with the arms that the Japanese had surrendered.

It was this army that defeated Chiang's forces in 1948 and early 1949. On October 1, 1949, the Communists proclaimed the People's Republic of China, which was recognized the next day by the USSR and its satellites.

The State Department began negotiations for recognition, but Chinese Communist intransigence delayed matters. The Senate took the matter under consideration in the spring of 1950. Then in June of that year, North Korean troops invaded South Korea, and negotiations broke down.

The Korean War made Communist China an outlaw. It was at war not only with South Korea, but also with the United States and the United Nations. No peace treaty was ever signed. Mao's China imposed an isolation on itself that lasted until 1971, when Richard M. Nixon opened his negotiations with Peking.

The Chinese Communists now occupy the China seat on the U.N. Security Council. President Nixon and Secretary Kissinger fashioned the Shanghai Communiqué which became the basis of China policy for the next two administrations. This document is not a joint understanding. The U.S. version differs from that of the Chinese. Moreover, it is a purely executive agreement. To the extent that it conflicts with our Mutual Defense Treaty with the Republic of China (Nationalist), an accord which has been ratified by the Senate, the latter prevails under international law and the Constitution.

The Shanghai Communiqué is a diabolical document. If implemented, it would make Taiwan a mere province of China and place the millions of Chinese who have sought and found freedom and prosperity on that island totally at the mercy of the Chinese Communists.

Nor is there any practical reason why the United States

should allow Nationalist China to be absorbed by Peking. To do so would mean abandoning a staunch and powerful ally. It would mean condemning one of the most free, prosperous, and modern states in Asia to servitude. The People's Republic of China desperately needs the United States' support against the Soviet Union. Yet in this situation, the United States makes concessions. The Chinese Communists concede nothing.

Peking has made no effort to conceal its bloodthirsty intentions toward Taiwan once the Shanghai Communiqué is carried out. In a statement to the editors of the *Wall Street Journal* published on October 4, 1977, Chinese Communist Vice Premier Li Hsien-nien said: "Chairman Mao told [U.S. Secretary of State Henry Kissinger] there are such a heap of counterrevolutionaries on Taiwan that it cannot be managed without a fight. Whether the fight takes place in five years, ten years, or even longer, that is another matter."

The *Wall Street Journal* dispatch reads:

> In a further extension of China's hard-line position, Mr. Li said it would be "inappropriate" for Taiwan to receive arms supplies, including replacement arms, from the U.S. or from any other country or private company following normalization of relations between China and the U.S. This would be "manifest interference in China's internal problems," he said.
>
> He followed this by citing Chairman Mao's views on the inevitability of a violent takeover of the island.
>
> Referring in general to formulas by which China might somehow promise to "liberate" Taiwan peacefully, Mr. Li said, "We say this won't do. We say it once. We say it ten times. We say it one hundred times."[3]

[3]Reprinted by permission of *The Wall Street Journal,* Copyright © Dow Jones & Company, Inc., 1977. All rights reserved.

Free China is and has been an unwavering friend. It has a superlative army. It provides a firm anchor for our Western defense perimeter. Its survival is a measure of our reliability as an ally, of our integrity as a nation, and of whether or not we stand for freedom in Asia. Taiwan is one of the economic miracles of the post-World War II world. Its success trumpets the system of free enterprise, whereas the grimy poverty on the mainland blazons economic failure for totalitarianism. Taiwan's foreign trade is more than double that of mainland China though the latter's population is fifty times greater. We are dealing with the fate of a loyal ally and also of warm and gentle human beings. Taiwan is a beacon and magnet for millions of overseas Chinese scattered throughout the world.

Our abandonment of all of this for the mirage of Chinese Communist friendship would be an abandonment of moral principle, of military prudence, of national interest, of ordinary decency, and of common sense.

After this chapter was finished and after this volume was put to type a diplomatic thunderbolt crashed over the world. In the shadow of Christmas week and after he declared Human Rights Week, President Carter announced he was normalizing relations with the Chinese Communist government, thereby consigning seventeen million Chinese living on Taiwan and the offshore islands to the totalitarians on the mainland. Even though the Senate and the House resolved that it was "the sense of Congress" that the Mutual Defense Treaty with the Republic of China not be changed without consultation with that Congress, the president announced that he was forthwith abrogating that treaty.

Let us look at this move in the context of this volume. While President Carter continued to invoke the doctrine of human rights, he nonetheless embraced the world's most repressive (with exception of its ally and surrogate Cambodia) totalitarian regime, teeming as it is with political prisoners.

By abrogating the treaty and committing us to withdrawing our troops, he surrendered a firm defensive anchor, Taiwan, and a strategic waterway, the Strait of Taiwan, to a regime that is now tactically adopting a cooperative front. In so doing he has drawn our defense line thousands of miles eastward in the Pacific Ocean.

The president has knuckled under to Chinese Communist demands by complying with their three provisions—cutting ties with the ROC, withdrawing our troops, and abrogating the treaty—without even getting an assurance that they will not use force to annex the province of Taiwan. The president has thus added still another ally to the lists of those whom we have abandoned in the fatuous hope that our enemies will become our friends.

He has used the words "reality" and "normalization" as a cover for nullifying the diplomatic existence of a stable and friendly government that has been a model of economic stability and growth, and a bastion of political and spiritual freedom. He did this needlessly, for there was no justification in international law for the claim of the PRC that it has jurisdiction over Taiwan, the Pescadores, Quemoy, or Matsu. The act of the president was totally gratuitous and unilateral, based on no principle of international law, no consideration of future security, and no sympathy and compassion for seventeen million people who have come close to being exemplars in today's strife-torn world.

21

Chinese Communist Propaganda and Espionage

FOR A MEMBER of the United Nations, the People's Republic of China has an unusually large delegation in New York which provides an excellent base for intelligence operations against the United States.

There is also a liaison office in Washington between Communist China and the United States. This serves as an unofficial embassy and also as a base for espionage.

Both delegations were organized by Huang Hua, now foreign minister of the People's Republic and a veteran Chinese intelligence officer. It is difficult to determine the number of officials and employees assigned to these two offices, but I learned that in 1977 there were one hundred and nine Chinese Communists assigned openly to the U.N. delegation and fifty-five to the liaison office in Washington. In addition, the Peking regime has resorted to duress, blackmail, and duplicity to recruit most of the Chinese working at the U.N. Secretariat to serve as its agents.

The Chinese Communist regime is led by men who served in the Chinese secret police. Hua Kuo Feng, the chairman of the Communist Party and prime minister, was promoted from head of the Chinese equivalent of the KGB to his present position.

Huang Hua, the foreign minister of Communist China, previously served as his country's ambassador to Ghana. Under

Nkrumah, the pro-Chinese dictator of that African country, Huang Hua abused his diplomatic position to set up networks of espionage agents throughout Africa. When Nkrumah was overthrown, hundreds of Huang Hua's operatives were expelled. Hua later operated from Canada, a vantage point from which he directed Chinese Communist intelligence in the United States. When the U.N. admitted Red China to membership, Huang Hua was assigned there.

On Hua's promotion to foreign minister, control of the Chinese espionage organizations in the United States fell to Kao Liang, who used the New York office of the New China News Agency as his front. When he came to the United States, his official title was second secretary of the Peking liaison office in Washington.

The Chinese counterpart of the KGB is the Ministry of Public Security, which was headed by Hua Kuo Feng until he assumed the leadership of the regime. This department supervises, monitors, and controls 850 million Chinese with ruthlessness and efficiency. It operates forced labor camps that have held millions of people—some estimates run as high as fifty million. It also runs the so-called rehabilitation centers in which political prisoners are brainwashed.

While not as notorious or as flamboyant as the KGB, the Chinese Ministry of Public Security has purged millions of Chinese citizens, ranging from political dissidents to so-called rich peasants whose living standards were inferior to those of Southern sharecroppers in the great depression of the 1930s. The total human cost of Chinese Communist rule is unknown, but it admittedly runs into the millions and, according to the estimates of some eminent Far Eastern political scientists, may have totaled sixty million human beings.

Following the promotion of Hua to leadership of the Chinese Communist Party, Wang Tung-hsing is believed to have taken over at the Ministry of Public Security. He is also reportedly in command of the 8341st Army unit, originally the bodyguard protecting Mao Tse-tung, which has, since his death, been expanding into the nation's security police force.

Under Wang, both organizations are fusing and becoming

dominant forces in Chinese political life. It was Wang who arrested Chiang Ch'ing, Mao's widow, and her three associates —the "gang of four." The nationwide purge of these dissidents was directed by the Chinese internal security organs.

The power which the secret police wields in China is illustrated by the fact that Wang holds one of the four vice chairmanships of the Chinese Communist Party and is a member of its all-powerful Politburo. In addition, he is believed to be in charge of the department of the Central Committee of the Chinese Party which handles all intelligence matters. Wang probably ranked fourth in power as of 1978, behind Prime Minister Hua, the former Chinese KGB head, Teng Hsiao-p'ing, who controls the armed forces, and Li Hsien-nien, a vice premier of Red China.

The strength of the internal security apparatus can be inferred from the fact that the 8341st Army unit, or palace guard, is an elite, highly-trained, combat-hardened force of 50,000 officers and men. Clearly, the Chinese KGB has at least as great an influence over China as the KGB has over the Soviet Union —perhaps greater.

The *New York Daily News* assigned two veteran reporters, Paul Meskil and Frank Faso, to do an assessment of Chinese Communist intelligence in the United States. They uncovered an extensive network, including diplomats, journalists, military officers, scientists, university professors, businessmen and, in great numbers, merchant seamen. These people have infiltrated every Chinese community in the country and are especially zeroing in on electronic research and computer technology.[1]

I cite these findings, but they are only surface findings. It should not be the responsibility of the media to bring evidence of subversion to light. The Committees of Congress, charged

[1]The Department of Commerce has issued export licenses for Control Data Corporation's advanced Cyber series of computers sold to Communist China even though our Defense Department states it can be used for missile targeting and other military purposes. It is being sold on the condition that the People's Republic give verbal assurances that it will not be so used.

with learning the facts about internal security, bore that responsibility, but, alas, they have been virtually abolished. The Senate and House Foreign Affairs Committees, whose area of interest is the "normalization" of relations with this still aggressive and subversive regime, should probe and publicize the depth and scope of Chinese Communist intelligence and subversion in the United States. To deny ourselves these facts is an act of "know-nothingism" that provident men should deplore.

When Clarence Kelley was director of the FBI, he repeatedly warned of espionage by operatives assigned to the Red Chinese U.N. mission and the liaison office in Washington. The FBI estimated that the Chinese Communists more than doubled the scope of their spying operation in the United States between 1976 and 1978.

The People's Republic maintains many front organizations in the United States. The most influential of these is the United States-China People's Friendship Association. Private organizations devoted to closer American ties with the Chinese Communist regime include: American-Chinese Friendship Alliance, Committee for China Reunification, Tiao-yü-t'ai Committee, Committee on Scholarly Communication with the People's Republic of China, National Council for U.S.-China Trade, and National Committee on U.S.-China Relations.

Just as a vast apparatus of cultural, educational, diplomatic, scientific, scholarly, and literary organizations combined to pressure the United States to embark on its disastrous policy of aiding the Chinese Communists to take power, so another such coalition, featuring some of the same cast of characters, is importuning the United States to embark on an appeasement policy that could have equally disastrous consequences.

As stated above, the United States-China People's Friendship Association, with over a hundred branches scattered through the United States, is the most powerful Red Chinese propaganda organization in this country. One of its leaflets asks: DID YOU KNOW THERE'S JUST ONE CHINA? and concludes with the thought: U.S. OUT OF TAIWAN.

The organizer and leading spirit of this society, a tireless

202

propagandist who moves from campus to campus extolling the virtues of the Chinese peasant and proletarian paradise, is a certain William Hinton, to all appearances an honest toiler in the vineyard of peace and a man as American as apple pie.

We had the pleasure of his company as a witness before the Senate Internal Security Subcommittee on several occasions. At all of these meetings, he invoked his privilege not to incriminate himself under the Fifth Amendment of the Constitution of a country he despises.

Unfortunately for Hinton's mask of secrecy, the customs authorities seized his footlocker when he re-entered the United States from Red China in August 1953 and searched its contents.

This apostle of American-Chinese friendship wrote to his sisters, Joan and Jean: "That great beast, America, looks down upon the world and licks its lips." However, he found some aspects of the Chinese workers' fatherland disappointing: "So far I have seen no evidence of the anti-American feeling this [sic] is supposed to be rampant here. This worries me a little since it indicates the people have not yet learned who their enemies are."

Many of these semi-literate expressions of hatred for his country were penned at a time when Chinese troops were killing American forces in Korea.

In Red China, William Hinton rose in the Communist Party to become one of those who had the sacred duty to "purify the Party." In other words, he became a small-time, two-bit inquisitor.

"We organized," he boasts in the notes that were seized in his footlocker. "We purified. We sent directives. We treated different cases differently." And then, with simulated piety: "The upper cadres must take the blame."

And thus the little man who hated his country became "upper cadre"—a super-ant in the Chinese antheap.

The Hinton family, in part at least, followed in the footsteps of their brother. Sister Jean was a friend and co-government worker of Gregory Silvermaster, a man who took the Fifth Amendment when charged with wartime espionage for the

Soviet Union. Sister Joan was an atomic research assistant at Los Alamos where she had access to classified material. She went to China, worked on the Chinese atomic bomb, married a fellow renegade, and vanished with her mate into the depths of Inner Mongolia. She came out of obscurity long enough to make a bitter speech seething with hatred of her native country before a Communist front called the Asian and Pacific Peace Conference.

That the Chinese Communist regime is interested in getting all the information it can from the United States, while giving little or nothing in return, was made clear by a surprising statement on cultural exchanges between the two countries by Dr. Robert M. Lumiansky, president of the American Council of Learned Societies. According to the *New York Times* of June 28, 1976:

> Dr. Lumiansky reported that there had been growing "uneasiness" in United States universities and among individual scholars and scientists over the "seemingly increasingly superficial trips" that are now all that is allowed.
>
> He said that some institutions, such as the Massachusetts Institute of Technology and Bell Laboratories, were also unhappy that they had been asked to receive numerous Chinese delegations while being turned down in their efforts to send groups of their own to China. Bell Laboratories has played host to eight Chinese delegations, he said, and M.I.T. to six groups.
>
> Another member of the scholarly group that went with Dr. Lumiansky added that there was some concern that the Chinese wanted to send a number of delegations to study particular advances in United States technology, often with commercial applications, that did not really fall into the scholarly category. In addition, he said, the requests are embarrassing to the American companies involved since

the providing of information about their technology infringes on patent rights. He noted that the delegations sent by the Chinese had been almost all scientific and technical groups, with few delegations from the arts, literature, history, or the social sciences.

Dr. Lumiansky said that there had also been a problem with achieving parity in the number of delegations from the two sides, since the Chinese had sent twenty-five groups to the United States and permitted only nineteen from America to visit their country. Last year the committee gave Peking a warning that it was prepared to call off the exchanges entirely unless parity was achieved, Dr. Lumiansky said. Next year each side will dispatch six groups.

Exchanges between the two countries are also arranged under auspices of the National Council for U.S.-China Trade and the National Committee on U.S.-China Relations, both private groups.[2]

There is a Chinese Communist Party of the United States. It bears the designation Communist Party USA (Marxist-Leninist), and it is headed by Michael Klonsky. Klonsky owes his fealty to Peking just as Gus Hall, the chairman of the Communist Party USA, owes his fealty to Moscow.

When Secretary of State Cyrus Vance visited Peking on his exploratory visit in August 1977, he was accorded a short visit with Hua Kuo-feng, the Communist Party chairman. The *New York Times* dispatch of August 25, 1977, reported the event as follows:

When Secretary of State Cyrus R. Vance shook hands with Hua Kuo-feng, chairman of the Chinese Communist Party, in the Great Hall of the People today, he became the first active American official to meet China's highest ranking leader.

In the year and a half since Mr. Hua first sprang to prominence, the progress in Chinese-American relations has been so slight and the Chinese so preoccupied with domestic politics that there was no earlier chance to meet the 57-year-old chairman.

Former President Richard M. Nixon saw him in February 1976 when Mr. Hua had just become acting prime minister. The only other Americans to talk with him have been two Chinese-American scientists and Michael Klonsky, head of the Communist Party USA (Marxist-Leninist), which is a small pro-Chinese rival of the pro-Soviet Communist Party USA headed by Gus Hall.[3]

The Vance visit revealed a continuing commitment on the part of the Carter administration to adhere to the Shanghai Communiqué in working toward "normalization" of relations with the People's Republic of China.

In a remarkable expression of candor, President Carter, when meeting Henry Kissinger to obtain his support for the Panama Canal Treaty, came right out and said that he was adopting the policies of the Nixon-Ford-Kissinger administration on China, Southern Africa, the Middle East, and the Panama Canal. The president was quoted on that occasion as saying to Kissinger, "We've got obviously just an absolute continuum of what you and he started that we are trying to proceed with."

It is interesting to note that when the State Department voted the credentials of "China" to the People's Republic in the United Nations in 1971, it continued to contend that "Taiwan" should not be expelled from the world body. Yet if the issue then was one of expulsion, the United States ambassador to the

U.N., George Bush, had only to invoke Article Six of the Charter which makes expulsion subject to the veto.

While United States policy bends to the relentless demands of Peking, Chinese Communist policy remains inflexible. Hua told Secretary Vance that "Taiwan" was an internal issue and the People's Republic of China would brook no interference in its internal affairs. Even more significant was the editorial of the official Communist Party newspaper *Jenmin Jih Pao,* while Vance was in Peking, which quoted Hua's invocation of Lenin's guideline that a country should take advantage "of every, even the smallest opportunity of gaining a mass ally, even though this ally be temporary, vacillating, unstable, unreliable, and conditional."

A dispassionate observer viewing this scene would search in vain for evidence of mutuality. Obsequious offers come from our side. They are requited by scorn and implacability. President Nixon visited Peking twice (once while president), President Ford once, Secretary of State Henry Kissinger nine times, and Cyrus Vance once. No Chinese Communist advisor deigned to visit Washington, until Teng Hsiao-ping, having captured the great prize, came to the United States in triumph in January 1979.

22

Communist Psychological and Political Warfare

OF ALL THE many expert witnesses who appeared before the
Senate Internal Security Subcommittee Suzanne Labin gave
the most comprehensive, concise, and insightful exposition of
the Communist strategy and tactics of political and psychological warfare. She made this presentation in testimony before
the Subcommittee on June 12, 1967, and it was published as a
Senate document.[1] Much of her research and analysis is as
valid today as it was when she testified. I have added material
on the same subject which I have compiled independently.

Mme. Labin is a graduate of the Sorbonne and a journalist
of international reputation, whose many books include *Stalin's
Russia, The Secret of Democracy, The Ant Hill* (a study of Red
China), *The Unrelenting War*, and *Must We Grant Freedom to
the Enemies of Freedom?* The last-named earned a French literary award for "the book which best defends the principles of
liberty."

Mme. Labin demonstrated the important role of Soviet propaganda in world policy:

> The proliferation of representative governments has
> ushered the Western world into a primarily political

[1] *The Techniques of Soviet Propaganda*, Senate Document No. 34,
90th Congress, 1st Session.

era, in which molders of public opinion are more influential in the shaping of events than are industrial managers or military leaders. But by a strange and significant paradox, this crucially important evolution has been better comprehended by the enemies of democracy than by its patrons.

United States armament has little effect when the Kremlin decides to orchestrate ideas and influence. Iraq, for instance, was originally an integral part of the Baghdad Pact; the Iraqi armed forces were important to that organization. Moscow was able to foment internal disorders which forced Iraq out of the pact.

Panama is likely to become an even more striking example of the weight of Soviet influence. Communists have already acquired key positions in the Panamanian trade unions, the university, the free professions, the civilian administration, and the police and military. It will be a simple matter for these people to turn the Canal into a Soviet-dominated waterway regardless of any treaty provisions to the contrary. Then the United States will be confronted with the alternatives of allowing this strategic area to remain in hostile hands or resorting to armed invasion.

We have already seen the inability of the United States to counter Communist propaganda during the Vietnam War. President Nixon and some of his advisors thought that the peace movement was Communist-inspired, but the American press wrote off their suspicions as paranoia. Mme. Labin's analysis was demonstrated step by step as American troops were withdrawn and our allies left to the mercies of the North Vietnamese, according to the wishes of the "pacifists." It was not until 1976 that FBI investigations showed the part played by foreign and domestic movement Communists in the disturbances of the sixties. Cuban intelligence agents in particular, attached to the Cuban mission to the United Nations, were found to have created a core of terrorists in the peace movement. Promising candidates were trained in weaponry and the organization of violent demonstrations, spirited out of the country in 1970 when they were wanted by the FBI, and given further training and new identities in Eastern Europe.

As the *New York Times* revealed on October 9, 1977, North Vietnamese intelligence agents directed the hardcore element in the Students for a Democratic Society (SDS) on the organization and execution of the Days of Rage in 1969. Militant elements were chosen to provoke violent clashes with the police which would be publicized nationally, the coverage being slanted to depict the assault squads as victims. North Vietnamese control agents insisted that the demonstrations be escalated from verbal protest to physical confrontation and combat.

Communist influence on our foreign and military affairs is that easy, and our press will continue to call suspicion paranoia. More and more of the world falls each year to such psychological and political warfare, and we are helpless because the enemies of liberal democracy understand its uses so well. Unless we learn to discern the reality of Communist control behind the false façade of these operations, the Free World will perish like a languid colossus, gorged with unused atomic super-weapons, mortally wounded by the myriad flea bites of Moscow-trained agents.

We may in the end perish from what might be termed the Mars complex. This consists of visualizing, comprehending, and fearing only the "hot war," while neglecting our protection on the decisive political and psychological front.

Manning these ramparts is the task of internal security. If we continue to dismantle our internal security defenses, we may find that we have made preparations to confront the enemy on a field where he has no intentions of risking combat.

In saying this, I want to add that building up the retaliatory and defense capabilities of the West in opposition to Communist armament is also of vital importance. The Communist strategy is to strike at the enemy's weakest link. Therefore, every link in the entire chain of our security must be strong and invulnerable.

Although a student radical here and a Weatherman there may become conscious Communist revolutionaries, aware of

210

the chain of command that binds them to Moscow, by far the bulk of Communist inroads on the Free World is covert. Political warfare "uses indigenous personnel," too, Mme. Labin reported; but it is more complex and insidious than the recruitment of terrorists.

The objective is to capture, or at least subvert to the purposes of the Kremlin or Peiping, the command posts controlling national policy: administration, press, radio, television, universities, parties, unions, etc., while carefully concealing from the captured elements any awareness of their service to Communism.

It is this last characteristic which distinguishes Communist political warfare from normal political activity. While normal political activity tends to win agreements around objectives as clearly defined as possible, Communist political warfare tends to manipulate allegiances to favor objectives which are as thoroughly disguised as possible.

The term "political warfare" is often used as a synonym for the "war of minds," which frequently leads to a confusion of concepts. The use of the word "mind" often evokes the idea that what is involved is a confrontation of ideals, doctrines, and motivations; a contest played on the field of intellectual activity. However, Communism today aims primarily at the emotionally conditioned part of the mind. It seeks alignment, not enlightenment.

Propaganda of this type is not aimed at recruiting members for the Communist Party, but rather at the dissemination of views openly or covertly serving Soviet foreign policy, regardless of their compatability with any social doctrine.

Bolshevism has always been fond of underground activities. It has always attempted to spread its influence by the use of "transmission belts": individuals or organizations which would conceal their allegiance. This phenomenon is repugnant to Westerners, who prefer to air political differences openly, based on professed ideas and declared allegiances. But it would be not only foolish, it would be disastrous if free people chose to ignore secret allegiances because they find them repellent. This reality which must be faced is the Communist world as made by Moscow, rather than as we would prefer it to be.

Mme. Labin went on to describe the functions of Communist "auxiliaries," who spread opinions and information slanted in favor of Soviet policy. These auxiliaries work in much the same ways wherever they are active.

The various auxiliaries customarily maintain their contacts in clubs, salons, cafes, bars, and semipublic gatherings such as young people's church groups. Communist propaganda is matched with the channel through which it is to be disseminated. There are few social, political, or religious doctrines into which, with an appropriate dialectical twist, some elements favorable to Soviet foreign policy cannot be insinuated, especially since there is no need to maintain consistency with Communist ideology, which has nothing to do with the undertaking.

This technique works well in newspapers and other periodicals, in news agencies, in schools and universities, and in churches. Mme. Labin's description of its implementation in the case of the press is particularly instructive.

There are few publications in the world, even including some ostensibly conservative ones, into which the tentacles of the Soviet apparatus have not reached. The primary tasks of the auxiliary in this medium include manipulation of the editor or, if this

212

is impossible, of the reporters without the editor's knowledge. The auxiliary will be indefatigable in slanting news stories and all other material in a Communist direction. Whether he does this subtly or blatantly depends on the circumstances.

Characterizing one newspaper as "conservative" and another as "Catholic" is no longer adequate to define their policies vis-à-vis the Soviet Union. The managing editor may actually be unaware that his newspaper has been penetrated.

The most heavily infiltrated departments are international news and commentary and book and film reviews. Reviewers have an especially important propaganda role. By their favorable appraisals, many readers will be influenced to attend film showings and read books favorable to the Soviet line, while ignoring others less biased, because of unfavorable reviews or the "silent treatment."

An effective Soviet technique for manipulation of the Free World press is the "letter brigade." Auxiliaries representing themselves as "devoted readers" write quantities of outraged letters when a paper has printed something anti-Communist, and messages of approval when it has favored some concession to Moscow or Peiping. Since the anti-Communist community is far less effectively organized, the preponderance of correspondence received from the auxiliaries exerts a significant influence on the policy of newspapers whose editors honestly believe they must be attuned to their readers.

In his autobiography, *The God That Failed*, Arthur Koestler relates how, as a young journalist employed by a large conservative newspaper, he went one day to offer his enthusiastic adherence to the Communist Party. He believed this membership would entail resignation from his "counter-revolutionary" position to serve the publications of the Communist Party regardless of salary. His surprise can be imagined when he was told, by the *aparatchik* who received him, that this was a childish impulse; that he would serve the cause far better by staying with the conservative newspaper, carefully concealing his Communist affiliation, while spying and reporting to the party all that occurred in the editor's office and at the same time attempting to subvert the newspaper's policy to favor Moscow.

Political and psychological warfare, then, is a striking instance of Lenin's famous dichotomy between the attitudes and practices of Marxism and the West. For the Marxist or auxiliary, every phase of day-to-day life is politicized into a weapon of subversion; the goal of world Communism is ever in view. The thought of the average citizen of a Western democracy is far more diffuse, so he is highly vulnerable to what Mme. Labin characterized as "the bluff that an unscrupulous specialist can easily impose upon amateurs."

23

The Stratagem of Eurocommunism

IN 1975 A new word swept across Western Europe—Eurocommunism. It was created to summarize a new line of the Western European Communist parties. The change had three components:

(1) The Western European Communist parties refused to accept responsibility for the crimes of Stalinism and took a more critical attitude toward the Soviet Union.

(2) They asserted that they were independent national organizations and that they rejected monolithic control from the Kremlin.

(3) They claimed that Communism was compatible with political liberty and a multi-party system of government.

The reasons for this change in propaganda approach were self-evident. The appeal to nationalism and the verbal espousal of the democratic process made them more attractive to the electorate. Being known as a lackey of Moscow was hardly an asset in Western Europe where the people have sufficient contacts with Soviet and East European satellite people to know that those countries are poor, backward, incompetently governed police states.

I can well remember the day in 1943 when the Stalin regime announced the dissolution of the Communist International (Comintern). I was in the wardroom of a destroyer in the middle of the Atlantic Ocean. But even from this inadequate observation post, I expressed my profound skepticism. When I returned to New York and talked to my associates who were close to the Communist Party, they told me that it was all a hoax and that the comrades were ignoring "the piece of paper" and proceeding exactly as before.

Not so the world leaders. Our statesmen greeted Stalin's announcement with jubilation. They were straining to put aside whatever doubts they might have that the Soviet dictator was going to join them in building a brave new world.

We know now that it was all a fraud. In this case, we learned something from experience. When in 1956 the Communist parties of the United States, France, Germany, and Italy declared their "independence" of Moscow, no responsible Western statesmen took the assertion seriously.

Eurocommunism, however, *is* being taken seriously.

Before dealing with its origins and development, let me quote from what I wrote on the subject on April 15, 1976, from the vantage point of Rome, where I was teaching on the "College of the Air" for the University of Plano:

> The current government of Prime Minister Moro is simply not governing. His Christian Democratic Party is organically split several ways, with each faction holding separate caucuses. . . .

> The Communists have made spectacular gains in the last series of municipal elections. They are the controlling party in Naples, Turin, Milan, Florence, Venice, and Bologna. Rome was the only large city they did not capture, and that is because municipal elections will be held this year, not 1975.

> They are a powerful legislative sector which all parties must court to get any kind of bill passed.

> In other words, they are doing very well now. Their goal is to come into the government in what they call an "historical compromise." This is a voluntary union with the Christian Democrats who, with all

216

their shortcomings, still reflect the heart of Rome and of most of the country.

If there are to be new elections (and the odds are now that there will be), the Communists will have to campaign, and campaign vigorously, against, rather than with, the Christian Democrats, and if they win they will inherit a colossal mess. This will impose on them a responsibility they do not have now.

The columnists I read here in the two American journals are alluding to the "liberalization" of the Italian Communist Party. . . .

All the evidence points to the fact that the move is one for campaign purposes. It was pointed out to us this morning that [Italian Communist Party leader] Berlinguer made the same statement in Moscow seven years ago and the Party nevertheless continued, with its inherently totalitarian structure, to follow undeviatingly Moscow's foreign policy everywhere. And they continue to do so now even in such flagrantly indefensible adventures as the Soviet thrust in Angola.

Another deceptive element is the Communist pledge not to seek Italy's unilateral withdrawal from NATO, which is hailed as a symptom of moderation. When an experienced newsman, however, asks the wily Communists "How about multinational withdrawal?" the answer is that they favor the dissolution both of NATO and the Warsaw Treaty Organization. (With mutual dissolution, NATO would be gutted with U.S. forces and weapons withdrawn, but the Warsaw Pact troops and weapons would simply stay in place "unorganized.")

Jay Lovestone was the head of the American Communist Party until he was removed by Stalin. He has been until recently a senior foreign policy advisor to George Meany, president of the AFL-CIO. Let me quote from his penetrating article "Eurocommunism—Roots and Reality":

> Throughout their history, all Communist parties have denounced the Western democratic form of government as an instrument of the capitalists to hold down the working class. After the Bolsheviks seized power in 1917, Communists everywhere hailed the "proletarian dictatorship," the Russian Soviet system set up by Lenin, as "the highest form of democracy" ever attained by man.

> However, in recent years the Communist parties in the Western industrialized countries and Japan have stopped deriding "bourgeois democracy" as a fraud. British, French, Italian, Japanese, and Spanish Communist leaders have made a revolution in their rhetoric in order to demonstrate their dedication to democratic institutions. They have even replaced their once sacred slogan of "proletarian dictatorship" with a call for democracy, plain and simple, which they formerly rejected as "bourgeois democracy." At the same time, it is true, they also call for working class hegemony, a term which, in Communist parlance, is synonymous with dictatorship of the proletariat. But this term sounds innocuous, and not many people know its true meaning in Communist doctrine. . . .

> The emergence of Eurocommunism has aroused no little acceptance among academic experts on Communist affairs. Journalists have hastened to condemn American official efforts "to deny West European Communists respectability." In *Le Monde*, André Fontaine, a consistent critic of the U.S., pleaded: "The Communists will change even more if they are again given a share of power." He recalled the celebrated observation that a Jacobin turned minister is not necessarily a Jacobin minister.

Proposals have been made for U.S. cooperation with Communist parties that have broken ideologically with Moscow. . . .

Eurocommunism has already brought handsome dividends to Communists on both sides of the Iron Curtain. In Italy and France, their respectability and influence have risen sharply. . . .

What is more, the non-ruling Communist parties learned to be more flexible in their tactics while firmly adhering to their final goal. Their present call for "social transformation" has far more popular appeal than the cry for "social revolution" which frightens not only the "bourgeoisie" but also many intellectuals and other middle class people whose support is indispensable—especially for Communist electoral success. They now realize that they can get much further and faster by speaking of the "hegemony of the working people" than by shrieking for the "proletarian dictatorship." Semantic acrobatics? . . .

Berlinguer, Carrillo, and Marchais have fully comprehended and ably complied with the course worked out for them by Brezhnev when he explained:

"Experience teaches, in particular, that the 'Cold War' and the confrontation of military blocs, the atmosphere of military threats, seriously hampers the activity of revolutionary, democratic forces. In conditions of international tension in bourgeois countries, the reactionary elements become active. The military raise their heads; anti-democratic tendencies and anti-Communism are strengthened.

"And conversely, the past few years have shown quite clearly that, in conditions of slackened international tension, the pointer of the political barometer moves left. Certain changes in relations between Communism and Social Democrats in certain countries, a noticeable falling off in anti-Communist hysteria, and the increase of the influence of West European Communist parties is most directly correlated with the reduction in tension which has taken place in Europe" (*Address to the Conference of European Communist Parties in Karlovy Vary,* April 24, 1967).[1]

What is the evidence that the policy changes announced by the leaders of Western Communism are insincere, mere tactical maneuvers to attain power by parliamentary means?

Consider, first, independence from Moscow. In an interview with the British periodical *Encounter,* published in May 1977, Italian Communist leader Lucio Lombardo Radice was asked the crucial question: If war broke out between the NATO alliance and the Soviet Union, which side would the Italian Communists take? In the taped version of the interview, Radice replied: "We would choose the Soviet side, of course, and we would do so on grounds of principle."

Probably under instructions from his Politburo, Radice requested and received permission to change the published version of his reply to a softer formulation. But even in this version, he pledged that Italy, under a Communist government, would side with the Soviet Union if the conflict were an "imperialist aggression with the avowed object of rolling back socialism." Since any Western defense is "imperialist aggression" in the double-think language of Marxism-Leninism, the two answers are the same.

Consider, second, the pretended espousal of liberal concepts of free speech and parliamentary democracy by the Western European Communist parties. For the evidence on this point, I turn to an unusually perceptive article, "The Specter of Eurocommunism," by the distinguished British expert on world Communism, Robert Moss. It appeared in the Summer 1977

[1] *Free Trade Union News* (AFL-CIO), June–July 1977, p. 2.

issue of the authoritative journal on foreign affairs, *Policy Review.*

Moss points out that "French and Italian Communist Party leaders continue to attend closed meetings with the Soviet leaders in Moscow." The leader of the Italian Communist Party, Berlinguer, "praised the revolution of October 1917, the 'superiority' of the Soviet system over the West, and the 'irreversibility' of socialism in the East. He also lauded the principle of 'democratic centralism.' "

The Italian Communist Party promised at its Bologna conference in February 1969 to tolerate internal differences of opinion. Yet it ousted the supporters of *Il Manifesto*, a new-left organ. "If Eurocommunist parties cannot tolerate differences of opinion within their own ranks," asked Moss, "how is it possible to believe that they will allow political freedom for rival parties if they managed to take power?"

The basic question on individual liberty and democracy for any Communist party is this: What would you do if, once in power, you were voted out of office by a democratic majority? When Radice was asked this, he replied that "once the working class has acquired hegemony . . . it would be difficult to envisage anyone wanting a regression from a better state of society to a worse society."

A wise answer indeed! It must be because nobody who has ever lived under Communism could conceivably want to return to conditions of capitalist oppression that the Russians have had to build the Berlin Wall and the Iron Curtain across Europe!

Moss points out that Radice supported the Soviet military invasion and occupation of Hungary to crush the 1956 revolt that occurred there.

Finally, he quotes Lenin's justly famous letter to Chicherin in which the Bolshevik leader announced his discovery that "to tell the truth is a bourgeois prejudice. On the other hand, a lie is often justified by our ends."

Robert Moss gives numerous other examples of the lies, deceptions, flagrant violations of intra-Party democracy, and intentional perversion of Communist history by the leaders of

221

the French and Italian Communist Parties during the 1970s. Those interested in this tedious record of perfidious conduct and double-dealing are referred to his article.

A question frequently asked is whether, if either the Italian or the French Communists came to power, they should be allowed access to NATO. I think it is self-evident that the only reason a Communist-ruled France or Italy would wish to remain in NATO would be to steal its military secrets, disorganize it from within and, if possible, destroy it.

Finally, Ronald Waring pointed out in a 1977 paper for the Foreign Affairs Research Institute (British) why he believes that the Kremlin would not tolerate an independent, liberalized Communist power center in Western Europe. He wrote:

> It is inconceivable that Moscow could permit a new form of Communist heresy which would be so immensely attractive to the peoples of the Eastern European countries such as Rumania, Hungary, and Poland, not to mention the Russian people themselves. Both Russian imperialism and international Communism themselves would be in mortal danger.

It follows that the promises of Eurocommunism are deceptive. If the leaders of the French and Italian Communist parties were sincere and if they took power and attempted to put these more liberal policies into practice, the Soviet Union would have to use force to overthrow them. The Kremlin could do this easily by using the Red Army to invade the country in question and then calling on "a hard core within the [Italian] party after the overthrow of Berlinguer and his adherents to restore order in the interests of 'proletarian internationalism' and the upholding of the Brezhnev Doctrine."

In short, we would see the Hungarian and Czechoslovakian experiences all over again.

American policy toward Eurocommunism has been of the fatuous and bumbling sort that we have learned to expect. The

United States did indicate that it would prefer not to see the Communist party as part of a French government, and that tepid statement may conceivably have played some role in the rejection of the Socialist-Communist alliance by the French electorate in the spring of 1978.

24

Urban Guerrilla Warfare in America

WE IN THE United States are now in the early terror stage.We have seen, particularly during the Vietnam War, agitation and demonstrations. More recently, we have seen the beginnings of terror.

Let us listen to the testimony of former Attorney General Evelle Younger of California, the state that has borne the brunt of domestic terror thus far, testifying before the Senate Internal Security Subcommittee on September 23, 1974:

> In 1973 California terrorists commanded headlines throughout the nation and the world. The actions of the Symbionese Liberation Army, the Zebra killers, the Weather Underground, and imitative terrorists such as the Los Angeles bomber have provided a tough challenge to federal, state, and local law enforcement officers. During the past nine months California has experienced over fifty acts by known and suspected urban guerrilla and extremist activists. These are politically motivated terrorist attacks, and it is clear that the number is increasing. There were a total of thirty-five in 1973 in our state and so far this year in the first nine months there have been fifty.

Our prognosis of future actions in California stated in our June report remains unchanged. The trend of revolutionaries to organize into small, cohesive, and highly clandestine cells is also likely to continue. It would be unwise to characterize the SLA as an historic anomaly, not to be repeated. A similar group could arise again, and not only in California.

The SLA exemplifies the new breed of terrorist we will continue to encounter. He is better educated, resourceful, disciplined, and armed with a political ideology which serves to motivate him. Along with this, he usually has no interest in material or monetary gain; neither he nor his peripheral supporters can be easily bribed. In addition to these characteristics, the new breed of terrorist views himself in an historical perspective; time, he feels, is on his side. He views the revolutionary struggle as a protracted one, and he chooses where and when he will act with deliberation.

The domestic terrorist identifies closely with his foreign counterparts and their struggles abroad. The exploits of the Tupamaros, Al Fatah, and the IRA are studied and followed. Similar to foreign terrorists, U.S. revolutionaries are attempting to institutionalize their activity; to many it has become a full-time occupation.

Although urban guerrilla warfare is a new development in this country, it has been a way of life in Latin America and the Far East. Revolutionary sympathizers in this country eulogize the exploits of the SLA; however, their tactics were not original. True, they successfully carried out America's first political kidnaping; however, even this act was copied from abroad.

If we are to credit the SLA with originality, it can be found in the manner in which they achieved publicity. No other terrorist group has become so visible in so short a time. From the day their first communiqué was printed in full, to the day of their shootout—live and in color—they remained a media favorite. All this publicity tends to romanticize the terrorist in the eyes of the public and is instrumental in attracting additional sympathizers and supporters.

In examining various terrorist groups operating in our state, one common characteristic emerges—they all have an unmistakable Maoist basis. This is true of the Weather Underground, the SLA, BLA, and their predecessors, the Revolutionary Union and the Venceremos Organization. Although there are distinctive differences in how each group interprets its own role in bringing about a revolution in this country, their guiding political philosophy is Marxist-Leninist doctrine as interpreted by Mao Tse-tung. However, this Maoist philosophy has been augmented by the practical experiences of revolutionary favorites such as Che Guevara, Franz Fanon, Carlos Marighella, and Vo Nguyen Giap.

Attorney General Younger showed the Subcommittee an SLA target list which was a computer printout containing information obtained in an SLA safe house in Contra Costa County. Nine hundred targets were listed.

In an address in Lubbock, Texas on November 4, 1975, former FBI Director Clarence M. Kelley gave a good summary of terrorist activity in the United States up to that time. Let us listen to him:

An organization calling itself the New World Liberation Front has claimed at least fourteen terrorist bombings in California this year alone.

The self-styled Continental Revolutionary Army boasts of three bombings in Denver, Colorado this year—a government office, a bank, and the home of a government official were the targets.

The Weather Underground claimed it was responsible for the September 5 bombing of the Kennecott Copper building in Salt Lake City, Utah. This group declares it is waging war and will seize power. Its members claimed four bombings of government and corporate targets last year.

The Black Liberation Army, which grew out of the Black Panther Party, boasted in its first "communiqué" that the group had "no hangups about dealing with fascist pig cops."

Police officers have been the primary target of urban guerrillas. Since 1971, the deaths of forty-three officers and the wounding of one hundred and fifty-two others have been linked to these terrorists.

In 1971, attacks on police reached epidemic proportions. There were twelve ambushes, twenty-seven snipings, and fifty other shooting confrontations.

But you are more likely these days to hear about the number of doors an FBI agent breaks through in search of an armed fugitive revolutionary than statistics on terrorist activity. So let me cite a few more figures regarding the latter.

From 1971 through 1974 there were 634 reported incidents—such as bombings, fire-bombings, ambushes, and police killings.

In 1973 there were twenty-four bombings by New Left revolutionaries. Last year the number of terrorist bombings increased to forty-five. During the first six months of this year, there were forty-six such bombings, one more than in all of 1974.

New terrorist groups emerge as others pass into obscurity. And we face new challenges in combating their activities. Some of these groups have adopted tightly controlled cell systems to prevent infiltration. Some have become expert in fashioning false identifications. And they are able to vanish in an entire subculture of communes that extends across the United States.

Yet there was increasing pressure to take the intelligence role from the FBI and allow the latter to engage only in "criminal investigations."

When Director Kelley appeared before Senator Church's Intelligence Committee on December 10, 1975, he pinpointed the fallacy of that viewpoint:

> In short, if we learn that a murder or bombing is to be carried out *now,* can we truly meet our responsibilities by investigating only after the crime has occurred, or should we have the ability to prevent? I refer to those instances where there is a strong sense of urgency because of an imminent threat to human life.
>
> In this regard, I am troubled by some proposals which question the need for intelligence gathering, suggesting that information needed for the prevention of violence can be acquired in the normal course of criminal investigations.
>
> As a practical matter, the line between intelligence work and regular criminal investigations is often difficult to describe. What begins as an intelligence investigation may well end in the arrest and prosecution of the subject. But there are some fundamental differences between these investigations that should be recognized—differences in scope, in objective, and in the time of initiation. In the usual criminal case, a crime has occurred and it remains only for the government to identify the perpetrator and to collect sufficient evidence for prosecution. Since

the investigation normally follows the elements of the crime, the scope of the inquiry is limited and fairly well defined.

By contrast, intelligence work involves the gathering of information, not necessarily evidence. The purpose may well be not to prosecute, but rather to thwart crime or to insure that the government has enough information to meet any future crisis or emergency. The inquiry is necessarily broad because it must tell us not only the nature of the threat, but also whether the threat is imminent, the persons involved, and the means by which the threat will be carried out. The ability of the government to prevent criminal acts is dependent on our anticipation of those unlawful acts. Anticipation, in turn, is dependent on advance information—that is, intelligence.

25

Puerto Rican Terrorists

PERHAPS THE MOST vicious terrorist organization operating in the United States is the FALN, or Fuerzas Armadas de Liberación Nacional Puertorriqueña (Armed Forces of the National Liberation of Puerto Rico).

By the summer of 1977, this terrorist band had been linked by police and internal security organizations to no less than fifty-nine bombings, involving the murder or mutilation of scores of bystanders who had nothing to do with Puerto Rican politics.

The FALN has little popular support either within Puerto Rico or in the Puerto Rican communities on the U.S. mainland. Its demand for total independence from the United States is supported by only a minority of Puerto Ricans, and advocates of this position have been decisively defeated at the polls when they have ventured to run for office.

The FALN is an extremist revolutionary organization, the militant cadres of which are armed, financed, and trained in Cuba or by the Castro regime, as I shall show in detail. The organization is very similar to those European, Mideastern, and Japanese organizations of terrorism which have caused so much havoc and received so much publicity in recent years. The areas of similarity include complete repudiation of the democratic process and the use of indiscriminate terror against people who are in no way connected with Puerto Rican politics

230

as a means of destroying the confidence of the American people in the ability of their government to maintain law and order.

In its annual reports, the FBI has consistently called attention to the terrorist activities of the Puerto Rican Independence Movement and its military arm, the FALN. It has also revealed the extent to which this movement has become one of the tentacles of the Castro Cuban program to subvert and destroy the United States.

The 1973 FBI annual report stated:

> Terrorist organizations advocating independence for Puerto Rico have carried out over four hundred bombings or acts of incendiarism since the 1967 plebiscite in Puerto Rico, but only a negligible number occurred during the past year. Practically all the attacks were against United States military or United States-owned business establishments.
>
> A current tabulation shows that approximately one hundred and thirty-five leaders of subversive Puerto Rican independence groups have traveled to Communist Cuba for indoctrination and/or training. Many of them received extensive instructions in guerrilla warfare tactics, preparation of explosive devices, and sophisticated sabotage methods.
>
> A large majority of persons so trained have instructed others upon their return to Puerto Rico and have carried out acts of sabotage there. Dozens of these individuals are presently awaiting trial for violations of Puerto Rico's explosives law or are being sought as fugitives for such violations. It is commonly thought that vigorous police action against these terrorists is primarily responsible for the decline in the number of bombings during the past year.

Again in 1974, the FBI warned:

The Castro government of Cuba continues to champion the cause of complete independence of Puerto Rico from the United States. In June 1974, Juan Marí Bras, secretary-general of the home-based Marxist-Leninist Partido Socialista Puertorriqueño (Socialist Party of Puerto Rico—PSP), visited Cuban government officials to help marshal world unity in supporting Puerto Rican independence. In furtherance of its stated aspirations and in sympathy with the revolutionary government of Cuba, the PSP also maintains a permanent representative in Cuba.

The Nationalist Party of Puerto Rico (NPPR), another domestic revolutionary organization which has as its avowed goal Puerto Rico's complete independence from the United States, on June 12, 1974, commemorated the birth of the Puerto Rican flag and publicly reaffirmed its objective of total separation from the United States.

Then in 1975 its report read:

There has also been extensive activity by certain Puerto Rican pro-independence and anti-Castro Cuban organizations. Illustrative of such matters is the bombing of a restaurant in New York City on January 24, 1975, resulting in four deaths and personal injury to fifty-three persons, credit for which was claimed by the Armed Forces of Puerto Rican National Liberation.

The FALN struck again on August 3, 1977. Not only did it unleash two bombs and kill one man, but it caused the evacuation of scores of thousands of workers in midtown Manhattan.

Previous FALN bombings in New York City had struck at such heterogeneous government and business targets as the Gulf & Western building, the Pan Am building, and Citibank branches. Bombing attacks were also made on the State Department in Washington and on the Cook County building in Chicago.

The worst of these earlier atrocities was the lunch-hour blast that shattered Fraunces Tavern in lower Manhattan in January 1975, killing four people and wounding fifty-three.

"It was the tavern blast that dramatically underscored the group's potential for mayhem," asserted a *New York Times* report dated August 4, 1977. "Diners in the crowded restaurant, an historic landmark where George Washington bade farewell to his officers, were hurled from their tables. One man was decapitated, and other victims staggered bleeding into the streets. In many cases the blasts were followed by a 'communiqué' couched in radical rhetoric and calling for Puerto Rican independence and freedom for the five Puerto Rican Nationalists imprisoned for attempting to assassinate President Truman and for wounding five congressmen in the 1950s."

One of these messages read:

> We want to demonstrate by our action that the Yanki Imperialists' attempt at assimilating and annihilating the Puerto Rican nation . . . is not going to be taken sitting down by the liberation forces. . . . Any attempt to suppress the Puerto Rican liberation movement by the imperialist forces, the FBI and the Carter administration shall be met by revolutionary violence.

Police efforts to discover the identity of the Puerto Rican terrorists and to penetrate their closely-knit groups were frustrated by the wholesale destruction of police and internal security agency files on suspected subversives, a process which rapidly accelerated when Carter became president. Possible legal action against the authorities and against informants, based on information obtained by suspects and their attorneys under the Freedom of Information Act, served to protect the FALN and similar outlaw groups. Concerned citizens are reluctant to provide the authorities with information which may lead to lawsuits, publicity, and extra-legal harassment. Law enforcement agencies are reluctant to solicit or receive informant reports because of fear of lawsuits or reprimand by Washington officials.

According to the *New York Times'* summary article, most FALN bombings occurred "without prior warning, during the dead of night when injuries were unlikely. But it retained a willingness to inflict death, as in the case of the Fraunces Tavern blast and yesterday's explosion at a Citibank branch, both of which occurred during business hours in crowded commercial areas."

Following the Citibank terrorist attack, the FALN left a typed statement in Central Park which revealed that it had chosen "multinational corporations" as its targets because "they are the ones that strangulate us with their colonial yoke."

The FALN is believed to be an outgrowth of an older terrorist revolutionary group calling itself the Armed Independence Revolutionary Movement (MIRA), which launched incendiary attacks in both New York and Puerto Rico in 1969. The terrorist targets have included such department stores as Macy's, Gimbel's, and Lord & Taylor's, several of the largest New York City banks and insurance companies, and the U.S. mission to the United Nations.

The authorities picked up the trail of the Puerto Rican terrorists by accident in November 1976. An addict broke into a Chicago apartment and stole dynamite and other explosive materials which he sold for drugs. An undercover police agent made a purchase, whereupon police were led to the apartment where the explosives had been cached.

The sort of people implicated turned out to be middle-class Puerto Ricans of good education, connected with the Episcopal Church. "The apartment was rented by Carlos Alberto Torres, a quiet young man who was a member of the Episcopal Church's Hispanic Commission and who helped write hymnals and religious texts in Spanish. When the FBI searched the apartment, they found a piece of evidence more important than the explosives—a copy of a FALN communiqué."

Torres, his wife, and two other persons whose fingerprints

were found in the apartment escaped arrest and vanished. The director of the National Commission on Hispanic Affairs for the Protestant Episcopal Church, Maria T. Cueto, and her secretary, Raisa Nemikin, were jailed as recalcitrant witnesses.

As in the case of the Baader-Meinhof gang in Germany, the Popular Front for the Liberation of Palestine, and many other left-wing Communist terror brigades, the persons apparently implicated in FALN activities seemed to be well-educated, affluent, young members of the middle and professional classes.

In a symposium on multinational terrorism, telecast by the public television network for two hours on March 21, 1978, Robert Moss of the London *Economist* observed that the breakdown which had recently occurred in United States internal security made the U.S. far more open to the danger of multinational terrorism than in the past. There is good reason, Moss remarked, to believe that the Hanafis Muslim attack on the B'nai B'rith and on other institutions in Washington, D.C., could not have occurred if the responsible internal security organizations had not been compelled by politicians to destroy their relevant security files.

26

The Battle Against Skyjacking and Terror

IN SEPTEMBER 1977, five members of the Japanese Red Army hijacked a Japan Air Lines jet in Bangladesh and demanded six million dollars in ransom and the release of six terrorist prisoners held in Japanese jails. The Japanese government abjectly complied with these demands.

Inspired by this success, a mere two weeks later four terrorists, allied with the Baader-Meinhof gang, hijacked a Lufthansa 737 jet and held eighty-seven passengers and crew members hostage. They demanded six million dollars in ransom and the release of eleven terrorists in Germany and two terrorists in Turkish prisons. The terrorists murdered the pilot. When the plane landed in Mogadishu, Somalia, a West German commando squad, formed after the 1972 Munich Olympic Games massacre of Israeli athletes, made a lightning attack on the plane, using bombs that caused temporary paralysis, killing three terrorists and wounding the fourth.

The world, sickened by the repeated acts of terrorism that were poisoning the headlines, raised its voice in relief and gratitude. A West German spokesman hailed the raid as "a very serious lesson for some people around the world on how to deal with terrorism."

Japanese Justice Minister Mitsuo Setoyama, whose government had caved in to terrorist demands two weeks earlier, said that the West German action "showed how to prevent hijacking."

Immediately thereafter, the World Pilots' Association threatened a forty-eight-hour worldwide strike unless the United Nations called an emergency session of the General Assembly to take serious steps to prevent skyjacking. Since the U.N. contains member nations which condone, subsidize, or participate in terror, it did nothing. It was unrealistic to expect an organization which supports such murderous organizations as the Palestinian PLO and, in Africa, ZAPU, ZANU, and SWAPO to take any constructive steps in the interests of international justice or law and order.

In a study of international terrorism, Brian Jenkins of the Rand Corporation reports that "before 1976 there were hardly any attempts to storm hijacked planes or other vehicles or barricaded buildings when there were hostages at risk." Since then, however, of the forty-five incidents of international terrorism involving hostages during 1976 and 1977, twenty-three have been aircraft hijackings attempted by sixty-two terrorists; of those sixty-two, ten were killed by security forces, thirty surrendered or were captured, and twenty-three were given asylum.

During that period fifteen of the twenty-seven hijackers who did not use planes were killed by security forces and the remaining twelve were arrested.

Terror has many dimensions. In the context of this chapter, I want to talk about a specific type of political terrorism which is characterized by individual outrages designed to capture worldwide publicity and to destroy public confidence in the ability of the state to maintain law and order. These outrages are generally, though not always, accompanied by demands for ransom, release of imprisoned "comrades," or the like.

Characteristic acts of terror of this sort are the hijacking of planes and buses, kidnapings, individual assassinations, bombing of public places, and indiscriminate slaughter of civilians chosen at random. (These activities are obviously quite different from the systematic terror used by Communist guer-

237

rilla forces to intimidate native peasants loyal to the government, to force village leaders to furnish guerrillas with hideouts, food, and espionage, etc.)

We can make several generalizations about the new terrorism:

(1) Terror movements of this sort began in South America in the 1950s and 1960s and were conducted by such elite groups as the Red Brigades and the Tupamaros in such countries as Argentina, Brazil, and Uruguay. Methods often involved the capture or killing of prominent business or political figures, who were then held for trial before so-called "people's tribunals," which would almost invariably sentence them to death. On other occasions, these eminent people would be held for ransom and millions of dollars would flow into the coffers of the small terrorist groups.

(2) The political orientation of these movements was almost always Communist. There are exceptions, such as the South Moluccans in the Netherlands, whose only political demand is for the freedom of their island, Amboina, from Indonesia.

(3) The terrorists are generally revolutionaries who have lost patience with the parliamentary methods of the official Communist parties, particularly in such countries as Japan, Germany, France, and Italy. They are often motivated by a blind desire to destroy the power of the state, the social establishment, and the economic and political order.

(4) Their cadres are almost invariably composed of well-educated, affluent young people from the upper class and the upper middle class.

(5) Professor Wilfrid Rasch, a German court-appointed psychiatrist, studied the leaders of the Baader-Meinhof gang in depth because of their plea that their pre-trial confinement had made them mentally incapable of conducting their own defense intelligently. He found that they were neither psychotic nor neurotic, but normal. While the nineteenth-century pioneer in criminology, Cesare Lombroso, claimed that anarchist terrorists were suicidal types, this view was not confirmed by Israeli psychiatrist Dr. Ariel Merari, who believes that all psychological types are represented in terrorist ranks.

(6) Dr. Rasch believes that the terrorist commitment was a reaction against the materialism of Germany's miraculous post-World War II economic recovery and prosperity, and against the fact that their parents after the Nazi experience often refused even to discuss political issues. Dr. Merari points out that the PLO, which is led by Arafat and comparatively moderate, consists of lower class and lower middle class elements of rather inadequate education, whereas the more violent Marxist Popular Front for the Liberation of Palestine comprises upper middle class and highly educated cadres. Dr. Henry Kissinger pointed out in early 1978 that the rise of left-wing Communist terror in Europe and Japan was occurring at a time of unprecedented prosperity. He blamed the phenomenon on a vacuum of spiritual values.

(7) The relationship between the terrorist groups of this sort and the Soviet Union and the world Communist movement is much closer than the latter care to acknowledge. Peter Jahnke of the Institute for the Study of Conflict in London correctly pointed out that the Baader-Meinhof gang was armed with weapons smuggled in from Czechoslovakia. Since Czechoslovakia is a Communist state, smuggling of this sort is virtually impossible without the approval of the government. Moreover, the individual terrorists are Marxist-Leninists and generally former or present members of their Communist parties. Ulrike Meinhof, Germany's most notorious terrorist, was the editor of a German Communist magazine which was subsidized by the KGB, according to trial testimony.

(8) The terrorist movement is multinational. The nationalist demands of the Palestinians play a central role in the movement because the PLO and PFLP forces have almost unlimited funds at their disposal and a territory with a sympathetic population where the terrorist training camps are established. This attracts Japanese, German, Italian, and other terrorists to these bases. The cement that binds these groups together is primarily dedication to world Communism. The experience of training and fighting together also contributes to their solidarity, as do belonging to the closely-knit, semi-closed communi-

ties of wanted men and women, and a generally common class origin and educational level.

(9) The relationship of the Communist parties and of the Soviet Union to the terrorists is, as I have said, complex. In the Mideast, Soviet and Communist support of the terrorists and their outrages against innocent people is fairly open. In Italy, the Communist role has been ambiguous. In 1978 the Communist Party joined in the mass demand of the Italian people that the abductors of Prime Minister Moro be caught and punished. To have acted otherwise would have destroyed the middle-class and Catholic support that the Italian Communists were winning through their emphasis on Eurocommunism and their new façade of democracy. On the other hand, the Communists in the Italian legislature systematically delayed and sabotaged the adoption of even mildly repressive legislation against the terrorists. The motivation was to avoid creating a situation in which they would face the loss of their hard core of Stalinist support and be accused of betraying the revolutionary doctrines of Leninism. In short, the Communists support the terrorists in principle. Whether they support any specific terrorist action or not depends on political expediency.

(10) The literature of the Marxist-Leninist terrorist groups envisages an escalation of the terror struggle. At the initial stage, there are random assassinations and the murder of police officials, minor judges, foremen and factory managers, anti-Communist politicians, and the like. The purpose at this level is to create moods of fear and anxiety in the mass mind and to force the state to resort to openly repressive measures of a military sort. The terrorists believe, or state they believe, that by provoking this reaction they will rip the mask of democracy and civil liberties from the bourgeois state. The second stage is selective kidnaping and assassination of the leading business executives and political leaders of the nation. At this point, the terrorists believe that they will be able to polarize all political forces so that civil war will ensue between the Communists and that part of the population which is driven by its thirst for law and order to appeal for military dictatorship.

The destruction of this form of terrorism involves, as I have said, multinational cooperation. The first task is intelligence gathering. The wholesale destruction of intelligence files has been of inestimable value to the terrorists and a disservice to the American people and to the Free World in general.

The second vital task is penetration. Most conspiracies historically have been destroyed by massive penetration on a scale which created chronic distrust. Infiltration by outsiders is extremely difficult because the terrorists are the products of a long and intensive schooling in Marxism-Leninism, because most of them have backgrounds in the Communist parties and in the apparatus, because they have trained and fought together, and because they are security-conscious to an extreme degree and punish suspected spies with death.

Hence, the most effective means of penetrating their ranks is to transform members in good standing into double agents. Judging by the experience of the British SIS in destroying the Nazi espionage nets in Great Britain in World War II, the most potent instrument for this purpose is the death penalty, swiftly and routinely carried out. When agents face the choice between execution and betrayal of their organization, some will choose the latter. These are sent back to serve as spies within the ranks of the conspiracy.

The defensive measures involve the enormously expensive business of guarding vital and vulnerable American installations by electronic methods similar to those which have successfully protected American airlines from epidemics of hijacking. Finally, there are the private protective systems and trained squads, and the SWAT teams and special combat elements being readied specifically to meet this threat.

If, as appears probable, the wave of terrorism hits the United States with gale force, American liberals will have to choose between recreating the internal security systems they have so wantonly and irresponsibly destroyed and seeing this country plunge toward anarchy.

Not only should the suicidal campaign of destroying files and of restricting the FBI and other security agencies from investigating "domestic," "lawful political activity" being carried on by the Socialist Workers' Party and the Communist Party itself be stopped, but consistency in our opposition to terror must be adopted. We cannot deplore and at the same time condone, encourage, and even subsidize it as we are doing in Rhodesia, South-West Africa, and South Africa.

27

Communist Attorneys and Terrorism

LAWYERS ARE SUPPOSED to be officers of the court. As members of a profession which is supposed to have high standards of honor, they have a duty to uphold the law of the land.

When the lawyers are Communists, however, they become, in many instances, the advisors and co-conspirators of criminals and terrorists.

An advisory issued by the National Lawyers Guild, a Communist-front organization, speaks for itself:

Legal Street Sheet #6
Security—How Not to Get Busted

1. Operate on a "need to know" basis. Avoid information it is not necessary for you to know; don't spread information that others do not need to know.

2. Don't answer questions by the FBI. Legally you are not required to. If the FBI keeps bothering you, refer them to your lawyer; don't look at any pictures that the FBI tries to show you; don't admit to anything; don't confirm any information; if you have reason to think that the FBI is investigating you, warn your friends, parents, and employer if he's cool. Tell them that they are not required to answer anything and that they should remain silent.

3. Assume all telephones are bugged. Avoid unnecessary mysterious comments; never talk about dope or illegal activity over the phone; if you must talk over the phone, arrange a time when someone may call you from one pay phone to another. A good thing to say is, "We have a bad connection and I can't hear you. Can you call me back at this number?" That should be a clue to the person on the other end to go to a pay phone and call you at the pay phone that you are calling from.

4. Assume all mail may be opened and read. Be careful what you write. If you must use the mail for certain communications, use a public typewriter and don't sign the letter, or use a pre-arranged code.

5. If you need to type something that you do not want linked to you, use a public typewriter such as one at a public library.

6. In your home—Don't keep dope in the house. Keep your weapons hidden. Everyone in the house should know where they are. People who are visiting and strangers do not need to know that you have weapons. Keep a reasonable number of weapons. Larger stores of weapons should be in very safe places, like in a house that cannot be linked to the movement. Kim Il Sung says, "You should think of camouflage first of all when you build a house." If you don't want to be hassled or are into secret activity, don't put signs or posters or political slogans in the windows —otherwise you are advertising who you are.

7. In your car—Don't carry dope; if you don't want to be hassled by the pigs, don't put bumper stickers, NLF flags, or pictures on your car; keep your lights and other parts of your car in good condition so you won't get stopped; pay all parking tickets so you don't get stopped on a warrant.

8. Your person—Don't be carrying dope; don't carry phone numbers or papers that the pigs shouldn't have; don't carry any phone numbers or address books in demonstrations or situations where you might get busted . . . like postering, etc.

9. Don't sell dope to people you don't know. Don't buy dope from people you don't know well. Most people are busted on dope by informers or undercover narc agents.

10. Meetings—Don't meet regularly at the same place at the same time. Change the time and place, because people *and* pigs get suspicious when they see a group of people meeting at the same house a lot. You never know when the pigs are watching your house, or when a neighbor might want to know what is going on. If a meeting should be kept quiet, then only the people who need to be there should know about it. Don't discuss illegal acts, unless there is no possible evidence of conspiracy, and only with people you know well. If a meeting must be out of doors for protection against bugging devices, it should be away from all buildings. People should look casual and walk around to prevent lips from being read from binoculars. Don't act suspicious or mysterious. Unless necessary, only first names should be used.

11. Bugging devices—Telephones can be bugged whether they are on or off the hook. If you must talk in the house, keep an FM radio on, preferably with classical music which has the best interference, and talk lower than the radio. Assume that your car may be bugged. If you must talk in your car, move in a wide radius, between tall buildings for the best interference. Keep the radio on and talk lower than the music. Be extra care-

ful if people in the car should not be seen together. Don't act suspicious. Bugging devices can work up to five hundred yards, and sometimes more. If you don't want to talk inside a building, then don't go outside and stand next to it. The phone company works with the pigs. Be aware of telephone trucks parked outside your house or building. Notice if the phone company comes out to work on your lines. Be aware if the phone company is in your area often. The best protection against bugging devices is to write simple messages down. But remember to burn them afterward.

12. Don't give out names to people you don't know. Never say something that might implicate your friends in a crime, or infer that they know something about it.

13. Never talk to the pigs. Say: "I have nothing to say until I talk to my lawyer." Never talk about anything without a lawyer there.

14. Don't talk about illegal activity or secret information with people you hardly know. Don't let anyone involve you in such a discussion if you don't know them [sic] well. If you are suspicious of anyone, check out their [sic] background and references.

15. Maps, lists, and petitions—Don't sign anything that you haven't read thoroughly first. Don't put your name on a list unless you know what the list will be used for and who is going to keep the list. If you don't want everyone on the list to have your name, don't sign it. Don't let anyone mark your house on a map with your address on it. It is a possibility that the map could fall into someone's hands who will draw the wrong (or right) conclusions.

There is no such thing as security paranoia. Things are getting heavier, and undercover pigs are increasing. Always be cautious. Your brothers and sisters [*sic*] lives depend on you.[1]

[1]Reprinted in *Terrorist Activity Hearing before the Subcommittee to Investigate the Administration of the Internal Security Act and Other Internal Security Laws of the Committee on the Judiciary*, U.S. Senate, September 23, 1974, p. 8.

28

The Sabotage Potential

THE DANGER OF sabotage from terrorist groups and individuals is incalculable. The enormous destruction possible defies prediction.

Recently, New York City experienced a total power blackout that triggered outrageous looting and property destruction. The Trans-Alaska Pipeline has been sabotaged several times, causing great damage but no long-term interruption of oil flow.

Power plants, transformers, nuclear energy facilities, computer centers, airports, subways, railroads, pipelines, and all industrial installations are easy targets.

At this time of détente, Moscow and Peking agents in this country are concentrating on espionage and policy subversion. But if world trends should change, these professionals could easily wreck many of our facilities, particularly if we continue to dismantle our internal security.

The last act of the Senate Internal Security Subcommittee in 1977 was to issue a report on the vulnerability of the Trans-Alaska Pipeline to sabotage and acts of terror. The Subcommittee found the lack of security safeguards in the planning and construction baffling.

One of the more important findings was that no one agency had been given primary responsibility for assuring the security of the pipeline. The fragmentation of authority meant in effect that no one had responsibility.

One of the most serious weaknesses in the security of the Trans-Alaska Pipeline during the construction phase was inadequate personnel security. This was not due to any lack of recognition or diligence on the part of Alyeska, the construction agency; indeed, the Alyeska security department deserved high marks for its efforts to cope with a very difficult situation. Background checks on employees coming from all over the United States were virtually impossible because of the limitations of the Privacy Act. In addition, Alyeska had to yield to union insistence that dismissed workers be re-employed—even when dismissal was based on such charges as theft of company property or willful destruction of property. Because of union objections, there was no check on personal baggage brought into construction camps by workers, regardless of the amount. The unions also obliged Alyeska to back down from its original stand that trucks entering and leaving Prudhoe Bay and Valdez and construction sites along the line be subject to search.

The protection of the pipeline against the possibility of terrorist action is further complicated by the catastrophic erosion of law enforcement intelligence-gathering capabilities nationwide and the near stoppage of the exchange of intelligence information between the federal, state, and local law enforcement agencies.

While the Trans-Alaska Pipeline may be particularly vulnerable, its vulnerabilities are shared by other gas and oil pipelines in the mainland United States. One expert who had made a careful study of the problem told the Subcommittee in executive session that he could state unequivocally that if, "for some reason, tanker movement of oil to our eastern refineries were shut off to the extent that we would have to depend on our domestic supply of oil and natural gas moved by the pipelines, concerted sabotage by a group of less than fifty people could render the northeast portions of the country virtually without fuel."

Within a month of the issue of this report, the pipeline was the target of a series of explosions, bearing out the warnings of the Subcommittee.

Dr. Maynard Stephens, a pipeline safety expert, testified before the Senate Judiciary Committee and gave some instances of how terrorists could disrupt our oil supply.

One possibility was hijacking an offshore oil platform and holding it for ransom. Other terrorist options included a grenade attack on a Pennsylvania refinery and a blowtorch assault on pipelines in California.

Dr. Stephens stressed that an organized effort, such as we might expect at a time of crisis, involving only a few well trained men, could devastate the oil supply facilities of the nation.

29

If Terrorism Goes Nuclear

LIKE THE REST of the Western world, the United States faces the threat of rising terrorism, conducted with increasingly sophisticated weapons, including nuclear ones. As of March 1978, political terrorist groups were known to have antitank weapons and to have used surface-to-air missiles. Germans were arrested in Vienna trying to sell nerve gas. From these weapons to nuclear terror is merely a short step.

As Brigadier General Edwin F. Black wrote in a 1976 article for the prestigious American Security Council:

> Over a year ago, in January 1975, the FBI warned the government that thefts from nuclear facilities could provide terrorists with material to make a crude bomb. Such thefts need not necessarily occur within the U.S. They could take place abroad and the refined uranium or plutonium could be smuggled into the country. Although no weapon's grade material has been stolen thus far, terrorists have already demonstrated through actual attacks on nuclear facilities in France and Argentina that they are capable of raids against such sensitive, highly protected targets.

251

It does not take much to build a homemade device. Less than twenty pounds of plutonium will suffice. The know-how to build it is widespread. Senator Symington of the Joint Committee on Atomic Energy quotes "responsible nuclear scientists" as having testified that between 100,000 and 1,000,000 people throughout the world now have the basic information necessary to assemble nuclear explosive devices.

Studies conducted by the International Relations Center at San Francisco State University have concluded that the most practical way for terrorist groups to go nuclear would be to construct their own bomb from fissionable materials "stolen from the nuclear electric power industry." Dr. Ralph Lapp, a nuclear scientist and consultant to the Department of Defense, remembers vividly how he visited a commercial nuclear site in 1972 where a small force of armed men could easily have overpowered the unarmed guards and, with a little inside help, made off with one hundred pounds of plutonium—enough to make at least five crude weapons. In March 1973, members of the People's Revolutionary Army, a Trotskyite urban guerrilla force, seized a nuclear power plant in Argentina while it was still under construction. Fortunately they captured no fissionable material as the reactor was not yet completed, but they did paint political slogans on the walls, disarmed the guards, confiscated their weapons and threatened to return again.

The Joint Committee on Atomic Energy in their June 1975 report expressed serious concern that a determined band of terrorists might even be able to capture one or more nuclear weapons from the NATO stockpile of some 7,000 presently stored at various small sites throughout Europe. Senator

John O. Pastore, the vice-chairman, summed up the Committee's alarm:

"We have been talking for days and days and days about the possibility of terrorists stealing plutonium while it is being shipped. That is an insignificant problem when compared to the ghastly possibility of the theft of a complete atomic weapon. If a terrorist gang—and it is not that difficult breaking into one of these depositories—takes one of these bombs and it is heralded all over the world, I am telling everyone that we are going to be in a bad way."

Dr. Theodore Taylor, a former designer of nuclear weapons and co-author of a Ford Foundation report on the dangers of nuclear theft, sketched the grim consequences of a successful nuclear terrorist operation:

"A one-kiloton bomb, exploded just outside the exclusion area during a State of the Union message, would kill everyone inside the Capitol. . . . The bomb would destroy the heads of all branches of the U.S. government—all Supreme Court justices, the entire cabinet, all legislators and . . . the Joint Chiefs of Staff. With the exception of anyone who happened to be sick in bed, it would kill the line of succession to the Presidency all the way to the bottom of the list. A fizzle-yield, low-efficiency, basically lousy fission bomb could do this."

Dr. Taylor reminds us that since such an operation is acknowledged to be possible, the mere threat to fire a nuclear weapon by a capable, recognized revolutionary group would make it extremely difficult for responsible government officials to avoid meeting any demands the terrorists may see fit to make.

The London Institute for the Study of Conflict warns in a 1976 study that terrorism today has become an international phenomenon and that the number of leftist terrorist organizations has "increased dramatically." "Ideological mercenaries," willing to use their professional capabilities for violence anywhere in the world in support of a fraternal political cause, create entirely new problems for the security authorities. A classic example was the Lod Airport massacre in May 1972. In this case the ideological mercenaries were members of the Japanese United Red Army.

Nuclear terrorism against the United States would be a complex operation. It would require (1) acquiring the weapon's fissionable material; (2) assembling the nuclear device; and (3) establishing the credibility of the threat. Foreign clandestine services as well as "fraternal" terrorist organizations abroad may well be involved. Correct diagnosis of the gang's motivation would be the key in devising proper countermeasures and in subsequent negotiations with the terrorists.

Paralyzing blows can be struck against the United States through the use of sophisticated terror devices short of nuclear weapons, according to Dr. Robert Kupperman, the chief scientist of the U.S. Arms Control and Disarmament Agency and an expert on terrorism. Dr. Kupperman has organized White House staff research and planning in the strategic weapons area.

In a March 6, 1978, interview with *U.S. News & World Report,* Kupperman pointed out that international terrorists, working in concert, could smuggle a surface-to-air missile (SAM) into the United States and use it to knock out a jumbo passenger jet, killing over three hundred people. The probable result would be that pilots would refuse to fly the airplanes until the danger was stamped out.

Areas of a major U.S. economic vulnerability include gas pipelines and the most exposed areas in electric power trans-

254

mission grids. To the extent that "modern terrorism is theater," the blows struck against the United States would spread panic, create world headlines, and give the impression that the terrorists wielded gigantic power and that the U.S. authorities were helpless to control the situation.

This recommendation seemed bitterly ironic in the light of the drastic and irresponsible dismantlement of U.S. internal security agencies in the past decade which we have already described. Since there is an informed consensus that the levels of international terrorist activity will probably rise and that the United States has no rational reason to expect immunity from that trend, the FBI began organization of a special anti-terrorist department in the spring of 1978. Considerably before that time, both the army and the FBI had organized special anti-terror SWAT teams.

As these words are being written, Western nations are in the process of creating high-level crisis-management teams to handle terrorist confrontations. These went into action, for instance, after the kidnaping of former Italian Prime Minister Moro in 1978.

Terrorism has become multinational. The counter-terror measures are becoming multinational, but only in the restricted sense of cooperation among those victim countries which share Western concepts of individual freedom and due process of law. Libya and other Mideastern countries habitually provide safe haven for terrorist hijackers. The majority of terrorist forces are armed and supplied by either the Soviet Union or its East European client states.

The consensus of the experts in a recent two-hour television symposium on terrorism is that the danger is on the increase and that the reaction of victim states seems to be a trend away from conciliation and compromise toward the creation of special high-filter defensive systems and combat organizations.

An Israeli expert summed up the results of terrorism until 1974, adding that if the figures were carried forward to 1978, there would be little difference in the general result: Terrorists have a seventy-nine percent chance that the entire band will escape, an eighty-three percent chance of being offered safe passage to somewhere, and a one hundred percent chance of getting worldwide publicity.

Unless those percentages are drastically changed, the future prospects of anti-terrorist action look grim.

30

Demonstrations Against Nuclear Power Plants

THERE HAVE BEEN many demonstrations against nuclear power plants here in the United States. Thus far they have been peaceful. The anti-nukes, as they are called, have insisted that their protests have the aura of Mahatma Gandhi's passive resistance.

However, Ralph Nader has "wondered out loud" when anti-nuclear groups might use violence to achieve their purpose. He asked: "Shouldn't you destroy property before it destroys you?"

The Seabrook, New Hampshire, demonstrations are behind us. Former governor Meldrim Thompson, Jr., strongly asserted the authority of the state to remove the protesters after he had allowed them a forum to register their protest. I do not know whether an inquiry was undertaken to determine if Operation Clamshell had Communist support. I do not contend it did. But there is evidence that Communists in Europe are moving in on the cause.

John Chamberlain, a learned columnist, wrote on this subject on June 15, 1977:

> In West Germany the anti-nuclear demonstrators have been predominantly peaceful too. I have a correspondent in the German movement who insists that she and her friends will remain Gandhi disciples to the last ditch. But the "turn-the-other-cheek"

philosophy is already giving way in Germany to ugly physicality as Communists move in on the movement.

Die Welt reported the existence of a training camp maintained by the Communist West German Bund where an attack on the Grohnde nuclear plant construction site in Lower Saxony was elaborately and precisely rehearsed. An exact duplicate of one of the gates to the plant was set up, and Communist commandos in gas masks and motorcycle helmets attacked it in groups of three, using metal saws and bolt-cutters to complete the demolition.

When several hundred potential attackers had been trained while being subjected, for the sake of realism, to water cannon jets and tear-gassing, the group led 15,000 fanatical anti-nuclear demonstrators to the Grohnde site. There a three-hour battle was fought. The Communist commandos, using welding torches, bolt-cutters, and cable winches to tear down the steel fence around the site, were followed by a second wave of so-called peaceful demonstrators armed with spears and slingshots.

Thirty West German police companies had to be deployed against the attacking forces at Grohnde. The police were badly beaten up: 237 of them were injured by rocks and burning missiles. One policeman had to be evacuated by helicopter with an axe blade in his shoulder. The police used twenty water cannon trucks and tear gas against the invading mob, finally driving them out of the breach in the wall by calling on mounted forces. Of the protesters, eighty were injured—or about one for each three of the police. It was the police, of course, who were accused of "brutality."

The ironic thing about the whole business is that the Communists on the other side of the Iron Curtain go

serenely ahead with their own nuclear energy installations. It wasn't so long ago that I received an invitation to visit an atomic plant in Czechoslovakia as
part of an extended tour of European nuclear establishments.

James Burnham, who has been writing about what
he variously calls the Third World War and the Protracted Conflict for a generation or more, suspects
the Soviet KGB is behind the anti-nuclear demonstrations in the West. He may mistake a contagion
for a conspiracy, but if he is anywhere near correct
in his suspicion, the "Gandhis" of the U.S. anti-
nuclear movement will shortly be lobbied by Soviet
"sympathizers" to be a little more assertive in their
atomic site protests.

We have gone through the cycle before, with flower
children transmogrified into Weathermen. Do we
have to repeat the ugly pattern?

John Chamberlain's analysis speaks for itself.

31

International Terrorism— The Communist Connection

IN *INTERNATIONAL TERRORISM—The Communist Connection*, Dr. Stefan T. Possony, the distinguished international expert on Communism of the Hoover Institution at Stanford University, and L. Francis Bouchey have prepared a thoughtful analysis of some of the international implications of terrorism which is worth quoting:

> Maoists, anarchists, and the majority of the Trotskyite Fourth International have openly advocated terrorism and committed terrorist acts. The world Communist movement led by the USSR does not openly advocate terrorism and has even branded it as "adventurism," except when it is waged as part of a revolutionary campaign sufficiently promising to be designated a "national liberation struggle."

> In reality, the difference between the open support and frequent participation of the unorthodox radical leftist groups and the publicly expressed "opposition" of the Moscow-line parties and governments is a matter of degree—degree of secrecy and degree of direct involvement. Orthodox Communism always stands ready to take advantage of social disorder and political turmoil. Further, the Soviets appear to

260

have adopted a policy, dating from 1968, by which the Kremlin provides clandestine support and assistance to terrorists while they and their supporters, especially in Western Europe, profess to abhor political violence and put themselves forward as candidates for responsible participation in coalition government.

Clandestine Soviet support and assistance to terrorists is sometimes so direct that it involves the training, within the USSR, of Communists and non-Communist leftists as assassins, saboteurs, and guerrillas. Sometimes Soviet assistance on a large scale becomes known to the world at large, as in the case of the long-lasting terrorist campaign in Mozambique and the Popular Movement for the Liberation of Angola.

The PMLA is recognized by many today as constituting the government of independent Angola, but massive Soviet assistance existed before independence, indeed, as long ago as the late 1950s, at a time when partisans of the movement were operating as terrorists and guerrillas. After the seizure of power additional support was given to Angola for a variety of aggressive purposes.

The Soviets have additionally become adept over the decades at using second and third parties as conduits for their assistance to terrorists so that their own involvement becomes less direct or, rather, less directly obvious.

The Kremlin's caution is based on the need to avoid backlash against its successful policy of détente that has brought the Soviets such enormous benefit. They are not going to touch smoking guns, save in truly exceptional cases, because the backlash risk is simply too great. However, a terrorist group's "Moscow connection" can usually be uncovered through structural analysis; and once they feel strong enough they will not hesitate to touch the smoking gun.

Structural analysis begins with the *cui bono* test— i.e., does a terrorist act or campaign objectively advance Soviet interests? If it does, one should pursue the possibility that the Soviets have or will promote those operations.

Do the terrorists or their deeds receive favorable propaganda or political support? The Soviet press does not always praise an action or its perpetrator— support is usually more subtle and not always understood by non-Communists unschooled in Marxist jargon. Silence about, or a lack of willingness to support, for example, U.N. measures against terrorism are indirect assistance and may be interpreted as a policy to keep terrorism going.

If the answer to these first two questions is "yes," then the terrorist group should be investigated to determine:

What is its true ideological orientation? Where did members obtain their training and their weapons? What is known about the Communist past of the members? What is the attitude of the local Communist party? Where and how did the terrorists travel? What is the source of their finances? What is their relationship to various front organizations within the left radical and liberal universe?

It is important to remember that terrorists usually enjoy the support of "useful idiots," many of whom are not so idiotic as they appear to be, but are in reality "non-party Communists." If such supporters can be identified, the degree of a terrorist group's involvement in Communist party causes is easily determined.

In most instances the terrorist organization is not part of the Kremlin's strategic apparatus—i.e., not a covert operation of the KGB. The leader of a terrorist group may not know that he is being used, or that he is collaborating with a secret party member whose first loyalty is to Moscow. In the last decade international terrorism has been perpetrated mainly by radical (not orthodox) Communists whose Moscow connection is often only temporary and never complete. The situation is always in flux, and even though the Kremlin does not control or direct them, the Soviets encourage, manipulate, and assist terrorists because terrorist operations not directly attributable to Communist officialdom can advance strategic political interests of the USSR.

It also must be remembered that life is complicated. The Soviets may make a mistake or fall heir to an operation launched by someone else—any number of irregularities are possible. But structural analysis shows that in a cautious way the USSR has provided psychopolitical support to international terrorism. It has also made available most of the weapons and other logistics, and it is maintaining excellent relations with the non-Communist states more openly supporting terrorist activity.

In testimony before the Senate Internal Security Subcommittee in 1975, Brooks McClure, of the Defense Department's Policy Plans and National Security Council Affairs Directorate of International Security, cited an instance of Communist backing of a group that was avowedly Marxist but ostensibly anti-Soviet.

Klaus Rainer Röhl, editor of *Konkret*, a journal of the extreme left, has admitted that he and his wife were secretly members of the Communist Party from 1956 to 1964, years during which he was promoting the unorthodox Marxist movement. His wife was Ulrike Meinhof, a leader of the notorious Baader-Meinhof gang, who hanged herself in the spring of 1976 while being held in a West German jail. Via East Berlin and Prague, Röhl received a million marks in Communist subsidies for his publication ($250,000 at the then exchange rate).

In 1972, while Meinhof was a fugitive from the police, Röhl wrote in *Konkret*: "For ten years she greatly influenced an entire generation of young people with her typewriter and from her editor's desk: students, pupils, youth functionaries, ministers, social welfare workers, trade unionists, writers, and journalists. Her thoughts were adopted by student and youth newspapers, by youth group organizations, clubs, and work groups."

Thus it can truly be said that this Communist group evolved out of a circle inspired by an unorthodox Marxist journal secretly subsidized by the East Germans. This despite the fact that Meinhof's radical followers viewed orthodox, Soviet-line Communists as "chatterboxes who are only concerned about theory."

When she hanged herself with a makeshift rope of toweling, Meinhof stood convicted of attempted murder in a 1970 prison raid that freed the gang's other leader, arsonist Andreas Baader. *Der Spiegel* reported that "Ulrike was in a bad psychological state at the time of her suicide and had a history of psychological problems." Once a Christian pacifist, she is also reported to have had an emotional aversion to the sound of guns being fired, even after her conversion to violent radicalism.

After her death Meinhof received lavish praise from the East German press (i.e., the East German Communist government, since it controls all newspapers).

However, when three remaining Baader-Meinhof defendants asked that the East German Communists perform an autopsy, the East Germans declined, not wanting to be linked that directly to her.

Meinhof had served their purpose.

The case of Ulrike and Klaus Röhl is far from the only known, documented instance of Communist support and assistance to non-Communist or anti-Soviet terrorists and guerrillas. To cite another case, the Palestinian guerrillas who seized hostages on a Vienna-bound train in 1973 and compelled the Austrian government to close the refugee camp for Russian Jews at Schloss Schönau came fully armed from across the Czechoslovakian border. That frontier, like all Communist borders, is ordinarily known for its tight security.

Then there is the case of "Carlos"—Ilyich Ramírez Sánchez, member of a prominent Venezuelan Communist family. Carlos has been widely identified as the individual who led the international terrorist band that shot its way into the Vienna headquarters of the Organization of Petroleum Exporting Countries (OPEC) in December 1975 and kidnaped all the oil ministers present. Earlier in the year he killed two French counterintelligence officers in Paris.

Following that killing, the French government ordered the expulsion of three of Communist Cuba's diplomats. The French acted on the basis of evidence linking Cuban support to Carlos' operations—operations also involving members of the Baader-Meinhof gang, the Japanese United Red Army, and the Popular Front for the Liberation of Palestine (PFLP). It should be recalled that the Havana agency principally charged with the responsibility for lending assistance to terrorists and guerrillas is the DGI (*Directorio General de Inteligencia*) and that since 1968 the DGI has operated under the direct control of the Soviet KGB.

The *Sunday Telegraph* of London reported in February 1976 that Carlos had been relaxing in a seaside villa in Libya and that he had received two million dollars from Libyan President Qaddafi as a "reward" for the OPEC kidnaping. Carlos' father, José Altagracia Ramírez Navas, told French television interviewers that same month that Algerian President Boumedienne had given fifty million dollars "for the cause," but the sum seems excessively large, certainly for Algeria. Perhaps the father was suffering from exaggerated pride in the achievements of "my son, the terrorist." He granted other interviews amid signs that Carlos was becoming a glamorous media star. Even a right-wing Caracas newspaper compared Carlos to Simón Bolívar.

Señor Ramírez revealed that all three of his sons (named respectively Vladimir, Ilyich and Lenin) were taught Russian and sent to Moscow to study Communism. It is interesting to learn that the father believes his son's boyhood nicknames of "Fatty" and "Tub of Lard" help account for Carlos' aggressiveness.[1]

---

[1]Stefan T. Possony and L. Francis Bouchey, *International Terrorism —The Communist Connection*, Washington, D.C.: American Council on World Freedom, 1978.

32

Terrorist and Victim—
The Stockholm Syndrome

WE HAVE SEEN the direct results of terror—death, maiming, induced fear, forced compliance by the victim with the demands of the terrorists.

When Communist guerrillas raid a hamlet, whether in Vietnam, Angola, or Rhodesia, when they kill the mayor, the priest, and the schoolteachers and mount their heads on stakes for the horrified village to behold, they have made their point. The people of that village will be more prone to provide food and information to avert future forays. They will not be inclined to inform government security forces of the proximity of the guerrillas.

But apparently there are much more subtle after-effects of terror. One of the more intriguing of them is called the "Stockholm syndrome," so called because one of the most conspicuous instances of that phenomenon occurred in Stockholm in 1971 when bank robbers held four girls as hostages in a bank vault for six days. After their horrible ordeal, police were baffled to find that the hostages had developed a real affection for the bank robbers and kissed them goodbye after their capture.

In 1975, a young social worker named Louise Stratton was held hostage in a British Columbia penitentiary for forty-one hours. When she was rescued by the guards, they were shocked to find that she was angry at them, and not at the prisoners who had abducted her.

267

The situation was bizarre. A few hours before, a man named Wilson had held a butcher knife to her throat. Even if he didn't harm her, there was every chance in the world (as later events were to prove) that, like the eleven prison workers killed at Attica, New York in 1971, she would be gunned down by prison tactical squads.

But she could not hate him for what he had done to her. Indeed, over the two-day period the pair developed what she would later describe as a "loving, tender relationship." And after he told her about his life in prison, she began to hope that he and the others would make it out of the country to freedom.

At one point she began referring to the convicts as "we," which broke Wilson up. "What do you mean 'we'?" he laughed. "What is it now, 'the four of us'?" Their imaginations soared, and Wilson decided that he would add another to his list of demands—that Louise's children be put aboard the plane along with the hostages and convicts. And even though she realized at the time that the idea was mad—that no authority on earth would ever allow it—she joined in. Yes, they would all go off to a tropical paradise and live happily ever after.

Two years earlier, the pronoun "we" had been used in precisely the same way by another woman, this time in Sweden, when she described her part in a hostage-taking to her psychiatrist. "That was when," she told him, "we started firing at the police."

But the woman had never held a gun. She was a bank stenographer, not a robber, a hostage, not a criminal. The long siege, during which she, three other hostages, and two bank robbers shared a bank vault, had a strange effect on all concerned. The hostages and the robbers became allies, and the police became their common enemy. There was evidence of this "syndrome" in the case of Patty Hearst. Airline hostesses have fallen in love with hijackers who held guns at their heads.

What seems to be involved in this reaction is an emotional transference to, and identification with, the terrorists. Psychologists are studying it, and we can be sure that the KGB is analyzing this phenomenon for future strategic and tactical exploitation.

268

Discussing the problem with a panel of international experts on terrorism on a public television network show, *Terrorism—The World at Bay*, telecast on March 21, 1978, Dr. Frank Ochsberg, a psychiatrist with the U.S. National Institutes of Health, confirmed that "symbiotic relationships" generally develop between terrorists and victims. He considered this the main reason for prolonging tactical negotiations with terrorists. After three days, Ochsberg observed, experience has shown that the risk that the terrorists will kill their hostages is reduced almost to zero. The effect of living together in close quarters under extreme emotional and survival tension is that there develops some sort of human interrelationship.

Ochsberg defined the Stockholm syndrome as the "primitive need to link one's hopes for survival to dependence on some stronger person."

Louise Stratton had a knife at her throat, but her captor did not abuse her, while treating the other captives with abominable bestiality. Louise's anxiety was relieved in an emotion that involved elements of gratitude toward her captor.

As Peter Rowe, who was commissioned by the Canadian Broadcasting Commission, put matters in *Canadian Magazine*:

> Brian Jenkins, a Rand Corporation specialist in terrorism, calls kidnaping and hostage-taking "perhaps the most harrowing experience an individual can go through." He describes it as "a life-threatening, traumatic experience, like playing Russian roulette for an extended period of time. The victim is totally defenseless, helpless."
>
> Doug Dawe, the director of preventive security for the Canadian Penitentiary Service, and the man who has run the Ottawa crisis center during most of the penitentiary hostage-takings of the past two years, has studied 518 such incidents and has discovered some evidence of "survival identification" in all but two of them. "Whenever the hostage feels his or

her life is in immediate danger," he told me, "survival identification seems to be practically inevitable."[1]

The United States Senate Subcommittee on Criminal Laws and Procedures, which absorbed the role of the Senate Internal Security Subcommittee, held hearings on the terrorist and his victim on July 21, 1977. One witness was Professor H. H. A. Cooper, an expert on international terror. In analyzing the nature of terror, he testified:

> The victims speak of their terrorist captors in the most inappropriate terms: "He was very nice, basically a compassionate person, an idealistic, dedicated person," and so forth. The incongruity of these references to people who would dispatch them with no more thought than that required for plucking a weed from the ground is never apparent to those who utter them.

> It is not uncommon for victims to show expressions of affection for the terrorists and even to thank them at the moment of release for sparing their lives. These sentiments are often coupled with overt displays of anger against the government, and the condition can persist long after the victim is restored to the community.

> The operational consequences of this condition, which has now been well documented on numerous occasions, scarcely need underlining. Law enforcement must know that it can never rely upon the victim for help or even to help himself. However, a great deal more needs to be known about the Stockholm syndrome and its converse, a feeling of compassion sometimes generated in the terrorist for his vic-

[1]May 26, 1977, p. 6.

tim, which inhibits him from harming the victim at the crucial moment.

While the psychological mechanisms governing this behavior are understood, study is needed to discover the conditions under which the "syndrome" is produced and the extent to which different subjects might be affected by it.

The whole tangled web of relationships developed by the act of hostage-taking needs careful study, not only for what might be learned of operational significance but in order to cope better with the aftermath.

These words prompted the following exchange with Senator Strom Thurmond (R-SC):

SENATOR THURMOND. You spoke about the so-called "Stockholm syndrome" which sometimes causes the victims to identify with their abductors. Would you say that Patty Hearst was an example of the Stockholm syndrome?

MR. COOPER. I would say that she was certainly an example of a very exaggerated form of this. It is easy to understand how a person in the complete and total control of a kidnaper, as Patty Hearst was, would feel a necessity for doing whatever she was told to do. It is very difficult to explain, otherwise than by reference to the mechanism of the Stockholm syndrome, why she should have gone further than this—why she should have gone further than the merely protective aspects of identification and so completely subsumed herself under the leadership of those who had taken her captive. I think that that explanation can only be found in the mechanism of the Stockholm syndrome.

SENATOR THURMOND. Have you studied her case sufficiently to pass an opinion on whether you feel that she merely acted because she was ordered to do so, or was she convinced to join in their acts of terrorism feeling that it would help humanity, maybe?

MR. COOPER. I do not feel that she had any deep conviction on this matter at all. I feel that the change in her personality that was effected by her experience was a very superficial one. I feel that she had no deep conviction that the political line that she was led to espouse was either a correct one or a better one than that which had been instilled in her traditionally by her parents.

The Institute for the Achievement of Human Potential in Philadelphia, of which I am a director, has done extensive studies of the psychological changes that can be induced in the human personality by total sensory deprivation. Total blockage of the pathways of sight, touch, and hearing can cause breakdown and permanent impairment of reason. Patricia Hearst's abductors confined her in a dark closet for thirty-seven days and nights. She was completely immured there for that entire period of time. Her survival and eventual recuperation are evidence of her fundamentally sound psychic state and character structure.

Numerous studies of terrorist tactics show the extent to which these political kidnapers try to break down their victims into cringing, utterly dependent creatures or else Stockholm-type adherents to the terrorist cause by confining them for long periods of time in small spaces where they are unable to see, hear, or move about freely—in short, they suffer sensory deprivation.

Finally, so there should be no misunderstanding of the fundamental situation, the unanimous conclusion of the March 21, 1978, panel on terrorism cited earlier was that political negotiations with terrorists are always self-defeating.

"If you reward any type of behavior, you invite its repetition," Dr. Ariel Merari, an Israeli psychiatrist, commented. "Therefore never negotiate."

272

Conor Cruise O'Brien, editor-in-chief of the *London Observer,* summed up the consensus view by recommending that governments never engage in political negotiations with terrorists, but always encourage tactical negotiations. Political negotiations involve concessions to some or all of their demands and hence reward terrorists. Tactical negotiations are merely means of gaining time. They will involve such acceptable areas of negotiation as turning on lights and air conditioning in buildings held by terrorists, providing food, water, and needed medical supplies, generally on condition that at least some of the hostages be released. The strategy of such negotiations includes buying time so that symbiotic relationships between captors and victims may develop, decreasing the likelihood that the latter will be murdered.

The problem, however, is much larger than its tactical and psychological aspects, as I have attempted to show in other chapters.

33

Human Rights:
Crusade or Camouflage?

ONE OF THE great issues of the day is human rights. When Jimmy Carter was elected president of the United States, millions of Americans believed in the sincerity of his pledge that he would make respect for human rights a cardinal consideration in our foreign policy. They believed that the Carter administration was sincerely concerned with reasserting American moral leadership in the world and giving renewed emphasis to the universal character of justice and freedom.

Yet, after a few token gestures toward prominent Soviet dissidents, the human rights crusade seems to have been selectively directed for partisan purposes.

When a conference on human rights was held in Yugoslavia in the years 1977 and 1978 to assess the effectiveness of the Helsinki accord, a report was issued in March 1978 that omitted Soviet violations of their commitments. A United States delegation attended the conference but seems to have made no impact on the outcome.

The targets of our human rights campaign were generally either small countries which cannot retaliate or else anti-Communist regimes which left-wing elements in the administration desired to destroy.

There is resounding administration clamor and protest when the authorities use tear gas, shoot into, or otherwise forcefully disperse rioting protesters, often either Communist-led or Communist-infiltrated, in such places as Nicaragua and the Republic of South Africa. When Rhodesian forces raid terrorist bases inside Mozambique, which have been spreading murder, arson, and desolation throughout peaceful black communities, Washington reacts with official shock and outrage.

Strangely enough, these people, who claim such tender concern for the rights of mankind, have made no audible protests against the genocide and tortures in the People's Republic of China, in Communist Mozambique and Angola, or even in Cambodia, where up to a sixth of the entire population has been exterminated in the most ghastly butchery since the age of Genghis Khan.

The human rights crusade, as led by the president of the United States, has acquired a scriptural flavor. The relevant passage is Matthew 23:24: "Ye blind guides, which strain at a gnat, and swallow a camel." Then Jesus goes on to say: "Woe unto you, scribes and Pharisees, hypocrites! For ye make clean the outside of the cup and the platter, but within they are full of extortion and excess."

The late Bishop Cuthbert O'Gara, a kind and saintly man, was the Catholic chaplain of the University of Plano of which I was president. On many occasions he chronicled for me the long and bestial beatings he received at the hands of Mao Tse-tung's underlings. He was starved and beaten, his wounds were exposed to flies, and he was threatened with a savagery that was inhuman.

I have a statement from a good friend, Paul Cardinal Yü Pin, the archbishop of Nanking and the highest ranking Catholic prelate in Eastern Asia. In it His Eminence says:

> Communism is the moral enemy of God and man. It is atheistic and intrinsically evil. Communism is the total negation of everything that the Catholic Church ever stood for: justice, human rights, freedom of religion, personal freedom, and legitimate governments. It claims to promote a "classless society" but actually functions as a dictatorship of despots who exploit the toiling masses more viciously

275

than any other tyrannical ruling class in the history of the world. From a platform of absolute oppression, Communism unceasingly tries to mold the thinking of its victims. Communism has been provoking and conducting wars of oppression. In China alone Communism has slaughtered more than sixty million innocent people. There have been more Christian martyrs in Communist countries than in all history before the advent of Communism.

The Church can no longer remain silent. By default we are contributing to the enslavement of millions whose future is bondage without hope.

You cannot be a Christian and a Communist. You cannot enter into détente with the devil. A Christian cannot be an accomplice to terrorism.

We are standing at the turning point of history. The fate of mankind hangs in the balance. We must stop compromising with Communism. We must no longer indulge in the perversion of providing money and moral support for Communist ventures. We must reassert the meaning of Christianity against Communist atheism.

Communists with neckties are merely smarter, but not less dangerous, than Communists in Mao jackets.

Finally, we must insure that the Church realizes that it is responsible to the faithful everywhere, including those oppressed by Communist regimes. We pray for the suffering people of the whole world, especially for all the captive nations under the Communist yoke. As Chinese pilgrims from Free China, we cannot forget our brothers and sisters of mainland China.

The Senate Internal Security Subcommittee had an assessment made of the "human cost of Communism" on mainland China in 1971. The estimate, prepared by Professor Richard L. Walker of the University of South Carolina, an internationally known sinologist, was that the Mao regime had killed between thirty-four and sixty-eight million people. After its split with Peking, the Soviet government claimed that "during 1960 alone Mao Tse-tung's government exterminated more Chinese than were killed during the entire war against Japan."

In Cambodia more than a million people are believed to have been slaughtered when the country fell into the hands of the Communist Khmer Rouge. Aided by the *Reader's Digest* staff in neighboring Asian countries, John Barron, whose excellent book *KGB* I have already quoted, attempted to appraise the magnitude of the Cambodian holocaust. After interviewing hundreds of survivors in Asia, Europe, and the United States, he concluded that "at a minimum 1.2 million men, women, and children died in Cambodia between April 17, 1975, and December 1976." The details of this crime against the human race are contained in Barron's book, *Murder of a Gentle Land.* The following remarks were made by Barron at a press conference in Washington, D.C., in 1977:

> The murder of Cambodia began in Phnom Penh, the capital. After months of siege, the defending armies of Lon Nol collapsed. Their supplies were running out. And they knew that they would receive no more help from America. They also knew that South Vietnam was in its death throes. They saw the foreign diplomats fleeing the city. They knew the end had come.
>
> The Congress had cut off all funds for U.S. military involvement in Cambodia in the summer of 1973. (See S. 1544, introduced by Senator Walter Mondale, *Congressional Record* April 11, 1973, p. S7081.) Airpower support was halted on August 15. Finally the

Congress refused even financial aid to Lon Nol's forces in a series of actions during mid-March 1975.

The people of the city, particularly the children, greeted the first of the Khmer Rouge soldiers early on the morning of April 17 with shouts of: "The war is over! Peace! Peace!" Already 600,000 had died in the five years of fratricidal struggle. The people welcomed the end of the war that had brought so much bloodshed and which so few understood.

But then the word began to spread that the entire city of Phnom Penh was to be cleared. All three million of its inhabitants were to leave at once.

They made no distinction between bedridden and ambulatory patients, between the convalescing and the dying. Hundreds of men, women, and children in pajamas limped, hobbled, and struggled out into the streets, where the midday sun had raised the temperature to well over a hundred degrees. Relatives or friends pushed the beds of patients too enfeebled to walk, some holding aloft infusion bottles dripping plasma into the bodies of loved ones. One man carried his son, whose legs had just been amputated. The bandages of both stumps were red with blood, and the son, who appeared to be twenty-two, was screaming, "You can't take me like this! Kill me! Please kill me!"

When the people sought to find out why the city was being evacuated, the answer was that cities were evil: "There are money and trade in cities, and both have a corrupting influence. That is why we shall do away with the cities."

For days the bewildered and terrified people of Phnom Penh straggled out of the city, not knowing where they were going or what would become of them.

The same fate was in store for the other cities of Cambodia. Some three and a half million people were driven out of the cities and into the countryside.

The cities became wastelands, occupied only by corpses, stray dogs, pigs, ducks, and chickens, and Angka patrols standing guard to ensure that human life did not return.

Having "cleansed" the cities, the Angka Loeu commenced to "purify" the population by eliminating "corrupt" elements. The corrupt elements were people with formal educations, including teachers, and those who had owned or operated businesses. But the most corrupt element consisted of former government employees, those who had worked for the regime of Lon Nol.

The extent of the brutality against these people defies belief.

Two weeks after the fall of Phnom Penh . . . a former truck driver was commandeered to drive some sixty people comprising ten families to a banana grove. Another truck with Communist soldiers followed. The heads of the families were middle to senior-ranking civil servants. Each family was clustered in the banana grove. All members except the youngest babies had their hands tied behind them. And they began with the first family, having the father kneel. Then the soldiers on each side proceeded to bayonet him to death while the family watched. The mother then was made to kneel and she was dispatched either by being stabbed in the throat or having her neck broken with a hoe from behind. Next, the children were killed by being stabbed in the throat. Each family died in turn as the others watched. In all of the screaming and hysteria, the little children ran in circles, finally to be caught. The babies were the last

279

to die. They were torn apart by people who took their arms and legs and ripped them apart.

In addition to moving the corrupt elements from the population, the Angka Loeu had to purify the culture. Schools, temples, statues, and famous buildings were targets for destruction. Books were piled high and burned—and the older they were, the surer they were to be destroyed. Having emptied and vandalized the cities, the Angka Loeu proclaimed the birth of a new Democratic Cambodia and proudly declared, "More than 2,000 years of Cambodian history have been virtually stamped out." It is difficult to dispute that claim. Within a few days, the Organization on High had advanced faster and further than any other revolutionaries of modern times toward the obliteration of an entire society.

The story of Cambodia under the Angka Loeu is difficult for Americans to believe. Some are inclined to wonder how reliable were the accounts given by those Cambodians who escaped to Thailand. The testimony of Angka Loeu leaders is therefore of importance.

Khieu Samphan, Cambodia's new chief of state, attended the Colombo conference for non-aligned nations last August, and while there he was interviewed by the Italian weekly magazine *Famiglia Cristiana*. These are Khieu's words: "In five years of warfare more than one million Cambodians died. The current population of Cambodia is five million. Before the war the population numbered seven million."

The interviewer asked: "What happened to the remaining one million?"

"It's incredible," Khieu replied, "how concerned you Westerners are about war criminals."

The theme of this volume is that vast human tragedies such as those that occurred in China and in Cambodia are caused by a combination of failures on the part of the Free World. First and foremost among them are faulty intelligence and defective internal security. The former defect makes it possible for policy-makers to misjudge grossly the consequences of their decisions. The latter enables agents or dupes of the Communist enemy to enter the ranks of the decision-makers.

I entitled this chapter *Human Rights: Crusade or Camouflage?* I ask the reader to look at what President Carter did on December 15, 1978, for the answer.

On that day, just after he had declared Human Rights Week, the President announced that he was recognizing the People's Republic of China. That regime had committed genocide against Tibet. It was aiding its surrogate, Cambodia, in its genocidal war on the Cambodian people. Its own government was one of the most repressive in the world, not with thousands but with millions of political prisoners. We have chronicled all of these things in this chapter.

Yet President Carter endowed this regime with diplomatic recognition under the pretext of "realism." But he did more than that. He, needlessly and without justification in international law, consigned seventeen million Chinese on Taiwan to the sovereignty of this repressive regime by declaring Taiwan to be a mere province of the People's Republic.

When you analyze it, he seemed to use normalization, with all its flouting of human rights, as a cover for ceding jurisdiction over a strategic island to the Communists.

As these words are written, there is reason to fear that Southern Africa is being driven by forces that are either blind or evil toward a tragedy comparable to that which engulfed Cambodia.

Mr. Carter has apparently entrusted the policy of the United States in Africa to U.N. Ambassador Andrew Young, the man who praised the Cuban invasion elements in Angola as a force for "stability and order" and who asserted that he sees no danger in African Communism. Among Young's qualifications for his responsible office is the fact that he insulted Mr. Carter's four immediate predecessors, Presidents Ford, Nixon, Johnson, and Kennedy, by calling them "racists."

He has made equally offensive, irresponsible, and witless remarks about Great Britain and other allies of the United States.

Mr. Young claims to represent the United States and not merely the black minority which provides him with his political support domestically. Yet he remarked: "It may take the destruction of Western civilization to allow the rest of the world to emerge as a free and brotherly society."

What Young means by "free and brotherly" may be indicated by some of his past affiliations. He has been active in the National Mobilization to End the War in Vietnam, in the People's Coalition for Peace and Justice, in the National Peace Action Coalition, and in the Peace and Freedom Party. American internal security and counterintelligence organizations have accumulated abundant evidence that these high-sounding organizations are all Communist fronts.

In 1977 and 1978, Mr. Young was given what appeared to be carte blanche in the direction of U.S. policy toward Southern Africa. While claiming to be crusading for a multiracial democracy, his chief effort in Rhodesia was to ensure that the transition toward black majority rule was kept in the hands of the Communist-armed, Communist-financed, and Communist-indoctrinated terrorists. He consistently conferred with the terrorists while denouncing the governments they assault. These bands have spread a wide swath of murder and havoc through Rhodesia, torturing and mutilating men, women, and children in the most ghastly ways imaginable. Most of their victims are black people who simply want to be left alone.

Young argued that the Communist-backed terrorists must be brought into the new multiracial Rhodesian government as a means of keeping out the Cubans and the Russians. This is the coalition government ploy that has failed in Poland, in Yugoslavia, in China, and in Laos.

When Prime Minister Ian Smith of Rhodesia agreed in 1978 to full political equality for blacks and whites and to the immediate establishment of a multiracial government elected by majority vote of all Rhodesians, Andrew Young was dismayed. If this plan should go through, power would be transferred to the moderate black leaders the Rhodesian people preferred, rather than to the bands of Communist assassins that both Moscow and Andrew Young supported.

34

Forced Repatriation— Operation Keelhaul

WHILE I WAS its counsel, the Senate Internal Security Subcommittee held hearings on the relentless drive of the Soviet Union and other Communist countries to repatriate forcibly those citizens of their nations who had managed to escape from bondage. I learned that no defector from Communism is ever safe from the KGB.

Communist repatriation of defectors means sending them to slave labor camps or even execution. It is one of the most flagrant violations of human rights occurring in the world today. Yet it is one concerning which our president has been strangely silent.

The importance to the USSR of capturing and bringing back its escapees is to convince the rest of the population that both resistance and flight are hopeless. Once these wretched people are hunted down and in the hands of the KGB or its Chinese counterpart, they are sometimes compelled to serve the secret police. Our Subcommittee hearings brought these matters to public light and helped block the repatriation program of the Soviet world.

Unfortunately, forceful repatriation continues today. When I was in Hong Kong in 1977, I saw terror-stricken Chinese, who had escaped from Communist China by swimming to the British colony, hiding out not from the Communists themselves, but from the Hong Kong police who were trying to turn them back to their jailers on the mainland. This occurred while Great Britain professed to support the Human Rights Declaration.

In my work with the Senate Subcommittee I came to know Julius Epstein well. Julius was an historian and a scholar who was appointed to the Hoover Institution in 1963 and later became a full professor at Lincoln University in San Francisco. He died a year or so ago, but not before writing *Operation Keelhaul* in 1973.

I had worked with Julius in his efforts to force declassification of the record on the shameful forced repatriation of Russian citizens carried out by Allied authorities after World War II.

The report had the appropriate code name Keelhaul, which the dictionary defines as follows: "To haul a person through the water under the keel of a ship from side to side—a method of torture."

Contrary to all standards for declassification, the stamp of secrecy was held and kept the wretched details from becoming known.

The essence of the story is that the United States, Great Britain, and France forcibly returned, against their will, and contrary to the Geneva Convention and all the international accords, except the secret Yalta Agreement, about two million screaming and beseeching men, women, and children to Stalin's security police, who proceeded to punish them in forced labor camps or by execution.

This egregious violation of human rights took place all over the world, even in the United States. The victims were beaten, bludgeoned, bayoneted, and doped as they were trucked off to their doom. And when Stalin received them, *Pravda* mockingly said, "It is a lesson all Russians must learn well. For it shows you cannot trust the capitalist states in the future."

The soldiers who surrendered to American troops, in response to our psychological warfare leaflets that denounced as "Nazi lies" the assertion that Soviet nationals would be forcibly repatriated to the Soviets if they surrendered or deserted to the

285

Americans, were all returned pleading and terror-stricken to the USSR.

Before dealing with Julius Epstein's moving account of this despicable episode, this American infamy, let me summarize the British side of the betrayal, as related by Lord Nicholas Bethell in *The Last Secret.*[1]

The Russians were handed over to Stalin by a secret clause of the Yalta Agreement. Since they were unwilling to fight the armies of the Western democracies, almost all Russians in German uniforms had surrendered to the British or American forces as soon as possible. Held in camps, they were given solemn assurances by responsible British officers, most of whom were ignorant of the secret Yalta clause, that they would not be forcibly sent back to the Soviet Union.

The Russians explained that they faced death there. Russian women had been executed by the Red Army for such offenses as taking in washing for German soldiers. The Russians said they would rather be shot than sent back.

On the British side, Foreign Secretary Anthony Eden staunchly defended the forced repatriation policy even while admitting that "we shall be sending some of them to their deaths." Eden (later Lord Avon) argued, whether sincerely or not, that prompt compliance with Stalin's wishes would ensure that Stalin promptly returned those British and American POWs in German prisoner-of-war camps that had been overrun by the Red Army. Field-Marshal Sir Harold Alexander was one of the minority of British generals who vigorously protested the repatriation policy. While the American official documentation on this affair is kept under a seal of secrecy, we know that Secretary of War Henry Stimson vigorously opposed the policy. General of the Armies Dwight D. Eisenhower, who had been carrying it out—reluctantly, according to Lord Bethell—terminated all coercive repatriation under direct orders from President Truman on October 4, 1945. But by then the damage had been done.

Thus, almost the entire European continent was swept clean

[1]New York: Basic Books, 1974.

of the two million Russians and people of Russian origin who had managed to flee Stalin's continental concentration camps or who had served in German labor battalions or with the German armed forces. Those two million vanished permanently into the vastness of the Gulag Archipelago or, if they were leaders, were shot, or, in a minority of cases, managed eventually to straggle back to freedom.

Let Julius Epstein in his searing account *Operation Keelhaul* tell how this crime against humanity was enforced right here in the United States—in fact, twenty miles from where I am writing this book:

> Among the prisoners of war at Fort Dix, New Jersey, in June 1945, there were some two hundred Soviet nationals who had been captured in German uniforms by the Americans.
>
> They had served as so-called *Ostfreiwillige* with Hitler's Wehrmacht and had surrendered to the Americans, but not without having received assurances that they would never, never be forcibly repatriated to the Soviets, their deadly enemies.
>
> As we know now, these solemnly given assurances were in full accordance with the Geneva Convention and the American policy as expressed in the Grew note.
>
> Most of the two hundred Soviet nationals at Fort Dix, who were entitled by law to be treated as German war prisoners, had already experienced the determination of American military authorities to violate the Geneva Convention and the traditional American right of political asylum. This had taken place at Seattle, Washington, where they were forced under threat of submachine guns to board a Soviet ship. But the two hundred put up such violent resistance that the American authorities decided to transfer them to Fort Dix.

287

At Fort Dix, the attempt to repatriate them was to be repeated. Again, the two hundred were ready to fight for their lives.

First they refused to leave their barracks when ordered to do so. The military police then used tear gas, and, half-dazed, the prisoners were driven under heavy guard to the harbor where they were forced to board a Soviet vessel. Here the two hundred immediately started to fight. They fought with their bare hands. They started—with considerable success—to destroy the ship's engines.

Since the disabled boat could not leave port, they were brought back to Fort Dix. This, however, did not mean that the military authorities at Fort Dix and in Washington had renounced their resolve to repatriate them by force.

After the failure of two attempts to repatriate these determined Soviet nationals in Seattle, as well as in Fort Dix, military authorities decided to try it for a third time. This time, the operation was more carefully prepared.

A sergeant, who will be a most valuable witness whenever Congress decides to investigate Operation Keelhaul, hit upon the idea of doping the prisoners. Consequently, he mixed barbiturates into their coffee. Soon all of the prisoners fell into a deep, coma-like sleep.

It was in this condition that the prisoners were brought to another Soviet boat for a speedy return to Stalin's hangmen.[2]

[2]Julius Epstein, *Operation Keelhaul* (Old Greenwich, Conn.: The Devin-Adair Co., 1973), pp. 103–104. Reprinted by permission.

Some of those forcibly repatriated were old emigrés who had lived in Germany or France for twenty years or longer and had never been Soviet citizens.

Probably the most treacherous of the episodes was the one that involved the Cossacks.

At the end of hostilities in 1945 there were 30,000 Cossacks assembled at Lienz, Austria. Their number included thousands of wives and children as well as old emigrés who had left Russia in 1917.

The British authorities gave the Cossacks repeated assurances that they would have a special status, allowing them even to keep their horses.

An English lieutenant who had gained the confidence of the Cossacks, however, came to the encampment and asked the officers to come with him to a "conference." To allay their suspicions he said, "I assure you on my word of honor as a British officer that you are just going to a conference."

All together 2,749 Cossack officers went to the so-called conference. Instead of a conference they were taken to a barbed wire camp and were told they were being shipped back to the Soviet Union.

Many suicides immediately followed. An account of what happened contains this report:

> The trucks that were to have arrived the next morning at four o'clock did not arrive until six and the Cossacks refused to board them. British soldiers with pistols and clubs began using their clubs, aiming at the heads of the prisoners. They first dragged the men out of the crowd and threw them into the trucks. The men jumped out. They beat them again and threw them onto the floor of the trucks. Again they jumped out. The British then hit them with rifle butts until they lay unconscious and threw them like sacks of potatoes in the trucks. Now the others gave up resistance and boarded the trucks.

Some British soldiers ground their teeth and closed their eyes. They loathed this massacre. Others beat the Cossacks with fury and madness. There was one British soldier who had tears in his eyes. Another one carried a basket and offered those in the trucks cigarettes for their wrist watches. They took the cigarettes and threw their watches into the basket.

At eight o'clock in the morning the loading was completed. In each truck were from thirty to fifty persons. Altogether four staff buses and fifty-eight ordinary trucks were used. The transport was accompanied by twenty-five light tanks, 105 KRAD sharpshooters, 140 drivers and co-drivers, armed with machine pistols, and seventy soldiers with the same arms, who stayed on the trucks with the Cossacks. In front of the transport as well as at the end armed groups of thirty to sixty soldiers drove in armed trucks. Altogether there were 310 machine pistols, 125 machineguns, and twenty-one light field pieces.

The convoy transported more than 2,000 officers from Spittal. Only thirty-two percent of them were former Soviet citizens; sixty-eight percent were old emigrés who had never acquired Soviet citizenship, and their status had never been changed. (No British-Soviet agreement covered these emigrés. Their extradition was even a greater crime than the repatriation of the others.)

The convoy drove in the direction of Judenburg. Later the story was told that two officers poisoned themselves during the transport and nineteen tried to escape. Probably only four succeeded in reaching the woods. Fifteen were shot by British soldiers.[3]

---

[3]Epstein, *Operation Keelhaul*, pp. 78–79.

That was the end of the "conference" at Spittal. As for the remainder of the Cossacks, let Epstein's *Operation Keelhaul* tell the shameful details:

Although deprived of their officers and leaders, the Cossacks decided to put up passive resistance.

They declared a hunger strike. They distributed placards throughout the camp with the English text: "We prefer to starve rather than return to the Soviet Union."

Black flags were hoisted. Emergency altars were built throughout the camp and priests began services which lasted all day and night. Everybody confessed and took Holy Communion.

Petitions were written and addressed to King George and the Queen of England, to the Archbishop of Canterbury, to Prime Minister Churchill, to the Pope, to King Peter of Yugoslavia, to General Eisenhower, and to the parliaments of all democratic nations. New addresses were constantly proposed. The British accepted the petitions, but Major Davis threw them into the wastebasket.

On May 31, the Catholic holiday of Corpus Christi, Operation Keelhaul was postponed for a day because the Austrian local priests pointed out to the British that all difficulties should be avoided on such an occasion, especially an action that offended divine and human rights.

On the evening of May 31, the British cut off the water in the barracks.

At dawn on June 1, a tremendous procession went to an altar set up on the main square of the camp. Priests, garbed in their most ceremonial vestments, preceded it. There were thousands of crosses, flags, burning candles, and holy books.

During the service, British tanks approached and heavily armed troops surrounded the camp. They belonged to the Argyll and Sutherland 8th Battalion, supported by the West Kent 5th Battalion. Both battalions belonged to the 36th British Brigade. The tanks used in this British Operation Keelhaul belonged to the 11th British Tank Division.

Suddenly, the British soldiers plunged into the Cossacks and their families and began beating them with rifle butts on their heads, shoulders, arms, and faces. The retreating crowd pressed against a wooden fence, which broke down. But there stood the tanks. The Cossacks tried to flee; shots at their feet wounded them. The injured were collected and thrown into the trucks. Shots from other nearby camps were heard. Many fled into the woods or jumped into the Drau River. Thousands of horses dispersed throughout the valley.

The Austrian peasants of the villages who witnessed the spectacle first made the sign of the cross, but they soon started looting the tents of the Cossacks and stealing the remaining horses and cattle. Church bells pealed. In nearby Dölsach, a black flag was hoisted on the church spire. The British ordered it taken down.

As Mackiewicz reports, there were many honest soldiers among the British. The story was later told that one of them said to a Cossack, in broken Russian: "Don't surrender. They have no right."

A British soldier reported that a little girl came to him with a note, saying: "Kill us, but don't surrender us to the Bolshevists." With difficulty, the soldier deciphered the note, put it in his pocket, and began to cry.

292

Many Cossacks threw themselves under British tanks. Along the Drau River from Lienz to Oberdrauburg, a real battle was waged. Those who tried to escape to the mountains were shot. Untold numbers of soldiers, women, and children drowned in the river.

At five in the afternoon, Major Davis appeared and addressed the few remaining Cossacks:

"Cossacks, I am deeply impressed by your heroic attitude. But according to the agreement, all those must be repatriated who were Soviet citizens on August 1, 1939. Those who are in the possession of documents to prove that they did not live on Soviet territory before that date should produce them."

Why didn't the British tell the Cossacks this in the beginning? Thousands of them, especially the old emigrés who had lived in Germany, France, and Yugoslavia for twenty years, or even longer, had never been Soviet citizens. They all left Russia between 1917 and the late 1920s. Even under the secret Vienna Agreement, they could rightfully claim asylum.

The next day, June 2, 1945, the Cossacks of Lienz and Peggetz were handed over to the Red Army.[4]

At least one American statesman did everything within his power to prevent the United States government from engaging in this shameful act of betrayal. The Yalta Agreement, which included the secret repatriation clause, was executed on February 11, 1945. The American secretary of state at Yalta was Edward R. Stettinius, a weak man with little understanding of world politics. President Roosevelt was ailing and near death. One of Stettinius' most energetic Yalta assistants was Alger Hiss.

[4]Epstein, *Operation Keelhaul*, pp. 78–81.

Undersecretary of State Joseph Grew became acting secretary at the time because his principal was at Yalta. Grew did everything in his power to prevent the United States from agreeing to the coercive repatriation and to persuade the administration, after it had been signed, that it should not be carried out since it was in violation of international law.

On February 1, three days before the Yalta meeting, Grew sent a note recommending categoric rejection of the Soviet demand.

As for turning over the so-called Vlasov soldiers, Grew pointed out that they were captured wearing the German uniform and therefore had every right under the Geneva Convention to be treated as American prisoners of war. Grew informed Soviet Attaché Novikov that "the clear intention of the [Geneva] Convention is that prisoners of war shall be treated on the basis of the uniforms they are wearing when captured and that the detaining power shall not look behind the uniform to determine ultimate questions of citizenship and nationality."

This was an important international precedent. Under the rule Grew cited, German citizens who had enlisted in the United States armed forces and were captured by the enemy could not legally be executed by the Nazis as traitors.

Grew had an additional reason to insist on his interpretation of the Geneva Convention: "There are among enemy prisoners of war held by this Government a number of prisoners who have claim to American nationality. This Government is not, however, screening out these persons for special treatment since it desires to avoid a violation of what appears to be the intent of the [Geneva] Convention and weakening its ability to protect every wearer of an American uniform who may fall into enemy hands regardless of his nationality."

This last clause may have referred to the status of American soldiers of Japanese birth or descent who had served valiantly as infantrymen in the European theatre of operations, but who might have to be shipped to the Pacific after Germany's defeat. Should some of them fall into Japanese hands as POWs, Grew wanted assurance that their American uniforms would protect them.

On February 8, 1945, Acting Secretary of State Grew sent a top secret cable to Secretary Stettinius in Yalta concerning the secret clause that Stalin demanded and that would lead to Operation Keelhaul.

Grew did not oppose the forceful repatriation of Soviet citizens who had voluntarily worked for the German state. He urged, however, that any agreement must not cover three classes of people whom Stalin wanted sent back to Russia. According to him:

(1) Soviet citizens captured in German uniforms should be protected by the Geneva Convention if they demanded such protection.

(2) Other Soviet citizens in the United States should not be included where the attorney general considered that they should be granted asylum.

(3) All people claimed by the Russians who were not Soviet citizens prior to the outbreak of World War II and who did not currently claim Soviet citizenship should not be turned over.

Grew's proposed policy would not have saved the Soviet *Hilfsfreiwillige* from deportation. These people were theoretically Soviet citizens who had volunteered to go to Germany to work in German war industries. The volunteer character of this decision was purely theoretical since over a million of the Russian captives who did not volunteer were starved to death in German prisoner camps.

It would have saved all those who fought wearing German uniforms. It would have saved all those prisoners in the United States considered worthy of political asylum. And, most important, it would have saved the great mass of anti-Communist Russians who had managed to escape to Germany or Western Europe and who had renounced Soviet citizenship prior to the outbreak of World War II.

"Stettinius' answer to Grew's warning," writes Epstein, "is contained in his top secret telegram of February 9, 1945, in which he rejected Grew's position and advice on purely pragmatic grounds." The most important of these pragmatic grounds was that the British were "most anxious" to have the forced repatriation approved *in toto.*

This ends my account of one of the most shameful acts in American history, an act of inhumanity which sealed the fate of two million human beings, and a gross violation of the Geneva Convention to which the United States subscribed and of accepted canons of international law.

Who was responsible for this infamous crime? The weakling Stettinius? The ailing Franklin Delano Roosevelt? Some advisor as yet unidentified? Or was this another of the contributions that Alger Hiss made to history?

We shall not know the answer until the relevant documents are declassified. It is high time that this be done. Secrecy should protect American security. It should not protect the reputations of men who disgrace the traditions of their country.

35

Abandoning Hungarian Freedom Fighters

THE YEAR 1956 marked a watershed in Soviet expansion. Stalin had been dead three years and Nikita Khrushchev was in power. After Khrushchev's dramatic secret speech to the Communist Party of the Soviet Union in which he exposed Stalin's crimes and moral enormities, the world began to accept the view that the Soviet Union and the international Communist movement had mellowed.

Then came the thunderbolt of the Hungarian revolution. Young Hungarians who had lived almost all their lives under Communist rule spontaneously exploded in mass demonstrations, overthrew the cruel Red regime, and executed the Hungarian counterparts of the NKVD.

With bare hands and improvised Molotov cocktails, these brave freedom fighters defeated their jailers and, for a few days, regained freedom for their country. Troops of the Soviet occupation forces soon realized that these insurgents were not fascist counter-revolutionaries, but fathers and sons who wanted to live in freedom. When Soviet troops began to join their ranks, Moscow reacted by withdrawing the Russian occupation forces and replacing them with Mongolian divisions that ruthlessly obeyed orders.

The uprising was put down bloodily. Later, Hungarian survivors testified before the Senate Internal Security Subcommittee hearings in Washington on this great convulsive event.

They told us that they received more help from soldiers and officers of the Russian occupation forces than from the entire West!

This shocking abandonment of the Hungarian freedom fighters occurred when Dwight D. Eisenhower was president of the United States and John Foster Dulles was his secretary of state. Eisenhower had successfully campaigned on a pledge to work for the liberation of the captive nations of Eastern Europe!

While the struggle for Hungarian freedom was still in progress, Monsignor Béla Varga, who had been elected head of the General Assembly of Hungary immediately after World War II but deposed by the Communists, led a delegation to Washington representing the Hungarian freedom fighters. The delegation asked to see President Eisenhower. The request was refused.

As counsel to the Senate Subcommittee, I undertook to obtain a conference for the Hungarian delegation with the Department of State.

The responsible official on duty was Robert Murphy, assistant to the secretary of state. He acknowledged the call and said that Senator Bill Knowland had also called for the same purpose but that no official of the Department was available to see the Hungarians.

This was the official State Department reaction to the most revolutionary popular movement against international Communism of the century!

We hurriedly set up hearings for Monsignor Varga. What did the Hungarians want?

What they wanted was only four United States Red Cross planes, bearing the U.S. insignia, to land at the four airports they had won with their blood and to bring medical supplies to their wounded! In short, they were requesting not military assistance, but a mere symbolic gesture to show that America still stood for freedom.

After this shameful refusal to help, all of subjugated Eastern Europe got the message: "Look not to the West."

298

At the time, the United States had a nuclear superiority over the Soviet Union of a hundred to one.

During this period of widespread acceptance of the illusion that the Soviet Union had abandoned its aim of world domination, Frank S. Meyer testified before our Subcommittee. Educated at Princeton and Oxford, Frank had joined the Communist Party in his college days and become educational director of the American Communist Party for the Illinois-Indiana district. A man of unusual erudition with a deep knowledge of the nature of the Communist conspiracy, he analyzed for our Subcommittee the new forms which the Soviet challenge was assuming under Khrushchev.

The report of the Senate Internal Security Subcommittee had this to say about his testimony:

> The witness, Frank Meyer, presented some observations on the Twentieth World Congress of the Soviet Communist Party: "Far from being strategically a retreat," he felt that its outcome "is the most forward and aggressive strategic statement that has ever been made by the Communist international movement."
>
> "Previously," he pointed out, "Moscow had always complained about living 'in a world of capitalist encirclement.'" But now, according to Mr. Meyer, "for the first time in all the years of the existence of the Communist movement the basic strategic point was reversed, and the constant talk was about 900 million people; the general tone was that of a period in which not socialism is encircled but capitalism is encircled, the free world is encircled."
>
> According to this view, the Communists can now afford to be extremely flexible, suiting their tactics to the given situation. Thus, according to N. S. Khrushchev in his report to the Central Committee of the

Communist Party of the Soviet Union, the following picture unfolds:

"There is no doubt that in a number of capitalist countries a violent overthrow of the dictatorship of the bourgeoisie and the sharp aggravation of class struggle connected with this are inevitable." And since the United States of America is the strongest "capitalist" nation, Mr. Meyer believes there is no doubt that it is the target of Communist violence.

36

The United Nations Peace Force

ON APRIL 1, 1978, President Carter recommended a United Nations peace force for Rhodesia and South Africa. Previous administration support of U.N. "peace-keeping forces" in southern Lebanon and the Middle East indicated a growing American commitment to substitute U.N. military authority for either NATO or United States contingents.

Under these circumstances, it becomes appropriate to examine the structure of the United Nations insofar as it relates to military and security operations.

The secretary-general's office in the U.N. has hardly ever been neutral—perhaps never. I have already referred to the anguished discovery of my friend Povl Bang-Jensen that the 38th floor of the U.N., which housed the Secretariat and the high command, was thoroughly Soviet-penetrated and that from 1963 to 1973 the confidential assistant to Secretary-General U Thant was a KGB officer. As far as I know, there is no evidence that this situation has changed for the better since Bang-Jensen's time.

When we consider the organization of the U.N., the key position is the Under Secretary of Political and Security Council Affairs who is in charge of such matters as the General Political Affairs Division, Outer Space, African Affairs, Conventional Armaments, and the vital Department of Enforcement Measures. The last of these serves the Security Council and various ancillary organs such as the Disarmament Commission and the Peace Observation Commission. It prepares position papers for the Disarmament Commission, advises on security aspects of trusteeship agreements for strategic areas, and participates with the Military Staff Committee Secretariat in the application of military measures. It provides senior staff for U.N. committees involved in investigation and conciliation and for the special committee which deals with apartheid and problems of South Africa. It also does whatever other tasks may be assigned to it by the secretary-general.

By agreement, this strategic post has always been held by a Soviet national. The 1978 incumbent was Arkadi Shevchenko. (I verified at the U.N. headquarters on April 6, 1978 that he held the position at that time, a few days after President Carter had recommended a U.N. peace force for South West Africa, Rhodesia, and South Africa.) His predecessors in reverse chronological order were:

Leonid Kutakov	1968–73
A. E. Nesterov	1965–68
Vladimir Suslov	1963–65
Yevgeni D. Kiselev*	1962–63
Georgi P. Arkadyev	1960–62
A. Dobrynin	1957–60

*Kiselev held the following posts before moving into this important U.N. post: He was Soviet consul general in New York during World War II, and our intelligence agencies learned that he carried on extensive organizational work with Communist front groups in this country. Later he was political advisor to Soviet Marshal Ivan S. Konev, commanding Red forces in Austria. The Associated Press story out of the United Nations in New York describing his appointment as assistant secretary-general stated that his career has been filled with tough assignments. He was Soviet ambassador to the United Arab Republic during the Suez crisis. He was regarded as the man who engineered the Soviet-UAR arms deal and demonstrated to President Nasser Soviet sympathy for his aims. He was ambassador to Hungary in 1949–54, when Stalinism was at its height in that country. In 1948–49 he headed the Department of Balkan Countries in the Soviet Foreign Ministry.

Dragoslav Protich	1957
Ilya Chernyshev	1954–57
Konstantin Zinchenko	1950–53
Arkadi S. Sobolev	1946–49

Trygve Lie wrote in his *In the Cause of Peace*[1] that the Big Five had entered into an agreement to give this "premier" post to a Soviet national. He interpreted the agreement as binding only during his tenure as secretary-general, but it has remained operative ever since. To assume that these Soviet nationals are in effect objective international servants would be naive in the extreme.

The actual situation is a good deal worse. Alger Hiss, a convicted Soviet spy, was the organizing secretary of the U.N. at its San Francisco conference. He was able to put his protégés in strategic positions in the organization. Some are probably still there today.

When our Senate Internal Security Subcommittee probed the U.N., we found it to be heavily infiltrated. Our investigation was limited to the loyalty of American employees of the United Nations. We assumed no authority to probe the Secretariat itself.

Our first witness to appear in open session was Alfred J. Van Tassell, who held the position of chief of the Economic Session of the U.N. Technical Assistance Administration. Prior to that, he had held a variety of positions in the U.S. government, the last of which was director of Reports Division of the War Assets Administration.

We had heard evidence in executive session that Van Tassell had been a Communist. When we asked him about that, he invoked his privilege against self-incrimination. He was to be the first of twenty-six United Nations officials who pleaded the Fifth Amendment when asked about their participation in the Communist conspiracy.

Our Subcommittee had employed no investigators. The evi-

[1]Trygve Lie, *In the Cause of Peace* (New York: Macmillan, 1954), p. 456.

dence that we turned up had been readily available. As we were to learn later, it had been already disseminated by the FBI through all the security agencies.

Before the grand jury on April 1, Van Tassell also invoked his privilege under the Fifth Amendment. He told our Subcommittee that he had, first orally and later in writing, given a full report of his conduct to his superiors at the Secretariat, A. H. Feller and Byron Price (both American) and H. L. Keenleyside (a Canadian). Not only did Van Tassell stay on his job after telling his superiors about his claim of privilege, but, according to his testimony, Keenleyside gave him an expression of support. Keenleyside continued as head of U.N. Technical Assistance. Only after Van Tassell appeared before the Subcommittee in open session did Secretary General Trygve Lie act against him.

Some of the more important United Nations officials who could not deny the Committee evidence of their Communist membership were Joel Gordon, chief of the Current Trade Analysis Section, Division of Economic Stability and Development; Jack Sargent Harris, senior officer, Research Section, Division of Trusteeship of the Department of Trusteeship and Information for Non-Self-Governing Territories; Irving Kaplan, economic affairs officer, Division of Economic Stability and Development; Frank Bancroft, editor, Document Control Division; Stanley Graze, project officer, Technical Assistance Administration; and Julia Older Bazer, editor of the Editorial Control Section of the Bureau of Documents. All of these people drew large salaries and were able to hire and direct the activities of scores of other individuals.

The most important case in this series of hearings was that of Frank V. Coe. He was not associated with the Secretariat, but was the secretary of the International Monetary Fund, a specialized agency of the U.N. Coe's salary when he was subpoenaed was $20,000 in 1952 dollars. Coe had entered government service in the Treasury Department; he had been financial advisor to the Federal Security Administrator; assistant director of the Division of Monetary Research, National Advisory Defense Council; executive secretary of the Joint War Pro-

duction Committee and assistant to the economic director of
the Board of Economic Warfare; economic administrator of the
Foreign Economic Administration; secretary of the National
Advisory Council on International and Monetary Problems;
and technical secretary-general of the Bretton Woods Monetary Conference. All were positions of tremendous power to
shape policy and control personnel.

Whittaker Chambers, we learned, had told the FBI in 1942
that Coe was involved in the Communist underground. In 1945
Elizabeth Bentley came forward and told the FBI that Frank
Coe had been a Communist subordinate of hers.

The FBI had prepared thirteen security reports through the
years, detailing this and other evidence to the various government agencies. And yet Coe was able to climb higher and
higher in the United States government and then in the International Monetary Fund. On December 2, 1952, we questioned
him and he testified:

> MR. MORRIS. I see you were the technical secretary
> at the Bretton Woods Conference?
>
> MR. COE. That is correct.
>
> MR. MORRIS. Now, would you describe the duties of
> the technical secretary at that time?
>
> MR. COE. The duties of the technical secretary were
> to see that papers were in order and ready for the
> committees, that the meeting places for the commit-
> tees were arranged, and that all of the administra-
> tive work of the Conference proceeded.
>
> MR. MORRIS. Well now, during that period of time,
> were you a member of an espionage ring, Mr. Coe?
>
> MR. COE. Under the protection afforded me by the
> Fifth Amendment, Mr. Chairman, I respectfully de-
> cline to answer that question.
>
> MR. MORRIS. Well, you will not tell this committee
> whether you, while acting as the technical secretary

of the Bretton Woods Conference, were then a member of an espionage ring?

MR. COE. I think that is the same question.

MR. MORRIS. I just wanted to be sure that you understood the question that you were refusing to answer.

The next day, December 3, Coe was dismissed as secretary of the Fund. The Committee had produced no evidence that had not been available for years to the appropriate government agencies. The FBI, Navy Intelligence and other security agencies knew who the Communists were, but were helpless to do anything. The nationwide publicity which our Senate hearings commanded forced the International Monetary Fund to take action. When I last heard of Coe, he was an official in Communist China.

In three cases, the action of the Subcommittee was later nullified by an U.N. Administrative Tribunal, which voted cash indemnifications to Jack S. Harris, Julia Older Bazer, and Frank Bancroft.

Harris was an OSS military intelligence officer in South Africa during the war. At the time of the hearings he was senior officer of the Research Section in the U.N. Trusteeship Division. When called by the Subcommittee, Harris refused to answer questions about his Communist membership. Julia Older Bazer, an editor in the Document Control Division, also refused under the Fifth Amendment.

This whole sordid history and its final chapter indicate the extent to which the United Nations was Communist-infiltrated and Communist-dominated at the time.

How can we assume with the president that the U.N. peace force, directed in New York by a Soviet national, will be a neutral force working for peace?

37

Brazil and South America

BRAZIL DOMINATES SOUTH America much as the United States dominates North America. It is larger than the continental USA without Alaska. It has an Atlantic Ocean coastline that extends for 4603 miles. It borders on every South American country except Chile and Ecuador. It is rich in minerals and other natural resources. It is the strategic center of Latin America. It has been our ally for almost a century. It has been called the "superpower of the future."

Yet the Carter administration has fabricated our foreign policy in such a way as to cause this loyal giant to terminate its mutual assistance agreement with the United States and its Joint U.S.-Brazil Military Commission.

These distressing developments have been given little coverage by our media and I did not realize the extent of this alienation until I visited the foreign offices of some of the allies whom we are rebuffing.

As the encirclement of the United States initiated by Nikita Khrushchev back in 1956—the encirclement reported in Frank Meyer's testimony—progresses, developments in Latin America become vitally important.

I believe that the testimony of General Gordon Sumner, Jr. USA (Ret.) before the Subcommittee on Inter-American Affairs of the House International Relations Committee on July 20, 1978, is most revealing and instructive. General Sumner was chairman of the Inter-American Defense Force for three years and his experience in that post makes him well qualified to assess this aspect of our security.

General Sumner retired so that he could tell the American people of the gravity of the situation making up "our southern retreat."

I have edited his testimony and set it forth here:

> First, some assessment must be made concerning the importance of the rest of this hemisphere to the security and well-being of the United States and of the dramatic deterioration of the inter-American defense security system. I contend that the Carter administration policy has failed miserably in this vital area so near our shores and borders. Mr. Carter, Mr. Vance, and Mr. Brown must bear this responsibility. The cover of collective security particularly in this hemisphere has been lost in an emotional orgy of rhetoric and hysteria which has alienated our friends and encourages our enemies. Under the guise of human rights, a small group of radical policy makers led by Mr. Robert Pastor of the National Security Council, Dr. Brady Tyson of Ambassador Young's staff, Assistant Secretary of State Pat Derian and Deputy Assistant Secretary Mark Schneider have, in effect, gravely damaged our security in the Western Hemisphere.
>
> Championing such causes as absolute world-wide arms sales ceilings, espousing the obviously bankrupt ideology that if there were no weapons, there would be no wars, and contending that U.S. military schooling is responsible for repressive governments, etc., this group, known around Washington as the "new left network," has effectively terminated most of the military relationships and seriously affected political relationships in this hemisphere. Working with like-minded staffers in the Congress, they have done a "hatchet job" on the long established security

apparatus of the Americas that grew out of World War II and was formalized by the Treaty of Rio in 1948.

Following policies advocated and formulated by these people, the Carter administration has polarized this hemisphere. This is, of course, thoroughly regrettable and from a geo-strategic viewpoint an absurd course of action. The message broadcast by the Carter administration is for the countries of this hemisphere to go left. By embracing the leftist governments and left-wing dictators such as Omar Torrijos, while taking punitive action against the right wing and conservative governments, we have departed on a path that the American people know nothing about and would, in my opinion, totally reject. As a matter of interest, state socialism has consistently failed in this hemisphere, and most of these governments, such as Peru, Chile, and Jamaica, are desperately attempting to find a way out of the problems brought on by socialism.

On one hand, while the Carter administration is against arms sales in principle, on the other hand, since sales are being made, they are using sale approval to pressure the anti-Marxist countries that the administration does not favor. In other words, they are using arms sales as a punitive weapon against allied Latin American countries in a way that constitutes a highly visible and emotionally laden symbol of U.S. paternalistic interventionism. Viewed globally, the percentage of arms flowing to Latin America is miniscule and that it has been constantly declining over the past few years is a persistent reminder of our neglect of our Rio allies and of our exposed southern flank.

Let me turn next to the training facet of arms sales in the Americas. Despite the campaign by the Carter administration to discredit this aspect of our military relationships, the historical record clearly demonstrates the moderating and liberalizing impact these programs have had over the past 30 years. By giving young South and Central American leaders and their families an opportunity to experience the U.S. way of life on a first-hand, and many times extended basis, our concept of democracy and human rights has been transferred at a very modest cost. The Carter administration has taken every step possible to terminate these programs, with great success. I consider this problem to be one of the easiest to correct and would so urge this committee to reverse the policy as a matter of priority.

I have mentioned third country sales. By utilizing a combination of bureaucratic bungling and pseudo-arguments concerning no arms/no wars, several of our closest friends, among them the most democratic governments in this hemisphere, have been denied alternate sources of arms. In the process we have brought the worst of all worlds. We are blamed in the first instance for not making cheaper, more reliable weapon systems available to governments who have traditionally used our systems. In the second instance, we take on the burden of forcing these governments to shop in Europe—or even the Soviet Union—for more expensive and sophisticated systems, thereby upsetting fragile economic plans. Finally, we incur the enmity of these people and their governments when, after they have located a free-world source, the Carter administration refuses to permit the sale, all the while publicly stumbling and fumbling to find an excuse on which to base its disapproval. The recent performance in the case of Ecuador makes a hollow mockery of our entire hemispheric policy concerning human rights. Gestures by Mrs. Carter can never paper over these factual disasters perpetrated by the Carter administration.

Before closing, allow me to discuss the geo-strategic element of arms sales and give a tragic example that may help you place the policy issues in proper context. This hemisphere is, after all, half the world, and it is the half in which we live. There is no reason to be forced to adopt a "Fortress America" mentality and stance if we utilize the enormous opportunities available to us today. The spirit of Simón Bolívar is alive and well today in this hemisphere—waiting for the U.S. as the leader of Western civilization and traditional value systems to demonstrate a willingness and a commitment to defend Western civilization as we in the Americas know it. But our trumpet is uncertain, and in some cases is blowing retreat. Our strategic life-lines in the South Atlantic corridor and the Caribbean basin are at risk and our supply of strategic materials is increasingly vulnerable.

We can no longer take for granted a secure southern flank—we must work in a positive manner for this security in our strategic back yard. The Rio Treaty has been allowed to fade into a background of bickering and suspicion—its military organization, the Inter-American Defense Board, is under attack by not only the Carter administration, but other elements in this hemisphere who perceive it as a stumbling block to Communist or vague leftist designs. In this regard, the Carter administration has failed totally by not making distinctions between authoritarian and totalitarian governments—creating through ignorance or design—a grievous geo-strategic error. To lump the Soviet Union—a totalitarian government with global objectives—together with an authoritarian government of say, Nicaragua, is geo-strategic folly of the first magnitude. Surely the people of this country deserve better.

Let me briefly summarize in the form of a "horrible example" what has happened since Mr. Carter has taken office. The country in question is Brazil—our firm friend through thick and thin, surviving many changes in both governments, and our fighting ally in World War II and the Dominican Republic in 1965. From a strategic viewpoint, it is the super-power of the future—a country of unlimited horizons —an open society—a fantastic mix of races and view-points in the best liberal tradition, positively catalyzed by the New World environment.

Special relationships have been the hallmark of our diplomacy—a mutual assistance treaty, healthy and growing economic ties. In fact, Dr. Kissinger, as one of his last acts, had signed a special memorandum of understanding on behalf of the United States which insured continuing consultations on all matters of mutual interest. The only cloud on the horizon was the impact of congressional restrictions regarding arms sales and military training. Still, offsetting this, we had the Joint U.S.-Brazilian Commission which was traditionally one of our strongest and most effective military relationships in the Free World. Our exchange programs were viable, and while other problems in our military relationships were appearing in this hemisphere, due mainly to congressional constraints, Brazil appeared to be a cornerstone of collective security. As a matter of fact, the Brazilian model was used in establishing similar commissions in the Middle East.

I believe the record is quite clear as to what happened. The group President Carter brought into the White House and State Department immediately initiated action to dismantle the Brazilian-U.S. relationships. First was the disastrous trip by Vice President Mondale to West Germany, who clumsily attempted to sabotage the nuclear supply agreement between Brazil and West Germany. This was followed by the now infamous human rights report proposed by the U.S. embassy in Brazil. Not only were these actions counter-productive in a substantive sense, the manner in which they were handled reflected a high degree of unprofessional conduct and personal animosity on the part of the individuals concerned, including the now retired American ambassador, John H. Crimmins. None of this was lost on the Brazilian people or the government. Explanations by the Carter administration were either more insulting or non-existent, and reluctantly the Brazilian government was forced to take actions that are normal under such strained circumstances—termination of the mutual assistance agreement, termination of the Joint U.S.-Brazilian Military Commission, withdrawal of all military students in this country, etc. At the same time, I understand actions were also taken on the political and economic fronts to reflect their displeasure with the "Carter-Mafia" policies similarly.

To summarize the Brazilian case study, nothing has been accomplished to enhance American interest—and I use the term American in its broadest sense. The alienation of Brazil and the United States is perhaps the most important strategic event of the decade—a major victory for the anti-American elements of the world.

Who has benefited from this fiasco? Certainly not the people of the Free World—nor the alleged victims of repression. Only the Communists and those who would destroy our value system have profited by this charade of the Carter administration.

Who is responsible? I think this question should be answered by the people I have identified during this testimony: Robert Pastor, now at the National Security Council, but formerly an employee and associate of the Linowitz Commission and of the decidedly leftist Institute for Policy Studies; Dr. Brady Tyson of Ambassador Andrew Young's staff, who was expelled from Brazil in 1966 after calling that nation's government "a front for United States foreign policy," which he obviously opposed; Assistant Secretary of State for Human Rights and Humanitarian

313

Affairs Patricia Derian and her deputy Mark Schneider, a former staff aide to Senator Kennedy who is also involved with the leftist Institute for Policy Studies.

These people and others in the so-called "network" are, it seems, part of nothing more than an informal New Left buddy system. However, many of them are linked to the Institute for Policy Studies and that organization's Transnational Institute program. Robert Pastor and Mark Schneider both had a hand in the preparation of a February 1977 Institute report entitled *The Southern Connection: Recommendations for a New Approach to Inter-American Relations.*

I call that report and its recommendations to your attention because it reads like a blueprint for present administration policies, policies that have been or are being implemented often by individuals like Mr. Pastor and Mr. Schneider who first had a hand in formulating them.

The Southern Connection is a remarkable document on a number of counts (I urge Committee members to read it closely).

1. Its central theme is that "apart from dropping paternalistic attitudes and practices, the new thrust of U.S. policy in Latin America should be to support the ideologically diverse and experimental approaches to development that are gaining support around the world. Underlying this recognition and response must be the acceptance of ideological pluralism in both economic and political affairs." Not once is it suggested or even implied that Communism or Communist expansion might represent a threat to freedom, human rights, or the peace and security of North and South America.

2. Specific recommendations included a) abandonment of the U.S. canal at Panama, b) normalization of relations with Cuba, c) abandonment of the long-

314

standing special relationships between the U.S. and
Latin America, and d) making the Caribbean what is
called "a testing ground for ideological pluralism"
where the U.S. supports "alternative models of development."

Does that not sound like what this administration
has done concerning Panama, Cuba, Brazil, and
Jamaica?

The report even called for the United States to
stop selling nuclear generating plants, which brings
us back to Brazil.

The U.S. Congress and the American people have
every right to demand an account of this matter
which is tragically typical of our policy in the Americas. As a matter of interest, it should be noted that
Brazil has been forced into developing its own arms
industry, which is proceeding very well indeed.
There is no necessity for me to discuss the implications of this very important strategic development at
this time, but it should be a matter of interest in
addressing arms sales policies.

In closing, gentlemen, I have presented to this
Committee just the tip of the iceberg which threatens our country. To paraphrase General Washington, when I laid aside my uniform to wear civilian
clothes, I did not lay aside my concern for the security of my country. This concern prompts my appear-
ance here today.

Our security has fallen into hands, which through
ignorance or misplaced loyalty, particularly in the
matter of arms sales, are pursuing policies which are
contrary to the best interests of this nation. The
American people and their representatives have a
right and need to know that military security relationships in this hemisphere are at the lowest point
since the late 1930s.

The geo-strategic vertigo demonstrated by the
Carter administration leaves our friends and neigh-

bors confused and apprehensive—our enemies delighted and encouraged. The Cuban involvement in Africa is the logical and predictable result of our policies in the Americas and the rest of the world. This Committee, by taking positive action to identify problems, and those in the Carter administration responsible for self-defeating policies, can take prudent steps to correct these dangerous trends.

38

And Now Southern Africa

I NOW COME to this final chapter. As I look about the world and
the nation, nothing seems to have changed in our outlook even
though that world and that nation have indeed changed, and
changed convulsively. Our leaders are deploring terror but we
are supporting terrorists in Rhodesia and South-West Africa
and encouraging terror in South Africa.

We have seen the diplomatic compromise called "coalition
government" fail disastrously in Poland, in Yugoslavia, in
China, and in Laos. Yet as I write this, President Carter is
demanding that Prime Minister Ian Smith, who has fashioned a government that insures black majority rule, protection of minority rights, and even amnesty to the terrorists if
only they put down their arms, take into that government
the Soviet-armed guerrilla leaders Nkomo and Mugabe. He
insists on this, even though the terrorists demand that they
control the policing of the forthcoming elections which they
say will take place after they have conditioned the country
to "truly anti-colonial democracy." They clearly do not want
black majority rule. They want a Marxist dictatorship. And
we are encouraging them as we wage war in the form of illegal sanctions* against the government that is struggling to

---

*The United Nations Charter expressly proscribes interference in
the internal affairs of any nation. Former Secretary of State Dean

form a democratic, constitutional nation.

I went to Rhodesia in October 1977 to see conditions there first-hand. I was alarmed but not surprised to learn that the United States, represented by Ambassador Andrew Young, submitted to Prime Minister Ian Smith a proposal, jointly with Dr. David Owen representing Great Britain, whereby the "liberation army," the term euphemistically applied by them to the terrorists, would be the "basis" of the new Rhodesian security forces.

When I returned home in November, I wrote the following:

> Prime Minister Ian Smith of Rhodesia recently took the peace initiative in Rhodesia from Dr. David Owen of Great Britain and Ambassador Andrew Young of the United States and followed through on his internal solution. He reiterated his offer of September 1976 to effect a transfer to black majority rule and ordered a devastating "hot pursuit" raid against the terrorist guerrilla bases across the border in Mozambique. Both have been successful thus far.
>
> Before then the world had been led to believe that Prime Minister Ian Smith of Rhodesia has been a stumbling block to a smooth transition from a harsh white minority regime to peaceful black majority rule for that lovely land.
>
> Dr. David Owen of Great Britain and Ambassador Andrew Young of the United States have been holding conferences all over Europe and Africa trying to effect the change of government, but always criticizing Ian Smith for his intransigence.
>
> The so-called front line states (although Tanzania and Angola do not border on Rhodesia)—Angola,

---

Acheson has described these sanctions as "barefaced aggression unprovoked and unjustified by a single legal or moral principle."

Botswana, Mozambique, Zambia, and Tanzania—dominated by the Communists in Mozambique and Angola, are made parties to the settlement. And two groups of terrorists, one operating out of Zambia and the other out of Mozambique, earn with Owen and Young the euphoric title of the "Patriotic Front" and are made prime beneficiaries of the concessions proposed.

The target of all these negotiations, the Rhodesian government which declared itself independent of Great Britain in 1965, is deemed illegal and is accorded the most contumelious treatment of all the parties involved.

Rhodesia has been a self-governing colony of Great Britain since 1923 and declared its independence after a long series of lengthy sessions in both London and Salisbury.

The individual who is most dedicated to a peaceful transfer to black majority rule is Prime Minister Ian Smith.

In September 1976 he entered into an agreement—some say belated—with the United States Secretary of State, Dr. Henry Kissinger, under which he agreed to transfer power, in two years, to a duly elected black majority on a one-man one-vote basis. There were several safeguards written into the agreement—the two-year interval for necessary preparations, and steps necessary to protect the interests of the minority from a precipitous change.

When the agreement was made, Smith was assured by Dr. Kissinger that the agreement had the approval of a majority of the "front line states." However, after it was made public, a shadowy figure who dominates the whole scene, Russian Ambassador to Zambia Vasili Solodovnikov, pressured the left-lean-

319

ing President of Tanzania Julius K. Nyerere to breach his oral agreement with Kissinger, and Nyerere voted with Presidents Neto of Angola and Machel of Mozambique to reject the agreement by a 3 to 2 count.

When Dr. Kissinger was asked to state publicly what had transpired, an account that would have been helpful to Ian Smith's reputation, he declined, saying it was an exercise in futility to call Nyerere a liar.

The world should have then recognized that Smith had done everything he had promised to effect a transfer of power to a black majority government.

But as he persisted in his efforts, he realized that Ivor Richards, Owen's predecessor, and Andrew Young were giving forth statements that implied that he rather than Nyerere was responsible for the failure to transfer power.

The British negotiators and Young, working closely with an Anthony Lake in the State Department, thereupon embarked on a long series of sessions with the terrorists whom they persisted in calling the "Patriotic Front," each time making more and more concessions to their recalcitrance.

I have seen the latest United States-British proposals submitted to Prime Minister Smith on September 1 of last year. They are severe enough, but at a press conference held simultaneously with the submission, Dr. Owen, speaking for the two governments, issued a statement saying that the "liberation army" would be "the basis" of the new Rhodesian army that would police the transition. In other words, the terrorists would become the policemen.

The terrorists are of two factions, one headed by Robert Mugabe, who educated himself while in Rhodesian detention and who operates out of Maputo, the capital of Mozambique.

Mugabe's defense minister is a grim character by the name of Josiah Tongonara who murdered his fellow terrorist leader, Chitepo, and was lodged in a Zambian jail for that crime. He was mysteriously released by the Zambians to attend the conference in Geneva that was to settle the fate of Rhodesia. Mugabe recently visited Peking for support. Machel, the Frelimo terrorist who came to power when Portugal abandoned its colony of Mozambique, was originally a proxy of Communist China, but of late he has been shifting his allegiance to Moscow. The organization these characters operate is called ZANU, or the Zimbabwe African National Union.

The guerrilla force operating out of Zambia is called ZAPU or Zimbabwe African People's Union and is headed by Joshua Nkomo. Nkomo has a 3,000-man force whose build-up was supervised by Ambassador Solodovnikov. Nkomo's forces, for the most part, are recruited by the terrorists' kidnaping fourteen- and fifteen-year-old blacks in western Rhodesia, some by bus loads, and sending them north for training as guerrillas. These abductions are understandably enraging the black Rhodesian mothers who, many believe, will dispatch Nkomo if he ever enters the country to stand for election.

The two guerrilla forces sometimes converge in their incursions, and when they do they clash, and the number of internecine killings is extensive.

The two terrorist forces are killing hundreds of Rhodesians, mostly blacks. I have seen the photographs taken after the terrorists have struck. Innocent farmers (black and white) and their families are slaughtered, often in the dead of night, with the guerrillas conspicuously maiming their victims in order to strike terror in the countryside. Even forced cannibalism is imposed on the victims—with women forced to eat the corpses of their murdered husbands.

Yet these are the people whom Andrew Young is proposing as policemen of Rhodesia.

Ian Smith should be applauded rather than besmirched for refusing to turn his people over to the mercies of these murderers. He would not be a leader worthy of the name if he surrendered his constituents, five million blacks and 270,000 whites, to these terrorists.

I have seen the mass of arms captured by the Rhodesian security forces. The cannons, mortars, machine guns, automatic rifles, and assorted weaponry bear the markings of Communist China, Yugoslavia, Czechoslovakia, East Germany, and Russia. The Western world which now professes to be outraged by acts of terror in the skies is not raising a voice in protest against these instruments of death being shipped into Rhodesia to kill innocent men, women, and children.

Rather than deploring these acts, men who are otherwise civilized are subsidizing them. While I was in Rhodesia, Judith Hart, the overseas minister of the British Labor Government, made a clandestine nine million dollar interest-free loan to the Frelimo government of Mozambique. Our State Department tried to grant that terrorist regime fifteen million dollars, but Senator James Allen (D-Ala) mercifully filibustered the effort.

The World Council of Churches has been regularly subsidizing the terrorists, making the thoroughly naive distinction that their funds are going to bandages and medicines rather than guns. I noted that the World Council of Churches recently made a ten thousand dollar grant to two Australian Communist organizations. The purpose of the grant was to prevent white Rhodesians from emigrating to Australia.

The man pulling the strings on this whole terror operation is Russian Ambassador Vasili Solodovnikov, who operates out of Zambia. When he was appointed he had no diplomatic experience but headed the African Institute of the USSR Academy of Science and was chairman of the Commission for African Countries. Intimately involved with the KGB, his formal mission is "to create an anti-imperalist solidarity front of African and Soviet peoples." At a reception in 1976 he declared that his country was "supporting the liberation movements of Zimbabwe (Rhodesia), Namibia (South-West Africa), and South Africa," a condition that Dr. Owen recently acknowledged in a London journal.

These terrorists do not want majority rule. They want a Communist dictatorship such as exists in Angola and Mozambique. Nkomo has almost no support from the black Rhodesians. The black national leaders, Bishop Abel Muzorewa, N. Sithole, and Chief Chirau, would, in the opinion of everyone here, receive the overwhelming majority of any votes cast. For that reason the "Patriotic Front" will not allow a peaceful transfer of power.

President Kenneth Kaunda of Zambia let the snake out of the bag on the day I was leaving Salisbury. He openly declared that he did not believe there was a need to rush into elections, and that they could be deferred for one or two years after the "liberation" forces took over the role of policemen. He pointed to the precedent set in Mozambique by Frelimo leader Machel.

The whole situation is so deplorable that I cannot comprehend why my country can support such a mindless policy. Andrew Young, Anthony Lake, and these men shaping this policy should account to the American people for these occurrences which are clearly driving another Western country into the Soviet orbit and subjecting five million people now living in relative peace and prosperity to an impoverished Marxist dictatorship.

Prime Minister Smith has since put together an interim regime that is planning general elections before the end of 1978. Suffrage has been granted to all adults over the age of eighteen. The interim government is presided over by a four-man executive council composed of Bishop Abel Muzorewa, a black nationalist, the Rev. Ndabaningi Sithole, a former guerrilla, Senator and Chief Jeremiah Chirau, a tribal leader, and Prime Minister Ian Smith.

Cabinet ministers have been assigned to the three blacks, with Ministries of Justice, Finance, and Transport going to Muzorewa, Defense and Agricultural portfolios to Sithole, and Internal Affairs, Education, and Water Development to Chirau.

I also went to South-West Africa, and there again I learned that we were using our influence to bolster another terrorist group, SWAPO—the South-West Africa People's Organization —led and directed by Communists. I interviewed some of the black nationalists and white natives in Windhoek, the capital, who had worked for years fashioning a democratic constitutional black majority government to be named Namibia. They all told me that they would have had such a government long ago if the United Nations and the Western nations, notably the United States, had not exercised a veto over the arrangement until the insatiable SWAPO was given more power in the framework.

Despite this thrilling development of a black majority-ruled democratic, constitutional government with protection afforded for minority rights, the United States continues to encourage the terrorists, not only not recognizing this exemplary effort, but declaring it illegal and continuing its war against Rhodesia that takes the form of sanctions.

When former Secretary of State Henry Kissinger shaped this crisis in 1976, he pressured the Congress to repeal the Byrd Amendment which had enabled the United States to bypass United Nations sanctions and import strategic chrome from Rhodesia.

Since this repeal, the United States has been purchasing chrome from the Soviet Union. Dr. Paul R. Parker of the University of California at Berkeley and a group of academic and industrial colleagues issued a report in April 1978 which concluded: "There are no substitutes for chromium in the fabrication of corrosion-resisting steels and high temperature alloys."

The report also concluded: "The United States is strategically more vulnerable to a long-term chromium embargo than to an embargo of any other natural resource, including petroleum."

These cogent considerations, however, are swept aside by our policy planners in their pursuit of the mindless policy toward Rhodesia that seems determined to destroy that healthy, vigorous, religiously-oriented country and put in its place a Communist-controlled dictatorship, repressive of blacks and punitive of whites, such as exists in Mozambique, Angola, Guinea-Bissau, and Ethiopia.

Even while our State Department is carrying out this policy, it is doing other inconsistent and senseless things. For instance, when I was in Dallas late in 1977, I learned that through State Department negotiations Bell Helicopter was conducting a training program for Idi Amin's pilots. Some of these trainees were to serve as the Butcher of Uganda's personal guard. We were aiding this bloody Marxist dictator while repressing the Rhodesians, black and white, who were agreeing to democratic, constitutional government.

I wrote of this situation, in October 1977, as follows:

South-West Africa is a sparsely settled territory, twice the size of California, on the Atlantic coast of Southern Africa. It is strategically situated just north of the Cape of Good Hope and below Angola. It is rich in diamonds and minerals.

South-West Africa is now on the center stage of the political drama. I was in Windhoek, the capital, in October and learned something of the situation there.

The Republic of South Africa has been administering this vast territory since 1915 under a League of Nations mandate. The U.N. has now declared this administration illegal and renamed the country Namibia. The South African government, recognizing the winds of change, has reconciled itself to surrendering the entire area except Walvis Bay, an excellent port on the Atlantic Ocean which has a separate identification because it was British rather than German at the time of the mandate in 1915.

I met some of the able people—black and white— who have been laboring, within constitutional guidelines, to effect a transfer of power to an independent country with majority rule. This could have been effected some years ago if the U.N. had not interfered by its support of SWAPO (the South-West Africa People's Organization). This may have been a nationalist organization in the past and there are many perceptive Africans around who were part of that organization. But it is now controlled by the USSR and directed by Soviet Ambassador to Zambia, Vasili Solodovnikov, who has KGB connections. Its headquarters is in Lusaka, Zambia. A few years ago when almost a thousand of the SWAPO field people went to the headquarters in Lusaka to confirm their suspicions that the present leader of SWAPO, Sam Nujoma, was not only a Soviet lackey but was enjoying extraordinary material comforts, they were seized and put into a Zambian jail. I learned that they have been transferred to a Tanzanian prison where they now languish. These are the political prisoners the South Africans are trying to bargain for in the current negotiations.

SWAPO cannot win the proposed elections without the use of force. The estimate I heard was that their support runs to about twenty percent. South Africa wants the elections held now, but the U.N. and now the ministers of five Western nations, including the U.S., are exerting pressure on South Africa to remove its troops before the election and allow the U.N. to supervise it. Since the U.N. openly champions SWAPO, South Africa has resisted this. This is the essence of the present confrontation.

But again the question arises: Why is the U.S., as it is doing in Rhodesia, intervening on the side of the USSR-led terrorists in their war of national liberation?

The prime target in that sector of the world is South Africa at the very bottom of the continent. I visited that beleaguered country, spending some time in Johannesburg, Pretoria and Cape Town, even going to the beautiful Transkei, the first of the tribal homelands. While I was there I wrote the following:

Cape Town, despite its majestic beauty, must be looked at strategically in this time of great turmoil when the United States, in a highly selective invocation of its human rights policy, is assaulting South Africa in the councils and the media of the world. Here at Cape Point, about thirty miles south of the city of Cape Town on the narrow peninsula that marks the confluence of the Indian and Atlantic Oceans, one can measure the importance of the Cape of Good Hope which Vasco da Gama sailed around in 1498.

Local sources tell us that 12,000 ships circumnavigate this cape every year and another 12,000 put into South African ports. When the Suez Canal was closed the numbers greatly exceeded these, as it became the only route between Western Europe and the Indian Ocean area. Most of Western Europe's and the United States' imported oil moves around this point. NATO is dependent on the strategic materials that pass here from the Indian Ocean to the Atlantic.

With Soviet geopolitical successes in Africa and Asia that have enabled them to set up naval bases or anchorages at Aden on the Persian Gulf, in Zanzibar, in Lourenço Marques (now called Maputo), Beira, Nacala, and Porto Amelia, all in Mozambique, this peninsula takes on added importance. Far on the Atlantic side now that Angola has been largely conquered, the USSR has Luanda, an excellent deepwater anchorage. Above Angola the Soviets are commencing to build anchorages in Guinea-Bissau, which includes the Cape Verde Islands, and even off São Tomé and Príncipe in the Gulf of Biafra. They also have air bases at Berbera in Somalia and at Conakry in Guinea.

This redoubt then is virtually the West's last naval bastion in this interesting part of the world. The British have abrogated their agreement to use the excellent South Africa base at Simonstown, about ten miles from here, and the United States, frightened by apartheid, will not move into the vacuum.

South African—as well as Rhodesian and South-West African—mineral reserves are tremendous. South Africa is the second leading producer of uranium, and it produces more than sixty percent of the non-Communist world's gold. It is responsible for more than fifty percent of African industrial production and twenty-five percent of its agriculture. It is ripe pickings indeed.

The Soviet navy is moving into the Indian Ocean to the east of us here, and Admiral S. G. Gorshkov, while commander-in-chief of the Soviet navy, openly declared, "The disruption of the ocean lines of communications, the special arteries that feed the military and economic potentials of the aggressor imperialist countries, has continued to be one of the fleet's missions."

Here from afar I can only wonder whether President Jimmy Carter has reckoned with all these considerations as he rather emotionally embarks on his vendetta, with all its double standards, against South Africa.

The purpose of foreign policy should be to establish successful relationships and form alliances with other nations who will work with us to strengthen our position in international affairs. With respect to South Africa, we are collaborating with the Communist nations to bring that country down. We are using a double standard with respect to human rights to isolate the Pretoria government from the commerce of the world. We have even voted for a military embargo. A day does not pass without one of our spokesmen denouncing the South Africans for some act or expression reflecting racial discrimination.

We talk of human rights for the blacks in South Africa—and that would be a good cause if it were universally applied—but we are silent and ignore the total eclipse of those rights in Mozambique, just to the north, in Idi Amin's Uganda, in Angola, and in the other Marxist and military dictatorships that abound in Africa, where black human beings groan in hunger, privation, and bondage.

Closer to home, just off our coast, we are not only tolerating a bristling Soviet military and naval base, replete with missiles, but we are straining to normalize relations with Cuba, despite its excesses abroad and its repression at home.

Castro's DGI or secret police infest Jamaica, Panama, and Guyana, all three governments collaborating with the bearded dictator. Yet under the prodding of Andrew Young we are giving substantial economic assistance to those regimes that Young calls "Caribbean democracies."

I believe that President Carter and the senators who voted for ratification of the Panama Canal treaties made a strategic error in ceding that vital waterway to Torrijos, who has all the earmarks of an inchoate Soviet and Cuban proxy, subsidizing him and his allies as we cede it.

When I see these things taking place today, despite the lamentable record of the last thirty years, I fear for my six sons, my daughter, and their progeny. An Africa pulsating with Soviet troops, Cuba an enemy bastion, Caribbean nations being drawn to Castro, and the strategic Panama Canal in the hands of hostile forces—all these make up a spectacle that has caused Admiral John S. McCain, Jr., formerly head of all Allied forces in the Pacific area, to observe: "They are building a Berlin Wall around us."

Indeed they are, and instead of resisting this encirclement, we continue to pursue all those practices and policies that have proved to be so disastrous over the years. Someone, watching us from above, would quite understandably observe that we are seeding our own destruction.

Epilogue

THE OCEAN BEFORE me here in Mantoloking rolls on, changing daily with the eternal tides but keeping the same seasonal cadences. We have had two great storms that cruelly eroded our dunes and threatened the foundation of our home. Though battered, they held and the house survives. It survives, however, only because we labored year after year to build up those dunes. Painstaking efforts, often derided, to weave a network of dune fences to catch the sands that sweep across the beach, and to plant and transplant clumps of dune grass that then hold fast the trapped sands, have been rewarded by our survival.

On the national and international scenes, the storms of the last twenty years rage on now, it seems, at an accelerated pace. I perceive little effort to ward them off. Instead we seem to be inviting the storm-tossed waves to continue their battering, under the fanciful hope, justified by no law of nature, that if we do not resist them, they will subside.

Let us draw back and try to deduce some conclusions from the chronicles of this volume, in the hope of reversing these tides.

Though the enemy remains implacable, now buttressing his implacability with military and nuclear might, we persist in the premise that if only we are reasonable, we can dilute or even annul his firm determination to destroy us all.

331

While Cuban troops move, without interference from us, over the African continent, our president and our secretary of state occasionally issue "warnings," but these "warnings" have a hollow ring. Everyone understands that they are meaningless and are meant only to break the monotony of our craven retreats. For where we do act, in Rhodesia, in South-West Africa, and in South Africa, our actions actually aid the Soviet and Cuban proxies, encouraging them in their acts of terror and aggression by our sanctions and our boycotts against the targets of the terror and by subsidies to those hosting the murderers.

Our government professes to champion human rights. Yet it accords White House receptions and state dinners to dictatorial heads of state whose subjects suffer great privations and repressions—Tito of Yugoslavia, Nyerere of Tanzania, and Kaunda of Zambia. And when our president goes abroad to trumpet human rights, he chooses Nigeria, still remembered for its genocide against Biafra, and Poland, whose brave people groan in bondage, to be platforms for his exhortations.

There are nations today that aspire to be friends of the United States—the Republic of China, South Korea, South Africa, Rhodesia, Nicaragua, Chile, and Brazil. These nations have fought with us for freedom and will do so again. Yet we wage variegated but relentless war against each of these.

On the national scene, our government indicts, censures, and intimidates our FBI officials, other counterintelligence officers, and outspoken military leaders in response to pressures brought by subversive forces. Yet if we had to fight for our country tomorrow, it would be those so harrassed, even dismissed, who would lead the effort while those we accommodate would be found in the ranks of our enemies.

Our Committees investigate Chilean intelligence, the South Korean CIA, and our own CIA and FBI, but not the most fearsome and formidable KGB or its Cuban and Chinese Communist counterparts.

The Republic of China, a wartime ally that is loyal to our traditions and constantly emulating our institutions, our system of free enterprise, and our extension of personal liberty, is a beacon of hope for all Asia. Yet our presidents, secretaries of state and national security advisors pliantly, monotonously, and without reciprocation journey to Peking to court its enemies even as they issue their threats, deliberately timing their arrivals to embarrass and insult the leaders of Free China.

Our spokesmen declare themselves bound by the Shanghai Communiqúe, which is an executive agreement and not binding, to deliver the Republic of China, with whom we have a treaty that does bind, to the jurisdiction of the Chinese Communists who warred on us in Korea and Vietnam, as well as on the United Nations that rapturously embraces them now. And as this is written, our president declares he will recognize the Chinese Communist regime.

Our president deplores terror in the councils of the world. He deplores it in Rome and in Munich, yet his policies encourage, incite, and subsidize it in Salisbury, Pretoria, and Windhoek.

There is a common denominator in almost all the acts of terror being committed today by the Baader-Meinhof gang, the Red Brigades, the Japanese Red Army, the PLO, the FALN, and others. They are motivated by a Communist ideology and an anti-imperialist orientation and largely armed by the Soviet Union and its satellites.

With the increase in the number of Communist nations entering the General Assembly of the United Nations, which more and more causes that body to list to the left, we nevertheless accept it as a neutral forum and look to it to settle international disputes.

Permeating all our actions is the impulse to be moderate and well disposed to our enemies, for they may become our friends, forgetting all the while that when we trample on our friends at the same time we approach the predicament that one day we will have no friends at all.

As we approach the SALT agreements, we have unilaterally and without reciprocal concessions jettisoned the B-1 bomber and the neutron bomb, all the while exporting to our adversaries the computers, ball bearings, and space techniques that enable them to erase the qualitative superiority we had that justified conceding them quantitative superiority.

An overview of all of this is not blurred. It is clear and in focus.

As the threat to our survival as a nation becomes greater, the more we tear down our ramparts, alienate our allies, strengthen our enemies, and weaken our army, navy, and air force.

It does not have to be thus. We can reverse these distressing trends. We must eliminate from our system what seems to be a neurosis that is forcing us to war on our security forces. We need them. We need the FBI, the CIA, and the counterintelligence forces in our armed services and in our police departments.

Congress must restore its Senate Subcommittee on Internal Security and its House Internal Security Committee. These committees must make a record of what subversives are now secretly doing in this country. These committees must keep files. They must publish their findings. The FBI must retain and strengthen its counterintelligence role. It must keep under surveillance the Communist party that is directed by Moscow as well as the Communist party directed by Peking and the FALN, the Socialist Workers' Party, the Symbionese Liberation Army, and other neo-terror organizations.

The FBI must infiltrate all these organizations. Informants are a valuable tool in preventing terror. Guidelines from the office of the attorney general that hold FBI and other counterintelligence officers financially responsible to defend actions undertaken in the line of duty must be revised.

There is need for a new Bricker Amendment that would prevent treaties from superseding our Constitution. Our relationship to the United Nations is that of a treaty, and Security Council resolutions are overriding acts of Congress. The United Nations is a threat to our sovereignty.

If the United States remains in the United Nations, it should adhere to its charter. It should oppose aggression and veto the admission of aggressor states. Even though its efforts would result in failure because of Communist vetoes, it should take the stand that aggressor nations should be expelled.

It should comply with the mandate of the U.N. charter which

334

prohibits interference in the internal affairs of other nations. It should remove the illegal sanctions from Rhodesia and South Africa.

The United States must strengthen its military forces, expand its navy, proceed with research and development of new weapons, create an effective civil defense, encourage armed forces' enlistments, abolish the Fulbright Memorandum, and designate as its spokesmen at SALT conferences and other strategic meetings individuals who are strong negotiators able to resist the aggressive demands of the Soviet delegates and their allies. All the while it should make the point that we stand for genuine disarmament and that we are against the arbitrament of war.

The United States must eliminate from its system what appears to be a neurosis causing us to war on our allies. Instead the United States should strengthen its ties with its allies and consolidate its defense treaties and other accords with NATO, ANZUS, OAS, Brazil, Israel, the Philippines, Spain, the Republic of China, and other friendly nations, particularly those in the Moslem world. The United States should develop its naval base in Diego García in the Indian Ocean, Clark Air Force Base and Subic Bay Navy Base in the Philippines, take over Simonstown, now evacuated by the British, protect the Panama Canal, retain our bases at Guantánamo Bay, the Marianas, and other Pacific outposts, and solidify our relationships with our neighbors Canada and Mexico.

But above all we must cease seeding our own destruction.

Index

336

338

340

Hoover Institution, Stanford University, 260, 285
Horn of Africa, 98, 122
Hornbeck, Dr. Stanley, 191–192
House: Appropriations, Committee on, 93; Civil Rights Committee, 62; Foreign Affairs Committee, 202; Government Operations Committee, 57; Inter-American Affairs Subcommittee of International Relations Committee, 307; Internal Security [Sub] Committee, 45, 46, 47, 54, 56–60, 79, 334; Judiciary Committee, 47, 56, 58–59; Un-American Activities Committee, 45–46, 47, 54, 55–56, 110, 132
Hua Kuo Feng, 199, 200, 205–206, 207
Huang Hua, 199–200, 201
Human Rights: Accord (Helsinki), 20, 274; Declaration, 285; Week, 197, 281
Hungarian Revolution (1956), 87, 297–298; Soviet suppression of, 181, 182, 221, 297–298

IBM, 44, 100
Ichord, Rep. Richard H., 57
"In a War Effectively Controlled by the United Nations," 90
In the Cause of Peace, 303
Indonesia, 238
Institute for Policy Studies, 313, 314
Institute for the Study of Conflict (London), 239, 253–254
Institute of Defense Analysis, 90
Institute of Pacific Relations, 33, 75, 107, 109, 133, 140, 162, 164–166
Institutes for the Achievement of Human Potential (Philadelphia), 272
Inter-American Defense: Board, 311; Force, 308
Inter-American relations, damaging of, 307–316
Internal Security Subcommittee hearings, Senate, 79, 177, 203, 263; on Bang-Jensen case, 183–190; on Communist infiltration of U.N., 303–306; on Communist threats in Caribbean, 115–116; on forced repatriation, 284; on Hungarian Revolution, 181, 182, 297–300; on Institute of Pacific Relations, 33, 75–77, 133–142, 191–195; on National Drive Against Law Enforcement and Intelligence Agencies, 72; on E. Herbert Norman, 162–167; on Soviet propaganda, 208–214; on terrorism, 224–226, 243–247, 248–250
International Monetary Fund, 304, 305
International Relations Center, San Francisco State University, 252
International Terrorism—The Communist Connection, 260–266
Iran, 36
Iraq, 209
Irish Republican Army (IRA), 24, 225
Irvine, Reed, 101
Israel, 36
Italy, 117, 216–217, 220, 238, 240

Jaegher, Father Raymond de, 35
Jahnke, Peter, 239
Jamaica, 16, 24, 120, 309, 315, 329
James, Gen. Daniel, 27
Jane's All the World's Aircraft, 92–93
Japan, 36, 98, 236–237, 238, 239
Japanese (United) Red Army, 236, 254, 265, 333
Jefferson School, New York, 141
Jenkins, Brian, 237, 269
Jenmin Jih Pao, 207
Johnson, President Lyndon B., 128, 155, 169, 176, 190
Joint Committee on Atomic Energy, 252–253
Joint U.S.-Brazil Military Commission, 307, 312, 313
Justice, Department of, 73, 74–75, 147; Internal Security Division, 16, 45, 52, 54, 55

341

342

343

270, 277, 284, 285, 297–300, 303–306, 334; Judiciary Committee, 33, 47, 74, 109, 112; Rules and Administration, Committee on, 52; Tydings Subcommittee, 107, 111

Setoyama, Mitsuo, 236–237

Shanghai Communiqué, 17, 23, 195–196, 206, 333

Shevchenko, Arkadi, 302

Silvermaster, Gregory, 203–204

SIS. *See* Special Intelligence Service (British)

Sithole, Rev. Ndabaningi, 323, 324

Skyjacking, 236–237

SLA. *See* Symbionese Liberation Army

Smith, Earl E. T., 34, 114–116

Smith, Ian, 282, 317, 318, 319, 320, 322, 324

Smith, Senator, 139–140

Smith, Walter Bedell, 157

Snyder, Richard E., 172, 173

Socialist Workers' Party, 74, 241, 334

Socotra, 122

Sokolovsky, Marshal V. D., 31

Soliah, Kathleen, 79

Solodovnikov, Vasili, 319, 321, 323, 326

Somalia, 122, 236, 328

Sourwine, Jay, 109, 135, 136, 183–189

South Africa, 36, 119, 180, 242, 275, 281, 301, 302, 317, 323, 326, 327, 332, 335; strategic importance of, 327–329

South Moluccans, 238

South Yemen, Republic of, 122

Southern Connection: Recommendations for a New Approach to Inter-American Relations, The, 314–315

South-West Africa (Namibia), 242, 317, 323, 324, 326–327, 328, 332

Soviet Union, 15–16, 22–24, 26–31, 34, 36, 75, 87–88, 91, 118, 122, 195, 220, 277, 321; disarmament suggestions by, 88; espionage conducted by, 124–130, 146, 150–160, 162–167, 168–176, 181–190; and Eurocommunism, 215, 216–222; forced repatriation to, 284–296; military buildup in Cuba, 93–94; nuclear superiority of, 15, 28, 91; peaceful coexistence defined by, 95–98; and political terrorism, 239, 240, 255, 260–266, 333; repression of Hungarian Revolution by, 297–298; strategic weapons of, 86

Soviet World Outlook, 96

Special Agents' Legal Defense Committee, 65

Special Intelligence Service (SIS), British, 150, 157, 241

"Specter of Eurocommunism, The," 220–222

Spiegel, Der, 264

Squires, Jim, 40

Stalin, Iosif, 22–23, 145, 215–216, 217, 285–286, 295, 297

Stalin-Hitler Pact, 75, 131

State Department, 33–34, 36, 42, 106–108, 115, 116–117, 143–145, 155, 177–178, 191, 193, 195, 206; Division of Far Eastern Affairs, 191

Stephens, Dr. Maynard, 250

Sterret, Judge Lew, 168

Stettinius, Edward R., 293, 295, 296

Stimson, Henry, 286

Stockholm syndrome, 267–273

Strategic Arms Limitation Talks (SALT), 28, 91, 333, 335; SALT 1, 99

Stratemeyer, General, 153

Stratton, Louise, 267–268, 269

Strong, Gen. Kenneth, 157

Students for a Democratic Society (SDS), 210

Subversive Activities Control Board, 16, 45, 52, 54, 55, 56

Sumner, Lt. Gen. Gordon, Jr., 307–316

Sunday Lorain Journal, 127

Sunday Telegraph (London), 266

Supreme Court, U.S., 66

Suslov, Mikhail, 119–120